Sabbats
ALMANAC

Llewellyn's Sabbats Almanac:
Samhain 2013 to Mabon 2014

Cover art © Carolyn Vibbert/Susan and Co.
Cover design by Ellen Lawson
Editing by Ed Day
Interior Art: © Carolyn Vibbert/Susan and Co., excluding illustrations on pages 37, 76, 113, 151, 185, 221, 258, and 295, which are © Wen Hsu

You can order annuals and books from *New Worlds*, Llewellyn's catalog. To request a free copy call toll free: 1-877-NEW WRLD, or order online by visiting our website at http://subscriptions.llewellyn.com.

ISBN: 978-0-7387-3197-1

Llewellyn Worldwide Ltd.
2143 Wooddale Drive
Woodbury, MN 55125-2989
www.llewellyn.com

Printed in the United States of America

2013

JANUARY
S	M	T	W	T	F	S
		1	2	3	4	5
6	7	8	9	10	11	12
13	14	15	16	17	18	19
20	21	22	23	24	25	26
27	28	29	30	31		

FEBRUARY
S	M	T	W	T	F	S
					1	2
3	4	5	6	7	8	9
10	11	12	13	14	15	16
17	18	19	20	21	22	23
24	25	26	27	28		

MARCH
S	M	T	W	T	F	S
					1	2
3	4	5	6	7	8	9
10	11	12	13	14	15	16
17	18	19	20	21	22	23
24	25	26	27	28	29	30
31						

APRIL
S	M	T	W	T	F	S
	1	2	3	4	5	6
7	8	9	10	11	12	13
14	15	16	17	18	19	20
21	22	23	24	25	26	27
28	29	30				

MAY
S	M	T	W	T	F	S
			1	2	3	4
5	6	7	8	9	10	11
12	13	14	15	16	17	18
19	20	21	22	23	24	25
26	27	28	29	30	31	

JUNE
S	M	T	W	T	F	S
						1
2	3	4	5	6	7	8
9	10	11	12	13	14	15
16	17	18	19	20	21	22
23	24	25	26	27	28	29
30						

JULY
S	M	T	W	T	F	S
	1	2	3	4	5	6
7	8	9	10	11	12	13
14	15	16	17	18	19	20
21	22	23	24	25	26	27
28	29	30	31			

AUGUST
S	M	T	W	T	F	S
				1	2	3
4	5	6	7	8	9	10
11	12	13	14	15	16	17
18	19	20	21	22	23	24
25	26	27	28	29	30	31

SEPTEMBER
S	M	T	W	T	F	S
1	2	3	4	5	6	7
8	9	10	11	12	13	14
15	16	17	18	19	20	21
22	23	24	25	26	27	28
29	30					

OCTOBER
S	M	T	W	T	F	S
		1	2	3	4	5
6	7	8	9	10	11	12
13	14	15	16	17	18	19
20	21	22	23	24	25	26
27	28	29	30	31		

NOVEMBER
S	M	T	W	T	F	S
					1	2
3	4	5	6	7	8	9
10	11	12	13	14	15	16
17	18	19	20	21	22	23
24	25	26	27	28	29	30

DECEMBER
S	M	T	W	T	F	S
1	2	3	4	5	6	7
8	9	10	11	12	13	14
15	16	17	18	19	20	21
22	23	24	25	26	27	28
29	30	31				

2014

JANUARY
S	M	T	W	T	F	S
			1	2	3	4
5	6	7	8	9	10	11
12	13	14	15	16	17	18
19	20	21	22	23	24	25
26	27	28	29	30	31	

FEBRUARY
S	M	T	W	T	F	S
						1
2	3	4	5	6	7	8
9	10	11	12	13	14	15
16	17	18	19	20	21	22
23	24	25	26	27	28	

MARCH
S	M	T	W	T	F	S
						1
2	3	4	5	6	7	8
9	10	11	12	13	14	15
16	17	18	19	20	21	22
23	24	25	26	27	28	29
30	31					

APRIL
S	M	T	W	T	F	S
		1	2	3	4	5
6	7	8	9	10	11	12
13	14	15	16	17	18	19
20	21	22	23	24	25	26
27	28	29	30			

MAY
S	M	T	W	T	F	S
				1	2	3
4	5	6	7	8	9	10
11	12	13	14	15	16	17
18	19	20	21	22	23	24
25	26	27	28	29	30	31

JUNE
S	M	T	W	T	F	S
1	2	3	4	5	6	7
8	9	10	11	12	13	14
15	16	17	18	19	20	21
22	23	24	25	26	27	28
29	30					

JULY
S	M	T	W	T	F	S
		1	2	3	4	5
6	7	8	9	10	11	12
13	14	15	16	17	18	19
20	21	22	23	24	25	26
27	28	29	30	31		

AUGUST
S	M	T	W	T	F	S
					1	2
3	4	5	6	7	8	9
10	11	12	13	14	15	16
17	18	19	20	21	22	23
24	25	26	27	28	29	30
31						

SEPTEMBER
S	M	T	W	T	F	S
	1	2	3	4	5	6
7	8	9	10	11	12	13
14	15	16	17	18	19	20
21	22	23	24	25	26	27
28	29	30				

OCTOBER
S	M	T	W	T	F	S
			1	2	3	4
5	6	7	8	9	10	11
12	13	14	15	16	17	18
19	20	21	22	23	24	25
26	27	28	29	30	31	

NOVEMBER
S	M	T	W	T	F	S
						1
2	3	4	5	6	7	8
9	10	11	12	13	14	15
16	17	18	19	20	21	22
23	24	25	26	27	28	29
30						

DECEMBER
S	M	T	W	T	F	S
	1	2	3	4	5	6
7	8	9	10	11	12	13
14	15	16	17	18	19	20
21	22	23	24	25	26	27
28	29	30	31			

Contents

Contents

Lammas

Mabon

Introduction

NEARLY EVERYONE HAS A favorite sabbat. There are numerous ways to observe any tradition. This edition of the *Sabbats Almanac* provides a wealth of lore, celebrations, creative projects, and recipes to enhance your holiday.

For this edition, a mix of up-and-coming writers— **Emily Carding, James Kambos, Diana Rajchel**, and **Suzanne Ress**—join more established writers—**Elizabeth Barrette, Deborah Blake, Ellen Dugan,** and **Melanie Marquis**—in sharing their ideas and wisdom. These include a variety of paths such as Garden Witchery or Green Witchery as well as the authors' personal approaches to each sabbat. Each chapter closes with an extended ritual, which may be adapted for both solitary practitioners and covens.

In addition to these insights and rituals, specialists in astrology, history, cooking, crafts, and family impart their expertise throughout.

Corrine Kenner gives an overview of planetary influences most relevant for each sabbat season and provides details and a short ritual for selected events, including New and Full Moons, retrograde motion, planetary positions, and more.

Linda Raedisch explores the realm of old-world Pagans, with a focus on customs such as ritual bread baking for Lammas and lesser-known facets of well-known symbols like the pumpkin and the maypole.

Dallas Jennifer Cobb conjures up a feast for each festival that includes an appetizer, entrée, dessert, and beverage.

Blake Octavian Blair offers instructions on craft projects that can also be incorporated into your practice.

Kerri Connor focuses on activities the entire family can share to commemorate each sabbat.

About the Authors

Elizabeth Barrette has been involved with the Pagan community for more than twenty-two years. She served as managing editor of *PanGaia* for eight years and dean of studies at the Grey School of Wizardry for four years. She has written columns on beginning and intermediate Pagan practice, Pagan culture, and Pagan leadership. Her book *Composing Magic: How to Create Magical Spells, Rituals, Blessings, Chants, and Prayers* explains how to combine writing and spirituality. She lives in central Illinois where she has done much networking with Pagans in her area, such as coffeehouse meetings and open sabbats. Her other public activities feature Pagan picnics and science-fiction conventions. She enjoys magical crafts, sabbat entertaining, and gardening for wildlife. Her other writing fields include speculative fiction and gender studies. One of her Pagan science fiction poems, "Fallen Gardens," was nominated for the Rhysling Award in 2010. Visit her blogs: *The Wordsmith's Forge*, http://ysabetwordsmith.livejournal.com and *Gaiatribe: Ideas for a Thinking Planet*, http://gaiatribe.geekuniversalis.com.

Blake Octavian Blair is an Eclectic Pagan Witch, ordained minister, psychic, tarot reader, freelance writer, Usui Reiki Master-Teacher, musical artist, and a devotee of Lord Ganesha. He holds a degree in English and Religion from the University of Florida. In his spare time, he enjoys beading jewelry, knitting, and is an avid reader. Blake lives in the Piedmont Region of North Carolina with his beloved husband, an aquarium full of fish, and an indoor jungle of houseplants. Visit him on the web at www.blakeoctavianblair.com or write him at blake@blakeoctavianblair.com.

Deborah Blake is the author of *Everyday Witch A to Z: An Amusing, Inspiring & Informative Guide to the Wonderful World of*

Witchcraft; The Goddess is in the Details: Wisdom for the Everyday Witch; Everyday Witch A to Z Spellbook; and *Witchcraft on a Shoestring*. Her award-winning short story, "Dead and (Mostly) Gone" is included in the *Pagan Anthology of Short Fiction: 13 Prize Winning Tales* (Llewellyn, 2008). When not writing, Deborah runs the Artisans' Guild, a cooperative shop she founded with a friend, and works as a jewelry-maker, tarot reader, ordained minister, and an intuitive energy healer. She lives in a 100-year-old farmhouse in rural upstate New York with five cats who supervise all her activities, both magickal and mundane.

Emily Carding (Cornwall, United Kingdom) is an author, priestess, and artist. An initiate of Alexandrian Wicca and a member of the Starstone network, she has been working with inner world Faery contacts since childhood. She has been trained in techniques of Celtic shamanism by John and Caitlin Matthews, and has worked with renowned Faery teachers R. J. Stewart and Brian and Wendy Froud. A respected and active member of the Faery and Tarot community worldwide, Carding's work has received international recognition. Visit her online at ChildOfAvalon.com.

Life is what you make it, and **Dallas Jennifer Cobb** has made a magical life in a waterfront village on the shores of great Lake Ontario. Forever scheming novel ways to pay the bills, she practices manifestation magic and wildlands witchcraft. She currently teaches Pilates, works in a library, and writes to finance long hours spent following her heart's desire—time with family, in nature, and on the water. Contact her at jennifer.cobb@live.com.

Kerri Connor (Chicagoland, IL) is the High Priestess of The Gathering Grove, and has been practicing her craft for twenty-five years. She is the author of three other books of magic, and her writing has appeared in *The Blessed Bee, Sage Woman, PanGaia*, and *New Witch*. She runs *The Pagan Review*, a website that provides reviews of Pagan products. She also recently started Nurturing Necessities, a nonprofit charitable organization. Her favorite sabbat is Mabon.

Ellen Dugan, the "Garden Witch," is an award-winning author and psychic-clairvoyant. A practicing Witch for more than twenty-five years, she is the author of ten Llewellyn books: *Garden Witchery, Elements of Witchcraft, Cottage Witchery, Autumn Equinox, The Enchanted Cat, Herb Magic for Beginners, Natural Witchery, How to Enchant a Man* and her latest books, *A Garden Witch's Herbal* and *Book of Witchery*. Ellen wholeheartedly encourages folks to personalize their spellcraft—to go outside and to get their hands dirty to discover the wonder and magick of the natural world. Ellen and her family live in Missouri. For further information, visit her website at www.ellendugan.com.

James Kambos spent much of his childhood on a farm in the Midwest. During this time, he developed a deep appreciation for the power and beauty of the changing seasons. This respect for nature is reflected in his writing and magic. Although of Greek ancestry, he was raised in Appalachia and was influenced by the magical beliefs of both cultures. He has fused each of these magical traditions into his spiritual practices. He enjoys writing for Llewellyn's annuals and holds a degree in education from Ohio University. Southern Ohio is where he calls home.

Corrine Kenner specializes in bringing metaphysical subjects down to earth. She has written sixteen books, including *Astrology for Writers, Tarot for Writers, Tarot and Astrology,* and *The Wizards Tarot*. Some of her work has been translated for a worldwide audience; her books are available in French, Italian, Japanese, Polish, Portuguese, Romanian, and Russian. A former newspaper reporter and magazine editor, Kenner has also edited five anthologies and several astrological publications, including *Llewellyn's Astrological Calendar, Daily Planetary Guide,* and *Sun Sign Book*. Kenner was raised on a farm in North Dakota. She has lived in Brazil and Los Angeles, where she earned a degree in philosophy from California State University, Long Beach. She currently lives in Minneapolis,

Minnesota, with her husband, a software developer. They have four daughters.You can find her at www.corrinekenner.com.

Melanie Marquis is the author of *The Witch's Bag of Tricks* (Llewellyn Publications, 2011), the founder of United Witches global coven, and a local coordinator for Denver Pagan Pride. She's written for many Pagan publications including *Circle Magazine*, *Pentacle Magazine*, and *Spellcraft*. She's a regular contributor to Llewellyn's annuals. A freelance writer, folk artist, children's book illustrator, tarot reader, nature-lover, mother, and eclectic witch, she's passionate about finding the mystical in the mundane through personalized magick and practical spirituality. For more, visit www.melaniemarquis.com, www.unitedwitches.org, or www.facebook.com/melaniemarquisauthor.

Linda Raedisch is the author of *Night of the Witches: Folklore, Traditions and Recipes for Celebrating Walpurgis Night*, as well as a forthcoming Christmas book for Lllewellyn. In between books and articles, she follows in the footsteps of her Great Aunt Anna who cleaned house for a Brazilian diplomat in Lübeck, Germany. Unlike Anna, who eventually married her Brazilian diplomat, Linda cleans much humbler abodes and remains the happily single mother of two. In her spare time, she likes to stroll through museums both here and abroad.

Diana Rajchel serves as the executive editor for PNC-News, and is the author of *Divorcing a Real Witch: for Pagans and Those Who Used to Love Them.* She is a third-degree Wiccan priestess in the Shadowmoon tradition, with seventeen years of practical experience as a witch. Diana lives in the Twin Cities with her partner, two robots, and a cabinet stuffed with herbs. She believes strongly in integrating the Pagan with the urban lifestyle, no matter how contradictory that may seem. You can find out more about her by visiting http://dianarajchel.com. Remember that.

Suzanne Ress has been practicing Wicca for about twelve years as the leader of a small coven, but she has been aware of having a special connection to nature and animal spirits since she was a young child. She has been writing creatively most of her life—short stories, novels, and nonfiction articles for a variety of publications—and finds it to be an important outlet for her considerable creative powers. Other outlets she regularly makes use of are metalsmithing, mosaic works, painting, and all kinds of dance. She is also a professional aromatic herb grower and beekeeper. Although she is an American of Welsh ancestry by birth, she has lived in northern Italy for nearly twenty years. She recently discovered that the small mountain in the pre-alpine hills she and her family and animals inhabit was once the site of an ancient Insubrian Celtic sacred place. Not surprisingly, the top of the mountain has remained a fulcrum of sacredness throughout the millennia, transforming from Celtic "Dunn" to Roman fortress, to its current form—Catholic chapel, and this grounding in blessedness makes Suzanne's everyday life especially magical.

Samhain

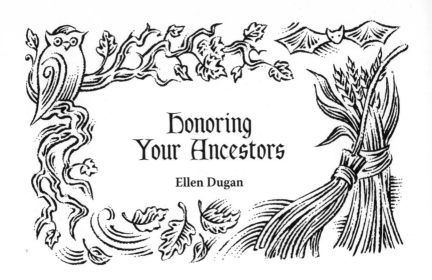

Honoring Your Ancestors

Ellen Dugan

Every man is a quotation from all his ancestors.
—Ralph Waldo Emerson

WHILE SEARCHING FOR SOME inspiration, I stumbled across an image on Pinterest for Samhain. It was simple image. A skull on a black background and the phrase, "Samhain is coming. Honor to your ancestors." These seven little words seem to really hit home with me and began to inspire the theme for this almanac article.

As you set up an altar to celebrate your ancestors and where you come from, stop and consider their stories. Every family has tales to tell, and if you do not know yours, then it is time to do some digging. These people are your roots and your connection to the past. For example, my paternal grandfather was born in 1901 and lived to be in his nineties. When I stop and think about all the things he saw and experienced—and how the world changed in his lifetime—it is staggering.

The U.S. Census Bureau defines the term "ancestry" as "a person's ethnic origin, or descent, 'roots,' or heritage" while genealogy is defined as "successive generations of kin." Also, we should note that genealogy also means "the study and investigation of family history." No matter what you call it—this is your family, your bloodline, and the ancestors you have literally descended from.

Sleuthing through your family tree is an interesting project. But before you dive into an online website, why don't you start with your oldest living relatives? See what they can recall about their family tree. Chances are, their memories are crystal clear when it comes to where they came from, and who their parents and grandparent were.

How well do you know your own family history? I'm lucky because in my case, my mother was really into genealogy back in the 1970s, so my family actually knows quite a bit of its history. As Samhain approaches, ask yourself, how well do you know your family's history? Everyone has a story to tell, and guess what? There may be some pretty interesting tales to uncover (as well as a few skeletons hiding in your own family's closet).

When my mother started to investigate, it was all done old school, going through microfilm and archives at libraries. It was the 1970s after all. One of her aunts had a good family tree from her own side of the family but from my own father's family tree—we had nothing. She joined genealogy groups and subscribed to magazines and placed ads in those magazines for clues to my father's family history.

As a young teen, I remember helping my mother a bit while she researched. The more my mother dug, the more interesting history she pulled up. Everything from Civil War soldiers to illegitimate children of one of my paternal great-grandfathers (seems he had a separate family across town). Pretty scandalous stuff for the 1900s era!

This actually finally explained my paternal grandmother's absolute hatred of her own father. She refused to talk about him. Only after my grandmother passed away and my mother dug deep into the family tree did we learn of my grandmother's half-brothers. Eventually, my mother made contact with one of the children of the half-brothers and the whole story came out.

My mother's paternal side of the family lived in the commonwealth of Kentucky as far back as the early 1700s, when it was one of four commonwealths that would eventually become the United States. Kentucky did not obtain statehood until 1792.

Rumor has it that my mother's paternal side of the family tree has some Cherokee in its branches, which makes sense, as my maternal grandfather was always very adamant about telling us the history of the Trail of Tears. Also, there are photos of my maternal grandfather, William, that even my husband commented on. William had the coloring and bone structure of his rumored ancestry, no doubt. As an adult, I asked my grandmother Dorothy about her husband's ancestry. To my surprise I got a very strong reaction.

She was livid at my asking. Then she announced that her grandmother had told her horror stories when she herself was a young girl, about what the "Indians" had done to "poor" General Custer. Yeah, my grandmother grew up hearing horror stories about the Wild West. Sometimes you forget that it wasn't that long ago.

I could only cringe at the politically incorrect, not to mention insensitive, comment. Grandma Dorothy was in her late eighties at the time, and no one lectures their grandmother—especially one who was six feet tall and on a tirade. When she came up for air, I quietly pointed out the atrocities that were done to the native peoples. It did not go over very well.

She fired back with, and I quote, "I will have you know young lady that there is none of that business in *my* side of the family tree!"

Whoa Grandma, me think thou dost protest too much. At any rate, it was an interesting bit to add to the family history. My kids, even as grown adults, still remember the time I asked their great-grandmother about great-grandpa's ancestry. It was a moment. So while we have no hard documentation of any Cherokee heritage, still we all wonder … and my intuition tells me, yes.

We know about my father's ancestors, thanks to my mother's enthusiastic and relentless investigation. My father's family mostly immigrated to the United States through Ellis Island during the early to late 1800s. We know that my father's paternal line settled in southern Missouri and one of my great-great-grandfathers, named John, fought during the Civil War as a soldier in the Union Army. My mother found the documentation. So if we wanted to, my sister and I and my own daughter, Erin, could be Daughters of the American Revolution. That tickles me.

Missouri was a border state, and the fighting here during the Civil War was guerilla style and not as organized as the bigger battles, such as Gettysburg. No regiments marching in line or formation across the fields here—you know, the scenes that most people imagine when they think of Civil War battles. According to the family history, my great-grandfather (Civil War soldier John's son) was born in the woods during a border skirmish, as the soldier's wife had fled her home with her other children in tow. Forced to hide in the woods to keep her family safe, she gave birth alone. But she was a scrapper, and once the fighting moved past, she took her children and newborn son back to their farm.

Soldier John was eventually discharged from the Union Army after an accident left him unable to use his legs. Believe it or not, he was helping push a cannon up a hill and it slipped and rolled back over him, crushing his legs. He returned home to his farm and fathered a few more children, but was left disabled. The son that was born in the woods, also named John, eventually moved to St. Louis where he met, fell in love with, and married a young immigrant named Anna.

Anna, my paternal great-grandmother, also has a fascinating story. We know that she and three of her friends left Copenhagen, Denmark, and sailed to America alone when they were only sixteen. (Think about that. Alone and travelling on a boat to another strange land knowing you will never see your family again?) That took moxie.

We know that back in Copenhagen, Anna's father was the conductor for King Wilhelm's private train in Denmark (we have an old photo of him on the train). There is also a photo of her family's home in Copenhagen.

While Anna kept in touch with her family via postcards, which my mother found and had translated, she never returned to Denmark. She and John stayed in St. Louis and had three children. My grandfather Edward was Anna and John's only son. Edward, my paternal grandfather was born in 1901 and loved to tease me when I was a little girl that he had indeed attended the St. Louis World's Fair, since his mother went while she was pregnant with him.

My maternal side of my father's family all came from Belfast, Ireland. There, Mary Dugan married a Coomer, and she and her husband immigrated to the United States, first living in Indiana, then coming to St. Louis, Missouri. We know Mary's husband was a coal miner and that Mary and her husband had four daughters—one of which was my great-grandmother, Laura.

Laura married and had two daughters, the youngest a feisty girl named Doris, who was my paternal grandmother. Doris adored her mother and hated her father. (He was the guy with the secret family across town.) He did eventually marry the other woman after Laura died. But my grandmother Doris never forgave him or spoke his name again. Grandma Doris was fiercely proud of her family's heritage and often remarked and spoke proudly of her "Black Irish" roots.

So, Anna and John's son Edward married Doris in the 1930s and they had one surviving son they named Edward Junior. My father. Edward married Judith, the daughter of William and Dorothy, in 1962 and their first born child was a daughter named Ellen. That's me.

It was from my paternal grandmother's side of the family tree that I chose my pen name, Dugan. Why do I use a pen name? Well because my married name is German, and ten letters long. It is confusing to pronounce and difficult as hell to spell. So number one author rule: If they can't spell or pronounce your last name, choose a pen name and stick with a first letter from the beginning of the alphabet. *Dugan.* Easy to spell. Easy to pronounce and easy to remember.

I'd like to think that great-great-grandma Mary Dugan, great-grandma Laura, and grandma Doris are proud that I honor the Irish part of my heritage. I know that my Grandma Doris would be thrilled with me using her grandmother's maiden name. It is a way for me to honor my roots.

As Samhain evening begins and you begin to set up your altars to honor your ancestors, stop and remember the history of your own ancestors and the fascinating stories of their lives. After all if it wasn't for them, you would not be the person you are today.

So in closing let me say to you,

Samhain is coming. Honor to your Ancestors.

Cosmic Sway

Corrine Kenner

Most of us think of Mercury as the messenger of the gods. This Samhain, we're reminded that Mercury was also a psychopomp—a guardian and conductor of souls. As darkness falls on All Hallow's Eve, we'll find him retracing an ancient journey through the sign of Scorpio and Pluto's realm of the dead.

Mercury in Scorpio

Mercury is usually pictured as a fleet-footed courier with wings on his feet. At times, however, he wears clothes that made him harder to recognize, such as a traveler's cloak and a broad-brimmed hat. In that guise, he's a god of boundaries and thresholds, and he guards transition points like crossroads and doorways.

Mercury is one of the few beings, mortal or immortal, who can pass in and out of the Underworld at will. Most of those who travel into the netherworld are condemned to remain there until their souls can be reborn.

Most people can't find their way to the Underworld by themselves, either. That's where Mercury steps in. Without his guidance, lost souls could be condemned to wander for eternity, both haunted by their memories of life, and haunting those who survive. It's those spirits we've been told to fear on dark nights—especially at Samhain, when the veil between the worlds is at its thinnest, and the boundaries between this world and the next seem to fade away.

Mercury, however, conducts the souls in his care with dignity and grace. He delivers them safely to Charon, the boatman who ferries them across the River Styx and into Pluto's realm.

Those are the same waters we tap into when we move through Scorpio, the sign of the dark mysteries of life. Scorpio is ruled by Pluto, the god of transformation and inevitable change.

As Mercury moves through the sign of Scorpio this month, he's in the depths of Pluto's realm. His travels are intensified by the fact that Mercury is in one of its infamous retrograde periods. From our perspective here on Earth, it looks as though the planet is moving backward through space.

Mercury started its retrograde movement on October 21. Mercury will turn around and move forward on November 10—when, symbolically speaking, he'll emerge from the Underworld and return to life on Earth.

Communing with Spirits

You can call upon Mercury to help you reconnect with lost friends, relatives, and loved ones. You might even want to invite them to dinner.

Prepare a meal of favorite foods you used to enjoy together. Set a place at the table, and set aside some of the food as a welcoming feast for the spirits you wish to call to your side. Eat by candle or firelight to serve as a beacon to those you'd like to join you. As you share your meal, you can also share stories and remembrances of those who have crossed over, and display the photos and treasured mementos that help you keep their memories alive.

If you'd like Mercury to help guide souls to your table, pull the Magician card from your favorite tarot deck and post it near a doorway. Astrologically, the Magician card corresponds to the messenger planet, and it symbolizes the easy flow of energy and spirit between two very different realms.

You can also call on Mercury in his capacity as an *oneiropompus*, or bringer of dreams. Mercury is uniquely suited to transmit images and messages from the subconscious to the conscious mind. At Samhain, he can also conduct messages from the spirit world, and bring loved ones to you in your sleep to communicate through dreams. As you probably know, dreams are some of the easiest routes for spirits of loved ones to return to our world for contact and communication.

Planetary Positions

Mercury isn't the only active planet this Samhain.

The Sun is in Scorpio, the sign of sex, death, and inheritance—both spiritual and financial. Scorpio rules the Eighth House of the horoscope, where astrologers look for information about shared resources, and how those resources are invested to provide for future generations. Scorpio also rules the reproductive organs, because sex, birth, and death are inextricably linked. At this time of year, especially, we're reminded that the old must pass away to make room for the new.

The Moon is exalted in airy, graceful Libra, the sign of partnership and balance. It's a reminder that we discover our own true nature and potential by weighing ourselves on Libra's scales, and measuring our actions against the actions and reactions of others.

Venus, the goddess of love and attraction, is in optimistic, outgoing Sagittarius, where she serves as a beacon to new people and new adventures. In a few days, on November 6, she'll glide into Capricorn, where she'll become more serious in her relationships and goals.

Mars is in earthy Virgo, in a cooperative trine with Pluto. The warrior planet is determined to reap the rewards of past campaigns before he moves on to new battles.

Jupiter, the expansive planet of good luck and good fortune, is in Cancer, the sign of home and family life. The Great Benefic is also in close contact with Mercury and the Sun. Tap into that energy to reconnect with family members over meals, and to make quick work of household chores. Get ready, too, for Jupiter to turn retrograde on November 7. For the next four months, the expansive planet will encourage you to count your blessings and share your own good fortune with others.

Saturn, the god of time, is in Scorpio—another reminder of endings and new beginnings. Saturn is also conjunct the Sun, emphasizing personal responsibility and clean breaks with the past.

Uranus, the planet of rebellion and revolution, is in fiery Aries—but it's lying low, moving in slow retrograde motion until December 15, in a protracted, irritating square with Pluto.

Neptune, the planet of spiritual connection, is in a watery Pisces dream world, where it's been floating in retrograde motion for the last five months. On November 13, however, Neptune will go direct—so you'll probably feel like you're waking from a lovely dream. Use that sense of gentleness and peace to move forward with your hopes and goals in everyday life.

Pluto is in earthy Capricorn, focusing on the worldly realities of physical existence.

Phases of the Moon

The last New Moon, in Libra on October 4, ushered in the month on a note of gentle grace and cooperation. That energy was disrupted, however, by an aggressive and fiery Full Moon in Aries on October 18—accompanied by a lunar eclipse. Eclipses always bring news of growth and change. Lunar eclipses herald personal developments, while solar eclipses signify public events. On Samhain, the Moon will look like a waning crescent in the sky, as it slowly fades away from its third quarter phase in regal Leo on October 26.

In the coming days, you can expect the smoldering energy of a New Moon in Scorpio on November 3, along with a solar eclipse. You can also look forward to a first quarter Moon in idealistic Aquarius on November 9, a bountiful Full Moon in Taurus on November 17, and the precision of a third quarter Moon in Virgo on November 25.

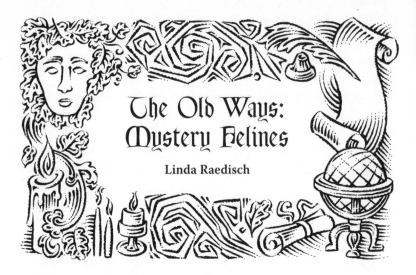

The Old Ways: Mystery Felines

Linda Raedisch

MY SEVENTH-GRADE FRENCH teacher insisted his cat could see spirits. According to Monsieur, Yasmin spent much of her day staring at a blank wall in their Greenwich Village apartment. We students listened intently to stories about Yasmin. To express doubt in the fluffy white Persian's psychic abilities was to risk a black mark in Monsieur's grade book. I never actually met Yasmin, but my teacher's opinion is supported by millions of cat owners, as well as by the folkloric insights of entire nations. There is even some hard evidence in the form of the "cat's eye," a greenish yellow chrysoberyl, the cutting of which reveals a slit-shaped mark like a cat's pupil. In Yasmin's native Persia, such stones were worn as talismans, the cat's eye protecting the wearer from those ill-intentioned spirits that human eyes cannot see.

In Celtic lands, the cat was on a par with the *Sidhe*: it was the only member of the human-run household allowed to sit in on the fairies nocturnal parties. And in English tales, talking cats surprise their keepers by zipping up and down chimneys on their supernatural business. Yasmin was an exclusively indoor cat, so I suppose she entertained at home.

At one time, cats were believed to adhere to the same social niceties as humans do. They were governed by a King of the Cats, to which post there was a clear line of succession. When the king died, they all turned out for the funeral. In Ireland, the reigning monarch was known as Irusan, and he held court in a cave in Knowth in the west of the country. Irusan was as large as an ox, but he liked to disguise himself as an ordinary housecat. In Scotland, he was the Cait Sith or "fairy cat," also known as "Big Ears." The Cait Sith was also a giant. He was long-eared with either dark green or black fur. The Cait Sith looked after his own: those humans who were foolish enough to roast and torture cats could expect a visit from this terrifying creature. From Lancashire, we know of one Mally Dixon, King of the Cats, as well as a King Doldrum who was succeeded by Dildrum. With a little bit of homework, one could probably construct an accurate "Genealogy of the King of the Cats of Great Britain," complete with Danish offshoots.

When a Cait Sith who went by the personal name of Peter expired in the Highlands, his funeral was held in a hollow oak. According to a curious human onlooker, a magical bending of space allowed the trunk to accommodate an entire church. The cats in attendance carried torches and were dressed just like human mourners while they set up a very unearthly wailing. King Peter's body was born out in a coffin, his crown and scepter placed on the lid, to be taken up by his successor.

The story of King Peter is clearly a folktale, but another instance of a cat disappearing into a hollow tree has a ring of truth. As a child in the late eighteenth century, William Cobbett was poking around the ruins of Waverley Abbey when he spied a spaniel-sized gray feline slipping inside the trunk of an elm. William's elders beat him for relating such a fancy, but he never recanted. As an adult, he would insist that the cat he saw at Waverley had looked just like the wild *lucifee*, or lynx, he saw in Canada while serving in the British army.

Cobbett's ruined abbey with its hollow elm lay in Surrey, a county which, two hundred years later, would gain brief notoriety for its alleged puma sightings. An actual puma was eventually trapped in Scotland in 1980 and had, according to the veterinarian who examined her, been living in the rough for some time. A handful of Britons believed she was a member of a beleaguered indigenous species, but it is more likely that she was a cast-off pet. As for Cobbett's tree-haunting big cat, it was probably a Scottish wildcat, albeit one far from home. The only problem with these explanations is the fact that sightings of "Alien Big Cats" are an ongoing phenomenon in the British Isles. Over the centuries, there has been no shortage of Black Dog and other "Mystery Animal" sightings, but the cat has demonstrated a crossover potential that the other beasts lack.

Take the Scottish Elfin Cat, which at first glance appears to be a purely mythological species. Believed to be shape-shifting Witches, Elfin Cats were described as dog-sized and black with a telltale white spot on the breast. When approached, the Elfin Cat would strike a pose with back arched, hackles raised and a fearsome display of teeth. In 1938, something closely matching the Elfin Cat's description began to appear in northern Scotland. Dubbed "Kellas Cats" after the village near which they were spotted, several of them, tragically, were shot, the latest in 1993. The cats were all indeed black and, at twenty pounds, both larger and toothier than the average housecat. There were no white spots on the breast, though one did have some silver-white patches on its flanks. The Kellas Cat's taxonomy remains uncertain. We can only hope they were not the very last of their kind.

It goes without saying that all cats lead hidden lives about which we humans know little or nothing, but the Scottish wildcat, who roams the Highlands to this day, is one of the most secretive of all. Classified as a subspecies of the European wildcat, he diverged from the continental stock over eight thousand years ago. He's the subject of the famous MacPherson Clan imprecation, "Touch not the cat but a glove," meaning you should not approach him unless his claws are sheathed. When this shadowy figure allows himself to be seen, he looks very much like a Maine Coon, but heavier-jawed and not so shaggy around the face. Weighing no more than seventeen pounds, he's not much larger than an overfed housecat. In prehistoric times, he was probably much larger. His reduced size is one of the reasons he has been able to hang on by tooth and by claw where other predators like the wolf, bear, and sea eagle have failed.

Unlike feral cats—escaped domestics and their progeny—who like to form colonies in abandoned buildings, *Felis silvestris grampia*, the Scottish wildcat, goes it alone. Only at midwinter do individual members of the tribe meet up in order to mate, swiftly going their separate ways as soon as the deed is done. Nowadays, these meetings are happening all too infrequently. In 2012, the pure Scottish wildcat population was estimated to be as low as thirty-five, the result of lost territory and an inflow of domestic feline genes. Replacing them are increasing numbers of wildcat/housecat mixes.

The wildcat, which once ranged all over Britain, has had the chance to interbreed with *Felis catus domestica* for about two thousand years—ever since the latter started wandering away from the comforts of the Romano-British villa. Consequently, it's almost impossible to say just who is and who is not a purebred wildcat. Now and then, an all-black kitten is spotted in an otherwise tabby-striped wildcat litter, including one plucky little fellow filmed in the Cairngorms in October 2010. Does this kitten's black coat indicate a smattering of domestic forebears? Was it a Kellas Cat in the making or a throwback to the Elfin Cats of yore? All in all, drafting that family tree for the King of the Cats would be a breeze compared to piecing together the Cairngorm kitten's ancestry.

🌾

I enjoy the sight of an inky black domestic shorthair popping out of a jack-o'-lantern as much as the next Witch, but this year I will have the Scottish wildcat—black, striped, purebred, or otherwise—much on my mind. Because the real mystery is whether or not he'll still be romping through the moonlit heather come next Samhain.

For Further Reading:

BBC News Highlands and Islands. "Black kitten among wildcat litter filmed in Cairngorms." October 14, 2010. http://bbc.co.uk/news/uk-scotland-highlands-islands-11540846. Accessed September 29, 2012.

Briggs, Katharine. *The Fairies in Tradition and Literature*. London: Routledge Classics, 1967.

Guiley, Rosemary Ellen. *The Encyclopedia of Witches and Witchcraft*, Second Edition. New York: Checkmark Books, 1999.

Leach, Maria, editor. *Funk & Wagnalls Standard Dictionary of Folklore, Mythology, and Legend*. New York: Harper & Row, 1972.

McEwan, Graham J. *Mystery Animals of Britain and Ireland*. London: Robert Hale, 1986.

Smith, Chris. "Touch Not the Cat But a Glove." January 2001. http://scotcats.online.fr/swc/touchnot.html. Accessed September 29, 2012.

Westwood, Jennifer and Jacqueline Simpson. *The Lore of the Land: A Guide to England's Legends, from Spring-Heeled Jack to the Witches of Warboys*. London: Penguin Books, 2005.

Feasts and Treats

Dallas Jennifer Cobb

As one year ends and another begins, there is a small crack between the years, the "crack in time." Tonight the veil between the worlds is thin and great magic can happen, especially with a sabbat feast. A time of death, we honor the dead and the wandering souls, so set an extra place setting at your table and offer a plate to the dearly departed. As you cook, imagine the ancestors standing around a large fire with their cauldron bubbling, looking into the future, divining what awaits them in the new year. Looking back and looking ahead, we pause for a moment, between the worlds before the New Year begins. And what here, happens between the worlds, affects all worlds.

Harvest Cauldron Stew

For a few years, I lived in rural Jamaica where all my food production was done outside, over a fire. After learning what "good coals" looked like and how to spread them out for even heat, I became a "one-pot wonder" cook. Night after night, I squatted by the fire, staring into the embers, gently stirring. Safe and warm around the fire, I cooked and processed the events of the day, and dreamed of what could be. In North America, many of us urban dwellers don't have access to a safe, accessible fire pit. But take this opportunity to cozy up around the stove and remember your ancestors, gathered close to their protective fires. Be sure to pause, giving thanks for the dead, and as you stare into the bubbling pot, look forward into the future.

Prep Time: 10 minutes
Cooking Time: 40 minutes
Serves: 4–6

2 pounds beef stew meat
1 cup of flour
Salt and pepper to taste (start with ½ teaspoon each)
¼ cup cooking oil
1 onion, diced
1 medium sweet potato, cubed
2 large Irish potatoes, cubed
3 large carrots, sliced
3 stalks of celery, sliced
1 cup frozen peas
1 teaspoon of dried rosemary
2 beef bouillon cubes (or replace 2 cups water with 2 cups beef stock)

On the stove top, put a large pot, with 4 cups of water, to boil. Cube beef and coat in flour with about ½ teaspoon of salt and pepper to taste. Heat oil in large skillet and fry diced onion, then add floured beef and brown on all sides. Pour contents of skillet into boiling water. Add all vegetables. Bring pot to a boil, add bouillon then turn it down to simmer for about 30 minutes.

Crack of Thyme Biscuits

I love fresh bread with dinner, but hate the long hours it takes to make it. These biscuits are quick and tasty. You can start the stew, then mix the biscuits, put them in the oven, and when the timer goes off, both stew and biscuits will be ready to serve.

Prep Time: 5 minutes
Baking Time: 12 to 15 minutes
Makes: 8 good-sized biscuits

2 cups flour
3 teaspoons baking powder
1 teaspoon salt
½ cup butter—cut to pea-sized pieces
Between ⅔ and ¾ cup cold milk, yogurt, or buttermilk (depending on the consistency you like)
2 tablespoons finely ground thyme

Mix flour, baking powder, and salt, then add butter and milk, mixing quickly to keep the dough cool. Shape into 8 generous-sized balls. Place on oiled baking sheet. Slit top of ball gently with a knife and sprinkle thyme in the slit. Bake at 400 degrees F for 12 to 15 minutes. Serve warm with butter.

Bloody Good Sparklers

Blood-red, and bubbling, like the cauldrons of old, these sparklers are easy to make. Easily adapted to kids and adults, this versatile drink is good at any gathering, but especially at Samhain. Kids, who are obsessed with the dead, will love the idea of drinking blood, and of course, the "eyeball" shaped cranberries floating within. For adults, this tasty, seasonal fruit drink has an added bonus—it is festive, indulgent, has minimal calories, and tastes great with alcohol added. Quick to prepare, Bloody Good Sparklers can be garnished with lemon, lime, or even a fresh cranberry bobbing merrily in the glass. (Note: Pure cranberry juice is very sour, so cranberry cocktail or cranberry-cherry juice is recommended.)

Prep Time: 2 minutes
Serves: 8 drinks

2 cups cranberry juice (or cocktail)
1 cup orange juice
Soda water
Ice cubes
Fresh cranberries
Lemon or orange slices

Mix cranberry and orange juice together to make a dark red "bloody" mix. Place ice in glass, pour ⅓ glass of "blood," fill glass with soda water, garnish, and serve. The adult version includes the addition of vodka to taste.

Dead Banana Bread

Death surrounds us as plants die off, blackened by frost. There is loss, and grief, but underneath there is hope because death also brings renewal—the dying plants will break down and compost into fertile soil. Usually the fruit bowl in my house holds fresh, sweet symbols of the earth's abundant fruition. But when a fruit gets beyond its prime, the kids draw my attention to it pointing out the wrinkled old apples and spongy oranges. Then these aged fruits go off to the compost pile. But not dead bananas. When they are brown or black, bananas have a high natural sugar content and make delicious banana bread. Use them fresh or freeze bananas that are past their prime for use in this recipe. I like to prepare the batter, and have it waiting. Just as the biscuits come out of the oven, I turn the heat down, and put the Dead Banana Bread in. After 50 minutes elapse while we serve and eat dinner, we can enjoy the warm dessert.

Prep Time: 5 minutes
Cooking Time: 50 minutes
Serves: 16 good-sized pieces

2 overripe (dead) bananas (fresh or frozen)
¾ cup honey or ½ cup sugar
1 egg
½ cup oil
½ cup milk
2 cups flour
2 teaspoons baking powder
½ teaspoon baking soda
1 teaspoon ground cinnamon
¾ cup semisweet chocolate chips

In a food processor, place all the wet ingredients, and puree until creamy. Add dry ingredients, but not chocolate chips, and mix. When you have a gooey batter, gently fold chocolate chips into it and pour into an oiled 8 × 8-inch baking pan. Bake at 350 degrees F for 50 minutes until golden brown.

Crafty Crafts

Blake Octavian Blair

THE CRAFTS PRESENTED IN this edition of the almanac are designed to help you celebrate and attune to the wheel of the year. Some crafts will accomplish this through spellcraft that is thematic to the magickal goals that traditionally correspond with the holiday, other crafts tap into the energy of the sabbat through observing and honoring the natural magick inherent in the changing seasons.

Some of the crafts are easier to complete than others and the span of time necessary to complete them varies. However, a fair number of them can be completed in about an hour, making them suitable for group gatherings or solitary celebrations. An estimated cost for each craft is included. You may have many of the tools and materials for the crafts already on hand among your magickal supplies. However, most of the supplies are fairly easy to acquire at local grocery, department, and craft stores. While having some materials on hand will undoubtedly save some money, the total cost for the majority of the crafts is generally fairly affordable, even when making multiples of an item.

Please remember to exercise proper safety practices when using tools, sharp objects, or adhesives. Tools and supplies are listed for each individual craft as are occasional safety reminders, however, it is generally a good idea to keep rubber gloves on hand for working with adhesives or any possible irritants. Work in a well-ventilated area when using varnishes and adhesives. It is also handy to keep sheets of newspaper available to cover your work surfaces.

Be safe, have fun, and enjoy making magick as the wheel of the year turns!

Samhain Crafts

While a major theme of Samhain is reflection upon and communion with our ancestors, as the season descends upon us we also are reminded of all things spooky and creepy. Bumps in the night also come to the forefront. Around Samhain, the diminishing light and shorter days become noticeable. Autumn colors are present, but dissipating, as trees begin to go bare and we hear the crunching of fallen leaves under our feet. Something about our nature causes us to playfully and knowingly work ourselves into a spooked frenzy. Did I hear an extra set of footsteps behind me or was that just the wind rustling? Late-night horror movie marathons (sometimes the corny ones are the most fun) and ghost stories around bonfires often are the entertainment du jour. Deep inside, we know there is no reason for worry, but sometimes we decide to leave the night-light on just in case!

Samhain, also being the witches' new year, is a perfect time for a functional spellcraft to add to your witchy décor in preparation for another turn of the wheel!

Witch Bottles

This witch bottle craft has the appearance of something that perhaps came straight out of a spooky black-and-white gothic film and serves as a nice energetic ward for your home while also adding ambiance to your décor! Historically, in many folk traditions it is often said that the witch bottle was used as protection against witches. This may be because bottle spells have also long been used by witches! One of the things I love most about witch bottles, besides the fact they have an awesomely fun witchy appearance, is their versatility. While one of the more traditional purposes for a witch bottle is protection, a witch bottle can be designed for virtually any purpose—money, love, luck, peaceful home, healing, etc. You simply adjust the ingredients to fit your goal utilizing principles of sympathetic magick. As mentioned earlier, this is the spiritual new year for many, so you can choose a bottle theme to fit a goal you may have for the year. The bottle ingredients suggested in the instructions will focus on the goal of a general home-protection bottle. One need not assume, suspect, or have foreboding thoughts that they are hexed, cursed, or under attack in order to create this bottle! The bottle is proactive and also assists with the natural stray energies that can be flung around the home and assist in transmuting them into neutral energy for more beneficial use. A witch bottle is good energetic home maintenance! Additionally, as with most of the other crafts in this book, the materials for creating the witch bottles are likely either already in your home or are easily obtainable.

Supplies

Clear glass jar or bottle of any size with lid or cork
Duct tape or taper candles (for the wax)
Dried herbs corresponding to your goal
Misc. other ingredients (see ideas later in article)
Thick gardening gloves (optional)
Funnel (optional)
Newspaper (to cover workspace and catch spills)

Instructions: Start out by covering your work area with sheets of newspaper. It is often said that a witch with an immaculate workspace is a witch that doesn't work! Working with loose herbs, possibly liquid, and melting wax can lead to a bit of mess on occasion. This will make cleanup a snap, and besides, the last thing you want is a stray pin or nail that didn't make it into your bottle to end up underfoot or for a household pet to consume spilled herbs. You can

also put on gardening gloves to help reduce the chance of getting poked with the shaper objects, if that's a concern.

Gather your chosen filling materials on your work surface along with your bottle. You have a lot of leeway in choosing the type of bottle. I recommend using something that has a lid or cork. Empty pickle and jelly jars work well, and empty wine bottles have a very witchy look that I just love. Even an empty glass soda bottle works well for a smaller option, but you'll need to find a cork (check your local craft store) that will fit the bottle.

Now begin to add your ingredients one by one, imbuing each with your intent for its purpose within the bottle. I myself like to recite a simple incantation, for example if you were adding sewing needles to the bottle I'd say something to the effect of "Needle of metal, I ask thee to deflect stray energies away from me." When adding the nonherbal ingredients such as coins, tacks, nails, strands of yarn, etc., I like to use numerology to determine the number of each object to add. For example, 5 is associated with protection and the pentagram, so I would add five sewing needles. For herbal ingredients, you can add as little as a couple teaspoons of each or you can add as much as you feel guided. For example, if you have a hectic home, you may add a cup of lavender buds to promote calm in the home. Use your intuition and remember, you do not have to add a large amount of an ingredient in order to get its energetic benefits. Often times a small amount will do!

What to Include in Your Witch Bottle

Ideas of just a few things you could include for this witch bottle include:

Nails, tacks, or sewing needles: The pointy nature of these objects sympathetically evokes protection. Good for warding off and deflecting detrimental energies.

Yarn, twine, or string: Scraps of these, included in various colors, types, sizes, etc., serve to form a tangled web that traps and confuses undesirable energies, preventing them from permeating the home.

Keys: We all have an old spare key or two hanging around that no longer goes to anything. Naturally associated with locks, in the context of the bottle they evoke a energy of security.

Tinfoil: Its reflective surface acts as a mirror sending any unadmirable mojo back to its source (much like a reversal candle). Slip a few torn-up strands into the bottle.

Vinegar: A potent cleanser. Neutralizes stray energies that aren't serving the Highest Good of your home.

Fingernails/hair: Having each member of the household donate a nail clipping or strand of hair for the bottle adds a bit of each person's energy into the bottle and adds the personalization of the bottles intent.

Rice: Protection. Great for filling empty space in the bottle.

Anise: Purification. Also said to ward off the evil eye.

I do not attempt to make layers, as the ingredients will naturally end up shifting and mixing together, and I rather prefer it this way. When your bottle is fairly full and you deem it finished, either duct tape the lid on or light a taper candle and drip the wax over where the cork/lid meets the jar, sealing it shut and effectively finishing your spell. Traditionally, witch bottles are buried, put in the back of a cupboard, or hidden behind a door. I suggest that you leave it someplace visible but where it will inconspicuously blend into your seasonal décor and lend a wonderfully witchy vibe to your home's atmosphere!

Time to complete: About 30 minutes.

Cost: $10.00 to $15.00 depending on supplies already on hand.

References:

Cunningham, Scott. *Cunningham's Encyclopedia of Magical Herbs.* St. Paul, Minnesota: Llewellyn Publications, 1985.

All One Family

Kerri Connor

THE LEAVES ARE CHANGING and falling from the trees, the heat has finally taken a break, the harvest from the garden is all in, and it's time to start the darker, quieter half of the year.

Samhain is a fulfilling and enriching sabbat. Between being the third and final harvest—the harvest of blood, the night the veil is at its thinnest, and the pagan/witches New Year—there are a variety of themes and activities that can be added into your celebration.

This is the sabbat when it is of extreme importance to remember and honor our ancestors and those who have gone before us.

"Fire Mail"

A simple, yet extremely effective, we use to do this is with "fire mail." Whether you have a bonfire or a decent-size cauldron with a few lit charcoal tablets, you have the means for sending fire mail.

For this activity you will need paper for everyone, writing utensils, and a surface in which people can write on.

This should be done outside (even if you are burning inside a cauldron), so set up an area with your fire source in one location, with the writing surface (a card, end table, or coffee table) close by but in a second location. Place the writing utensils on the table, along with the paper, which you can weigh down with a large decorative rock. If you are using a cauldron for your fire source, be sure to keep it safe by placing it on a ceramic tile on a table or even on the ground.

Plan to have a processional to your activity area. It doesn't have to be long—but a walk that takes about thirty seconds makes great timing. At the starting point of your processional, take time to smudge each person before they begin their promenade. You may want to use some music or chanting at this point too. "We all come from the Goddess" is always a good, easy chant to use and it is particularly fitting for Samhain as we visit the topic of death.

After each person is smudged, they will proceed to walk to the table, and using the given supplies, write a letter to a loved one who has passed on. This letter can be to anyone. It can be to an aunt who recently passed, a great-great-great-grandmother who was never met, it can even be written to a family pet—this is particularly a good choice for young children who may not have experienced any other sort of death yet. Children should also be allowed to draw a picture instead of writing, or if they want, to dictate a letter for someone else to write for them. If they are really young, you may want them to work on their letter or picture earlier in the day so they don't end up getting rushed or feeling pressed for time.

The processional serves several purposes. For starters, it allows you to take the time to thoroughly smudge each participant. Between the smudging and the actual walking, this helps greatly to focus mind-set. It reminds them of the seriousness of this activity. This is a solemn moment in time. It also allows time between people arriving at the table to begin their writing. Generally, the table will only be able to hold a few people, but this way, by the time the third or fourth person arrives, the first is usually done and ready to move on to the next step.

Once everyone has reached the writing area, if possible, use a different song, such as "Ancestor's Song" by Kellianna. This song is very fitting as its lyrics honor those who came before us. While some people sing along, others are able to finish writing their letters. Once everyone has completed their letter, take them to the fire source and "mail" them by throwing them into the fire.

After the letters have been sent, give time for everyone to privately meditate. For this part of the activity, you may want to use a song such as "Into the West" by Annie Lennox. This song from the movie, *The Return of the King*, was written as an Elvish song about those going on without us. This song is sad and moving, and fits the atmosphere created as people connect to their loved ones. After this song finishes, you may give a few more minutes of silence. That time can be used to say a final goodbye or to re-center and prepare for the next task at hand.

During this exercise, there is generally crying. Saying goodbye is difficult to begin with, and often people put in these letters things they never got to say, so emotions are brought the forefront. This activity brings a group closer together, even if you were close already. The shared vulnerability and pain that comes from losing a loved one, brings people closer together.

After the final quiet time, you will want to raise spirits and energy to prepare your minds for your ritual. Try using a musical selection that is upbeat and easy to learn such as "She is Crone," also by Kellianna. Sing this song and spiral dance your way to your ritual site.

We have been very lucky so far when our group does this exercise and while it may be chilly out, we haven't had a heavy rain. We do have contingency plans to use a cauldron set up in the garage, just in case we have to go that route. Our plans say unless it's pouring plan to be outside.

Sugar Skulls

Because the fire mail activity is so somber and emotional, we counteract it with a more lighthearted activity after ritual that is fun for everyone—young and old. Decorating Day of the Dead sugar skulls is not only fun, you can give a mini lesson about Day of the Dead while people work, making it educational as well.

You can buy either premade sugar skulls or a mold kit. If you are going to make the skulls yourself, be sure to leave plenty of time to get them all done. They do have to cure for several hours (at least eight) at a time. You should have the skulls either bought or made well ahead of your ritual time. Don't think you can put it off until the day before Halloween and then whip them up. Molds, recipes, and kits can be found easily on the Internet. You will also need the recipes to make different color frostings which you will use to do the decorating. Make sure to have several extras on hand for unexpected guests or emergencies in case some break.

Sugar skulls won't last forever, so take plenty of pictures to preserve these memories for everyone for years to come.

Adding in elements from other traditions to your own celebration is a great way to educate yourself and your group members. It helps to build diversity and respect in our own lives when we learn how other people celebrate and honor their traditions.

As the wheel prepares to roll on, the first activity helps us say goodbye to loved ones lost, while the second activity reminds us of the importance of keeping our hearts open to learning about others. These two concepts will help us as we work on our internal selves through the dark half of the year. These activities can be very beneficial to adults and children alike who are dealing with loss.

Samhain Ritual
Celebrate the Craft

Ellen Dugan

*In all of us there is a hunger, marrow deep, to know our heritage,
to know who we are and where we came from.*
—Alex Haley

I prefer to work my Samhain spells privately. Even though I am a part of a coven, this spell is ultrapersonal and I prefer to keep it quiet and private. This ritual often makes me a bit misty when I remember my dearly departed, but it is a happy sort of tears, as they feel especially close to me at this time of year.

This solitary ritual not only honors the memories of your loved ones, it also gives you a big boost of power at the most magickal time of the year as you will reaffirm your vows as a Witch. To begin, set up a memory altar. Make the ancestral and memory altar pretty by draping a dark fabric over the table surface and add any antique photos of your great-grandparents, your framed photos of grandparents, loved ones, relatives, or friends who have passed over. (Yes you may also include photos of any pets that have passed over, too.)

Items Needed
Fresh rosemary
Votive cups

Tealight candles
Fresh flowers
Jack-o'-lantern

Add sprigs of fresh rosemary for remembrance, and place several white tealight candles in votive cups. Light the candles reverently, one for each person or pet, whose memory you are honoring.

If you like, you can add fresh fall flowers from the garden and a jack-o'-lantern. Once you have all the candles burning away on your memory altar, take a few moments and recall stories of your departed family and friends. Then think about the history of your ancestors and remember where your family started and who it is that you come from.

When you are ready, call the quarters. I like to begin in the east.

Quarter Calls

Eastern Quarter Call: *Element of air, I welcome you into the circle tonight. Bless me with your inspiration, motivation, and the winds of positive change this autumn. Hail and welcome!*

(Now turn right to face the south.)

Southern Quarter Call: *Element of fire, I welcome you into the circle tonight. Grant me the gifts of transformation, may passion and energy burn brightly within me during the darkest days of the year. Hail and welcome!*

(Turn right to face the West.)

Western Quarter Call: *Element of water, I welcome you into the circle tonight. Bless me with your gifts of love and healing. May your gates open and allow my beloved dead to safely pass through and join me here for a brief time tonight. Hail and welcome!*

(Finally, turn right to face the north)

Northern Quarter Call: *Element of earth, I welcome you into the circle tonight. Bless me with the powers of stability and strength. Help me to be grounded and secure as I work my magick this Samhain. Hail and welcome!*

Cast the Circle

Now, turn toward the center and say:

As above, now so below. The elemental powers spin and my magick holds. The circle is cast.

Ground and center yourself. Place your hands upon your altar and then repeat this spell verse.

Ancestors circle around me on the eve of Samhain,
You are not forgotten, your stories come to life again.
With the light of these sacred candles, I stop and remember,
My most dearly departed at the Eve of November.
I know you are close to me, at this magickal time,
I honor your memory with candle flames that shine.

Take some additional time and remember these people or pets and the important lessons they brought into your life. If you find yourself shedding some tears, that is to be expected. Let the emotions wash over you. This is a gift and a blessing.

When you are finished, you may move onto the second portion of the spellwork.

Now, hold your arms out to your sides and really feel the magick that is ripe in the air. Smell that autumn air, embrace the mystery and ancient magick of this night. It's our New Year! Allow the magick of Samhain to fill you up and to remind you of the duty, honor, and joys of being a Witch.

Then imagine yourself surrounded by a bright orange halo of light. Envision that this light protects you, encourages health, promotes abundance, enchantment, and success in your life. See your ancestors encircling you and adding to your strength and wisdom. Hold this imagery in place for a few moments. Then say:

On this Samhain night, magick is heavy in the air,
May I be gifted with courage, success, and health so fair.

May my magick manifest in ways both strong and true,
The Lord and Lady bless my work and all that I do,
All around me now magick glows so warm and bright.
I am truly loved on this holy Samhain night.

Close the Samhain spell with these lines.

For the good of all, with harm to none,
By the magick of Samhain, this spell is done!

Close the Quarters

Start in the North and then continue widdershins around the circle.

Northern Quarter Call: *Element of earth, I thank you for joining me this night. Continue to bless me with your strength as I move beyond this Samhain circle. Hail and farewell.*

(Now turn left to face the west.)

Western Quarter Call : *Element of water, I thank you for joining me this night. Now I bid a fond farewell to my loved ones and request that they all now safely journey back through the western gates to the Summerland. Peacefully return there and go with grace. May the element of water continue to bless me with intuition as I move beyond this circle. Hail and farewell.*

(Wait for a few seconds make sure that you "feel" that the spirits of your beloved dead have all returned to the Summerland. You will know when they go. If you feel you should, then verbally coach them back through. If you do this with respect, they will go effortlessly. Now turn left to face the south).

Southern Quarter Call: *Element of fire, I thank you for joining me this night. Continue to bless me with your energy and passion as we move beyond this circle and into the darkest days of autumn. Hail and farewell.*

(Now, finally turn left to face the east).

Eastern Quarter Call : *Element of air, I thank you for joining me this evening. Continue to bless me with inspiration and wisdom as I move beyond this Samhain circle. Hail and farewell.*

Open the Circle

Hold up your arms and move to the center of the circle and say:

The circle is open but unbroken. Release the magick as my words are spoken. Merry meet, merry part, and merry meet again!

Allow the candles burn out in a safe place until they go out on their own. Keep an eye on them. Typically, you should allow tealight candles four to six hours of burning time. You may keep the altar set up in place for a few days. Then take it down and carefully clean up from the ritual.

Happy Samhain. Happy Witches' New Year!

Notes

Notes

Yule

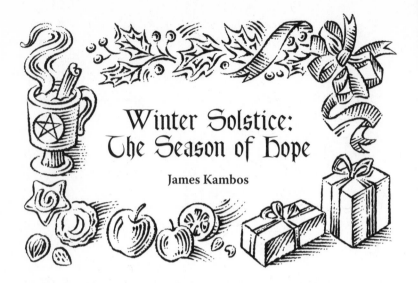

Winter Solstice:
The Season of Hope

James Kambos

THE GREAT WHEEL OF time turns and brings us to the Winter Solstice, also known as Yule. The word Yule is derived from the old Norse word *Jul*, which means "wheel."

The ancients viewed Yule as a time of wonder. As most of us know, the Winter Solstice is the shortest day of the year. From this day forward the hours of daylight lengthen until the Sun reaches its zenith on the longest day of the year, Midsummer, or the Summer Solstice. The Yule season was and still is a time of miracles. After the world reaches a point of almost total darkness, the spark of hope returns. The turning begins anew. The Sun—once again—starts its climb as it has done for eons, even before human or beast walked on our planet. It climbs toward another spring. Another summer. And with the light of the strengthening Sun hope and faith return. Order returns to the universe.

It's no wonder the Yule season was celebrated by numerous ancient civilizations. The Romans observed the Winter Solstice with a festival called Saturnalia. The Druids knew Yule as Alban Arthan and the Anglo-Saxons gave us the word Yule. This universal celebration to honor the rebirth of the Sun also found its way to Christianity. The Christians use Yuletide to observe the birth of Christ.

Christ serves as the Christian version of "The Child of Promise." Since this winter celebration was chosen to commemorate Christ's birth, it also symbolically links him with the young Sun God. There are many themes, messages, and symbols associated with Yule, but the main divine belief is the rebirth of the Sun God. No matter what your spiritual path or religion may be, the universal messages of Yuletide are hope, faith, renewal, giving, and sharing.

Our ancestors lived close to nature. As the Winter Solstice approached the days grew colder, the hours of daylight dwindled, and the earth became barren. People were naturally concerned if they could survive the coming winter. But Yule gave them reason to celebrate. The Sun—giver of life, light, and warmth was returning. There was reason to rejoice. Homes were decorated with pine and other greenery as symbols of everlasting life. Mistletoe, the herb of protection and love, was hung. The old songs of the season were sung, which we now know as Christmas carols. Sweets and pastries were made to bring good luck; small gifts were given. And, of course, after the Yule log was burned, a small piece of it would be saved to ignite the following year's Yule log. I'll discuss the seasonal symbols later, but the point is that these happy customs, taken from ancient Pagan traditions, brought our ancestors real comfort and joy.

The essence of Yule has been overshadowed by the commercialism of the Christmas season. Yule however, is a major nature festival which marks an important turning point of the year. As Pagans, we can focus on the original reasons for the season.

Symbols of the Season

The colors, scents, and decorations used during the Yule season are rich with symbolism and meaning. Most seasonal decorations are Pagan in origin.

Some of you may be observing the Pagan holiday of Yule for the first time. Learning about the significance of the seasonal decorations you are likely to be using will add enjoyment and meaning to the holiday. You'll also be better able to understand why and how they'll be incorporated into the ritual at the end of the chapter. If you already have your own Yule decorating traditions take, a moment and think about why you use those decorations. What do they mean to you?

For me, decorating for Yuletide is one of the best parts of the holiday. Each ornament, each decoration, and each accent has deep meaning. Perhaps it was a gift or was made just for me. Some ornaments are so worn with age the paint has come off, but I don't care because they connect me with my ancestors. I have some ornaments made by Native American children, which are special because the ornaments were one of the last gifts my mother gave me before she died.

And some decorations have special meaning because of their mystical associations with Yule. After reading this, hopefully you'll be able to decorate with feeling and magical intent.

The colors of Yule—red, green, white, and gold—are very symbolic. Red is the color of the life force and connects us with our ancestors. Green is the color that represents life everlasting and eternity; it's the color of many familiar decorations such as the Yule tree. White has several meanings. It's the color of newness and purity, and it represents a new cycle of life. It can also represent spirits, as the spirit realm is very active now. And white is also the color of winter and snow. Gold is naturally a solar symbol associated with the Sun God.

The scents I associate most with Yule are cinnamon, clove, orange, and bayberry. My mother's family was from Greece, so many of the cookies and sweets we prepared at this time of year are Greek. The kitchen was filled with fragrances of cinnamon, clove, and orange.

Cinnamon and clove were used in many cookies and, of course, baklava. Since my grandmother was Greek Orthodox, these spices represented the spices which were given as gifts to the Christ Child by the Wise Men. They are also scents associated with protection and prosperity. Oranges are used to flavor many syrups, which are made to pour over baklava and some cookies. Oranges have a strong link to Yule because they're associated with the Sun. They're excellent when used in spells for love and good luck. To enhance your Yule festivities, use oranges to make a pomander. Combining oranges with pine cones or needles in a bowl or on your altar is a simple Yule accent that is also magical.

To attract good fortune into the New Year light a bayberry-scented candle for a few minutes each night from Yule through New Year's Eve.

The Yule Log

Along with the Yule tree, the Yule log is one of the main visual elements of Yuletide. Most of us are familiar with the small Yule log set with three candles used as a centerpiece of most Winter Solstice observances. But the Yule log has a long history and can take different forms.

The Yule log is Germanic in origin and was originally not just a log, but was actually a large portion of a tree trunk—usually oak. One end of the trunk would be placed in the fireplace and the trunk would be slowly pushed into the fire until it was mostly consumed. The ashes (or a small piece) would be saved for the following year's fire. It was thought that by burning a Yule log, the home would be protected during the coming year, especially against fire and lightning. The light and warmth created by the Yule log represented the young Sun God. To Christians, it represented the light of the Savior.

I am Greek, but I was raised in Appalachia, so we have our own Yule log beliefs. For at least a week beginning before Yule and extending past Christmas, we would never let our fires go out. My father or grandfather, with me tagging along, would continuously feed our fire with large oak logs. As the wind roared over the Appalachian hills, and snowflakes as large as cotton balls drifted down, fragrant blue smoke would curl above our chimney for days. I continue this tradition by burning oak or hickory logs in my wood stove. And if I look closely at the flames, I can see the faces of my ancestors.

There also exists in Appalachia a very rare version of the Yule log known as the "backstick." The backstick was a large log placed behind the smaller logs of the Yule fire. The custom was that as long as the backstick burned the holiday festivities would continue. Keeping this in mind, the woodsman sent to bring in the backstick would usually soak the backstick in a creek, getting it wet so it would burn longer. Few people today have heard of a backstick, except for some old-timers in remote areas of southern Appalachia.

Whatever your tradition, the Yule log embodies the spirit of the Sun God and the warmth to come. Today the Yule log is usually a smaller log drilled with three holes to fit the ritual candles. In the left hole, I like to use a red candle to symbolize our ancestors. In the center, I use a white candle to represent the renewed light. And on the right, I place a green candle to honor the never-ending cycles of nature and eternity. All the candles represent the waxing forces of nature. I usually don't light the candles until Solstice Eve.

You may set your Yule log on your altar in your living room or ritual space early to enjoy it throughout the season. In a separate holder in front of the Yule log, I place a gold candle to represent the Sun/Sun God. Surround your Yule log with seasonal items. These may include holiday greenery: pine, holly, boxwood, ivy, and mistletoe. Pine cones, star shapes, or ornaments are also nice. Elf figures would be good to use as a connection to the fairy realm, and reindeer figures could represent the Horned One. Above all, include items that have meaning to you.

The Yule Tree

If there's one symbol of the season which embodies all the concepts associated with the Winter Solstice, it's the Yule tree (Christmas tree). The Yule tree is always some type of pine. The pines were already ancient before the human race appeared on earth. And since they remained green during the dead of winter, they symbolized eternal life, strength, hope, and promise. They're associated with masculine energy, so they also represent the young Sun God. The pine cones are a sign of fertility and new life.

Ancient people honored all trees but the pines were thought to be magical because they remained green while other vegetation had no foliage. To show their respect, our ancestors would attach small gifts to the pine branches such as ribbons, a bit of fruit, or small metal charms. These tokens of appreciation led to the Yule custom of bringing the pine tree indoors to be adorned with ornaments. The idea of placing gifts around the tree probably began with the Roman festival of Saturnalia, when small gifts showing love and friendship were exchanged.

As you decorate your tree, think of the true meaning of each ornament. They're more than just pretty. Ornaments shaped like nuts or fruits represent the coming season of abundance. Angels, stars, and the lights are symbols of heaven and light. Simple glass balls are an echo of the Witch balls which repelled evil. In recent years, I've faced death and grief, and for me the Yule tree has truly been a symbol of hope and light in the darkness.

Now is also the time to "hang the greens," and as you decorate your home it's good to remember the mystical significance of other holiday greenery. Holly is an excellent green to use for protection and luck. The berries represent the life force and it's believed that the points of the foliage catch any negativity. Holly will be included in the ritual later, since it contains cleansing properties. Ivy offers protection and is particularly effective when used with holly. It's a good plant to weave through garlands or wreaths.

We all know mistletoe is a love herb and is frequently hung above doorways at Yule. But it also repels evil, especially when burned.

No matter what greenery you use, when it's shaped into a wreath it also becomes a symbol of eternity, and the continuous wheel of the year. After enjoying your greenery, it should be removed and burned by Imbolc to cleanse your space.

Sharing the Light

One of the main spiritual themes of Yule is that the Sun God returns and shares his divine light with us. Each of us is a microcosm of Divinity, we are energy, we are light. Most of us feel good when we share our light with others. During this time of year we share our light by giving gifts.

I was raised in a poor coal-mining region of Appalachia. It's hard to explain the heartbreaking poverty I saw as a child. Even in the best of times this area has it rough. Many people lived—and still do—in gritty hardscrabble coal-mining communities. Every December my mother would go to the local welfare office and obtain a list of families who needed help. We'd spend days packing baskets of food, toys, and clothing before going out and delivering them. On crisp December nights after my parents packed the car we'd set out, driving deep into the back hollows. Snow crunched underfoot, and plumes of coal and wood smoke rose from the chimneys of the small coal company houses as we made our deliveries. Inside I'd see children too shy to speak, huddled around potbellied stoves.

Those December nights were long ago, but the faces of those children remain fresh in my mind. That is why the ritual will include a collection of food and any other supplies you can think of, to be distributed to the poor. In this way you and your coven will "share the light" in a very real way.

The Winter Solstice is a time to leave the darkness and move towards the light. Even if you don't plan to take part in a Yule celebration, or a Winter Solstice ritual, you can still observe this holiday by simply doing two things—caring and sharing.

Cosmic Sway

Corrine Kenner

AT THIS TIME OF year, two ancient planets of astrology come to life in the symbols of the season. We see Jupiter, the jovial god of good fortune, in modern-day depictions of Santa Claus—and we see his aging father, Saturn, as Father Time with the Baby New Year.

In fact, the Sun's movement into Capricorn marks the Winter Solstice and the start of Yule. On that date, the Sun reaches its lowest point in the sky, directly over the Tropic of Capricorn.

Jupiter and Saturn: Yuletide Synergy

Capricorn is ruled by Saturn, the ringed planet of boundaries, limitations, and restrictions. Ancient astrologers assigned Capricorn to Saturn because it was the most distant planet they knew—which meant it was also the furthest removed from the warmth of the Sun. As a result, Saturn became a symbol of cold, critical consideration. (Oddly enough, Capricorn also came to be associated with the hard, cold realities of our physical life, which seem far removed from the pleasures of existence.)

During this year's Yuletide celebration, we find Saturn in Scorpio, where it's associated with the dark mysteries of life. As luck would have it, however, Saturn also happens to be in an easy, flowing trine with its partner planet, Jupiter.

Jupiter was the Roman equivalent of Zeus, the king of the gods. He was known for his jovial good nature and love of celebration. In fact, ancient astrologers called Jupiter the "Great Benefic," because the expansive planet brings bounty and prosperity wherever it goes.

Saturn, on the other hand, was known as the "Great Malefic"— because whenever he arrives on the scene, he starts making cuts and imposing limits and restrictions. It's no coincidence that Saturn is often depicted as a wizened old man with a long beard, a heavy winter cloak, and a harvest sickle.

At first glance, Jupiter and Saturn might seem to be polar opposites. When they're considered in combination, however, Jupiter and Saturn make a pretty good pair. Jupiter encourages us to dream big, and Saturn insists that we bring those ideas down to earth and turn them into reality.

Right now, Jupiter is in Cancer, the sign of home and family life. Because Jupiter is so expansive, the Great Benefic has a tendency to enlarge both homes and families.

Jupiter is also in an uncomfortable square with the rebel planet, Uranus. When those two planets are at odds, you might feel unusually inspired—but you can expect some surprises when it comes to any plans you've made for growth and self-development.

Jupiter is retrograde, which means it seems to be moving backward through space—at least from our perspective here on Earth. Jupiter has been backtracking through Cancer since November 7. During this period, which lasts through March 6, you would be wise to quietly observe the dynamics of your family relationships before broadcasting your intentions to your relatives, or to the world at large.

On January 5, you'll have a great opportunity to see Jupiter for yourself. On that night, the planet of luck and good fortune will make its closest approach to Earth. You'll be able to see it easily, shining big and bright and fully illuminated by the Sun.

Beautiful, Useful, or Loved

The first two weeks of January are an ideal time to consider the relationship between Saturn and Jupiter in your own life.

Recognize that Jupiter's blessings can be a curse if you hold on to them too tightly. You can't add new riches to a space that's already full. Instead, make a determined effort to release anything in your life that's outlived its usefulness.

If you're surrounded by clutter, you'll need to clear your physical space. If you're overwhelmed by your responsibilities, you'll need to clear your head. If you're like most people, you'll probably have to do a little of both—because our external reality is a reflection of our internal beliefs.

Invoke the spirit of Saturn, and set aside a definite time to clean, clear, and organize your space.

Personal organizers will often ask you to keep only those things that are beautiful, useful, or loved. If something in your house—or your heart—doesn't meet at least one of those criteria, pass it along to someone else or throw it away.

Planetary Positions

As the Sun begins its monthlong march through Capricorn, the planets continue their movement through the other signs of the zodiac, too.

On the Winter Solstice, we find the Moon in Leo, moving into Virgo and shifting our focus from a mood of frolic and playfulness into more serious expressions of responsibility and attention to detail.

Mercury has been in Sagittarius since December 4. Mercury usually concentrates on routine errands and day-to-day responsibilities. In Sagittarius, the sign of vast horizons, he's distractible and unfocused—but the confusion won't last long. Mercury will regain his footing on December 24, when he joins the Sun in earthy and goal-oriented Capricorn. He'll slip into Aquarius on January 11, where he'll be received like an honored guest. The messenger's communication skills dovetail perfectly with Aquarius' rule of technology. You can tap into that energy, too: if you've been waiting to write an important email or make an important call, this is the time.

On December 21, Venus goes retrograde, prolonging her passage through Capricorn. The goddess of love isn't usually so serious, but when she makes her way through the wintry sign, her focus shifts to long-term partnerships and affiliations. This is a good time for you to assess your own alliances. Can you depend upon those who are closest to you? Can they depend on you? Venus will go direct on January 31.

Mars crossed into Libra on December 7. It's not a good fit. Libra is Venus' domain—and Mars, the ancient god of war, is weak and uncomfortable in the land of love. That discomfort is heightened on the day of Yule, when Mars will be in a stressful square with the Sun. He'll be on his best behavior, but don't be surprised if his temper flares up.

Mars is also squaring off with Pluto, which could exacerbate any aggressive tendencies in the room—and Pluto will also be square Uranus, the planet of unexpected developments. If you find yourself forced into a surprise power play at your holiday gatherings, take a deep breath, count to ten, and consider whether or not you really need to engage.

After five months each of retrograde motion, Neptune turned direct in mid-November, and Uranus turns direct on December 17.

Pluto continues its long, slow march through Capricorn. It moved into the sign in 2008; it won't cross into Aquarius until 2024.

The Phases of the Moon

The last New Moon, in fiery Sagittarius on December 2, introduced a mood of adventure, optimism, and enthusiasm. The first quarter Moon, in watery Pisces on December 9, softened the mood with a note of spiritual connection and dissolving boundaries. The Full Moon in Gemini on December 17 offered clear navigation for clear communication and conversation. Soon, the third quarter Moon in airy Libra on December 25 will lend a note of grace to relationships, partnerships, and social associations.

While New Year's resolutions don't always have staying power, this year is different. An earthy New Moon in Capricorn on January 1 will help ensure that your resolutions are grounded and realistic— and a fiery first quarter Moon in Aries will supercharge your resolutions with a burst of determination.

The Full Moon in Cancer on January 15 will be a good time to focus on home and family, with a special emphasis on your relationships with mothers and grandmothers. It's also a good time to give extra attention to the children in your life. The third quarter Moon in watery Scorpio will lend powerful insights and understanding.

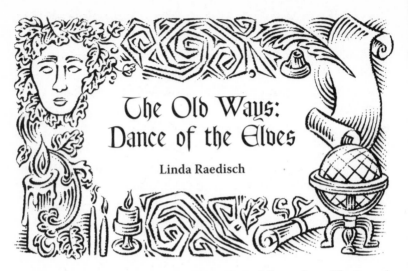

The Old Ways:
Dance of the Elves

Linda Raedisch

IT SEEMS LIKE EVERYONE'S getting married these days. If you and your partner have a Yule handfasting in mind, you might take a few tips from the elves, among whom such weddings are a longstanding tradition. Even if you're not about to tie the knot, the staging of an elfin wedding can add that extra sparkle to your Yule festivities. For both humans and elves, one of the highlights of the reception is, of course, the first dance.

Though he does not mention it in the context of a wedding, Olaus Magnus was the first to coin the phrase "dance of the elves" in 1555 in his *History of the Northern Peoples.* He borrowed the term from the Swedish peasants who used it to describe a circular rut within which the earth is either scorched or so compacted that no grass will grow. According to Olaus, the peasants shared his belief that these "elves" were the souls of those who had succumbed to the pleasures of the flesh and were thereafter doomed to dance in the night. Olaus was Sweden's last archbishop and perhaps a little out of touch with the actual beliefs of the Swedish countryside. Those who had named the dance of the elves were the same folk who left candles burning and set out bowls of porridge for the ancestral spirits on Christmas Eve and who poured offerings of milk into the cup-shaped depressions that those same ancestors had pecked into the boulders at the edges of their farms back in the Bronze Age. The elves and the ancestors were one and the same, and they were a tribe to be revered, not disdained.

Churchman that he was, Olaus may have equated the Swedish dance of the elves with "dance mania," a medieval urban legend that eventually spread throughout Europe and warned against enjoying oneself too much, especially at the old Pagan Yule. The earliest "account" of dance mania dates to 1012, when sixteen men and women performed a ring dance in a churchyard near Cologne during the Christmas morning service. When the priest stuck his head out the door and ordered them to come inside, they merely laughed at him. The priest then condemned them to dance for a whole year, whereupon their feet wore a deep ring in the churchyard.

Christmas was the time when the elves, too, were mostly likely to dance, or when mortals were most likely to catch them at it, for this was the season when the elfin community held its weddings. In Scandinavia, Midsummer was another popular night for elf/human weddings, for in summer, many teenage girls were sent to the mountains to look after the sheep. Left on their own, they might be easily spirited away as brides for eager elfin bridegrooms. But it was the tradition of the Yuletide Elf Dance that survived, just barely, into the twentieth century.

❧

In a typical tale of the late 1800s, a young Norwegian girl—we'll call her Gunhild Skjönne as in the Numedal version—went dancing on the Second Day of Christmas (December 26). She disappeared on the way home and nothing was heard of her again until the following Christmas when a tall, handsome young man appeared at the Skjönne residence and introduced himself as Gunhild's husband. Gunhild was well and about to give birth to her first child. She had been living with her new husband on a farm which, though not far away, was inaccessible by the usual roads. Judging by the young man's shiny black horse and the painted roses and gilt curlicues on the sleigh, Gunhild had made a good match. (Though her wedding is not described, other tales go on about the finely woven gowns, finger rings, crowns, and radiant, filigreed brooches, which the elves were capable of providing.) In response to the young man's invitation, Gunhild's mother packs up a few Christmas presents and departs with her son-in-law in a shiver of sleigh bells. There, on the well-appointed farm, Mistress Skjönne stays through Twelfth Night and witnesses the birth of her first half-elfin grandchild. Gunhild, we are told, is allowed to repay the visit, so long as she steers clear of the village pastor.

Gunhild's is a tale of elves and mortals living easily with one another. Less accommodating were the scores of Icelandic elves who crowded into the farmhouse on Christmas Eve to dance rings around the single maid or daughter left behind to look after the place while the rest of the family went to church. If only the girl could keep her eyes on her Bible, she would be all right. But if she joined in the dance, she might never be seen again. The Icelandic tale, "The Elves Dance on New Year's Eve," makes it clear that these elves have gathered for a wedding. Once they've assured themselves that the farmhouse is deserted, they spread rich cloths over the boards and set them with the finest silver. After the communal meal, the ceremony proceeds just as it would in a church, except that the vows must be exchanged before sunrise, and any non-elf caught spying will not escape to tell the tale. (In this case, the observer is watching through a crack in the paneled wall.)

✤

In the old days, it was not uncommon to pass a company of elves on the road or processing through one's living room. When those encounters became all too infrequent, people began dressing up as elves. The Yuletide Elf Dance survived for a time in the central Swedish "judge's dance" and the Smålander "angel dance." In the judge's dance, each dancer in the ring is confronted by a lighted taper and the statement, "If you dreamt of your dearest one last night/You'll smile upon the light." If the dancer allows a sheepish smile to spread across his or her face, that dancer must take the candle and circle widdershins outside the ring to taunt someone else.

The angel dance took place at the close of Christmas Eve dinner and signaled the arrival of the *julgubben*, one of the many Santa-like goblins who delivered the presents. The *julgubben* left as soon as he had passed out all the parcels, but the "angels" lingered on. Even after the human dancers withdrew, otherworldly spirits were believed to party on in the farmhouse until daybreak.

Meanwhile, Icelandic schoolteacher Holmfridur Arnadottir wrote in the early 1900s of the New Year's and Twelfth Night "fairy dances" of her childhood. These were led by a "fairy king" and "fairy queen" whose headdresses were reminiscent of the Nordic bridal crown, a chandelier-like work of art in gold, silver, or gilded brass from which hung all sorts of glittering pendants and trembling leaves to accentuate each inclination of the blushing bride's head. Holmfridur's fairies marched from the rocky cliffs down to the town's parade grounds where they dipped their flickering torches to light the bonfire. Round and round they danced and sang until the flames had consumed all, and the crowd repaired to the relative warmth of the dance hall.

This "fairy dance" appears to be a late incarnation of the *vikivaki* (possibly from Latin *vigilia*), costumed revelries that once took place throughout Iceland during the Christmas season. In many of the *vikivaki* dances, single men and women were paired off, and the lyrics of the accompanying songs left no doubt about what they were supposed to be doing with each other. Icelandic priests were already frowning on the *vikivaki* in the twelfth century, but the dances were still going strong in the seventeenth. In Stadarfell, Iceland, another bone of contention was the *Jorfa* dance, which went on all New Year's Eve and into New Year's morning. For some reason, this was when the parish babies were conceived.

It is interesting to note that half of Homlfridur's dancing fairies were always dressed in white—for purity, perhaps—and the other half in black, the most popular color for Scandinavian brides until the Victorian era. The color scheme brings to mind another famous case of white and black-clad women descending on an Icelandic farmstead, though it was not for a wedding. The episode comes from *Flateyjarbok* and takes place during the festival of winternights (mid-October). When three knocks are heard on the door, only the reckless Thidrand dares to answer it. As he steps out into the yard, nine women dressed in white come riding from the south. At the same time, nine women clothed in black sweep down on him from the north. It is not clear which company deals the mortal blow, but Thidrand does not survive the encounter. The author identifies the harridans as *disir*, female tutelary spirits, and suggests that they—or at least the black ones—were upset at having been stinted at the winternights sacrifice. The incident occurred as Iceland was poised on the brink of conversion, so one might suppose that the white-clad *disir* were riding out to proclaim the death of the Old Religion. We know so little about the *disir* or the festival of winternights that it is hard to say.

⚘

When the clock strikes twelve on the night of December 31, we will all become residents of an as-yet-undiscovered country. Like brides and bridegrooms, we will pass from one state of being to another. And like Gunhild Skjönne walking home from the dance, this is the time when we might most easily slip inside another world. Just as you can incorporate the magic of Yule into your nuptials, you might also inject the nuptials into your observance of Yule. Dress the dinner table in silver and white with white tapers and vases of pink tea roses or silk hydrangeas. When your guests are seated—chicken or fish?—raise your champagne flute and make a toast to Oberon and Titania. If you're not that ambitious, simply deck your halls in black and white in homage to those Icelandic *disir* and New Year's fairies. (Your neighbors already think you're weird, don't they?)

Wrap the presents under the Yule tree in wedding paper, or try your hand at making a Scandinavian bridal crown to hang from the ceiling or use as a centerpiece.

Besides the tinkling mini-chandelier, this might be a basketwork crown of pale birch roots for a Sami (i.e. "Lapp") bride or an explosion of gold wire, tinsel, and paper roses for the early twentieth-century Swedish country bride. Besides the crown, the medieval Swedish bride might also have worn an *ellakors* or "elves' cross," which was not a Christian cross at all but a piece of powerful magic. This pendant had to be forged from nine separate silver fragments that had been passed down through the family. There was no haggling with the silversmith over the price; when the *ellakors* was ready, the buyer had to pick it up and hand over the money without saying a word.

In addition to their power to protect, the crown, the *ellakors* and the other bits of bridal silver could transform even the most ordinary bride into an elfin princess, especially as she turned in the candlelight in the circle of the dance.

For Further Reading:

Arnadottir, Holmfridur. *When I Was a Girl in Iceland*. Boston: Lothrop, Lee, and Shephard Co., 1919.

Bjornsson, Arni. *Icelandic Feasts and Holidays: Celebrations, Past and Present*, translated by May and Hallberg Hallmundsson. Reykjavik, Iceland: Iceland Review, 1980.

Christiansen, Reidar, ed. *Folktales of Norway*, translated by Pat Shaw Iverson. Chicago: The University of Chicago Press, 1964.

Eskerod, Albert. *Swedish Folk Art*. Stockholm: Nordiska Museet, 1964.

Grydehoj, Adam. *The Dead Began to Speak: Past and Present Belief in Fairies, Ghosts, and the Supernatural*. www.islanddynamics .org. Accessed September 20, 2012.

Lindahl, Carl, John McNamara, and John Lindow, eds. *Medieval Folklore: A Guide to the Myths, Legends, Tales, Beliefs, and Customs*. New York: Oxford University Press, 2002.

Lindow, John. *Norse Myhtology: A Guide to the Gods, Heroes, Rituals, and Beliefs*. New York: Oxford University Press, 2001.

Simpson, Jacqueline. *Icelandic Folktales and Legends*. Berkeley, California: University of California Press, 1972.

Feasts and Treats

Dallas Jennifer Cobb

TONIGHT THE GODDESS LABORS, and after the longest, darkest night, she gives birth to the Sun God. From today forward the light will begin to return. A feast for this sabbat should be celebratory of the sun, and include lots of sun-shaped foods and a wide welcome to family and friends. Invoke love, peace, and positive energy, setting the tone for what is to grow in the waxing light. Plant the small seeds of change in relationships so you can continue to grow love, friendship, and loyalty. In addition to symbols of the sun, be sure to incorporate fire in your feast, decorating the table with tons of candles, radiating heat and warm, natural light.

Citrus Glazed Boneless, Skinless Chicken Breast

Citrus has always been a symbol of the sun, the same shape, and of course, a product of the sun's energy. This easy-to-prepare meal gives a tangy, zesty flavor to chicken and is accented by delicious wedges of grilled citrus.

Prep Time: 10 minutes
Cooking Time: 20 minutes
Serves: 4

2 tablespoons olive oil
1 cup orange juice
½ cup lemon juice
4 cloves of garlic, finely minced
2 teaspoons minced rosemary, fresh
2 teaspoons sea salt
4 boneless, skinless chicken breasts
2 oranges cut into quarters
2 lemons cut into quarters

Mix oil, orange juice, lemon juice, garlic, rosemary, and sea salt in a bowl. Marinate chicken for about 10 minutes. Heat a large, lightly oiled skillet. Pour chicken breasts and marinade in, cover and cook on medium for about 10 minutes. Turn chicken, and place orange and lemon quarters in pan, around it. Turn the heat up and "grill" chicken and fruit. Turn chicken a few times to keep coating it with marinade as it cooks. Serve chicken with grilled citrus and broccoli.

Broccoli with Slivered Almonds

I love to have colors on the plate at every meal, so I know I am providing a wide range of phytonutrients. Broccoli is high in antioxidants and almonds are rich in "good" fats, plus they provide a lovely contrast to the orange and yellow of the citrus. While it is dark outside, celebrate the return of the light with bright attractive food in an array of natural colors.

Preparation Time: 1 minute
Cooking Time: 4 Minutes
Serves: 4

1 head of broccoli, cut into florets
4 tablespoons of slivered, blanched almonds
1 lemon

Using a steamer, bring water to a boil, then add broccoli florets to steamer basket, cover and steam for 4 minutes, or until the color comes to a peak. Remove from heat. Sprinkle broccoli with almonds and fresh lemon juice before serving.

Ginger, Lemon, and Honey Tea

I love things that taste good and are good for me, too. This tea is especially helpful for dealing with colds and flu which are common at this time of year, but also the ginger stimulates the metabolism so that the body feels warm from the inside and adapts easier to the cold outside. Internalize the Sun God's energy with this warming drink.

Preparation Time: 3 minutes
Cooking Time: 20 minutes
Serves: 4

6 cups water
Fresh ginger, peeled (start with a thumb-length piece, to taste)
1 lemon
Honey

Set a saucepan on the stovetop and boil 6 cups of water. Chop the ginger in smallish chunks and add. Return to a boil for 10 minutes. Reduce to a simmer. Cut the lemon in half, squeezing the juice directly into the pot. Slice four rings of skin off of the squeezed halves, and discard the rest. Place the four rings in the pot. Serve tea in big mugs, with a lemon ring floating in each mug. Offer honey as a garnish.

Baked Brie with Cranberry Sauce

In France, dessert is often cheese and a bit of fresh fruit. For Yule, I love to splurge on a whole wheel of Brie, the shape so like the sun. When it comes out of the oven, warm, circular and glowing, I thank the Great Mother for giving birth to the Sun Child.

Preparation Time: 5 minutes
Cooking Time: 20 minutes
Serves: Many

One wheel of Brie cheese, 16 ounces
1 bag of cranberries
⅓ cup orange juice
¼ cup sugar
⅔ cup walnuts

Place Brie on an oven-safe platter, and bake at 350 degrees F for 15 minutes.

Rinse your cranberries and place in a saucepan with orange juice and sugar. Bring to a boil, stirring to "pop" the berries. Turn down to simmer.

Remove Brie from the oven. Use an oven mitt and gently touch the top of the wheel; it should feel soft and pliable under your hand. Pour cranberry sauce on top and bake for 5 more minutes. Garnish with walnuts, and serve warm with bread or crackers.

Remember, the platter is hot, so protect the table or you will end up with a permanent sun shape burned into the finish.

Crafty Crafts

Blake Octavian Blair

THE YULE SABBAT MARKS the Winter Solstice. Yule celebrates the returning of the sun, the triumph of the Oak King over the Holly King, and at a time when the trees are barren and the earth is asleep it promises the return of the green to the land. Yule's customs reach back into history for centuries and many of them are borrowed in modern Christmas celebrations. However, not all of our holiday customs are ancient, and it is perfectly acceptable to adapt modern additions for our own Yule celebrations. The exchange of holiday greeting cards, entering the winter holiday scene in the late 1800s, is one of these.

Our energetic connections to our family and loved ones (either by blood or by choice) are quite magickal when we think about it. Sending a holiday greeting card not only maintains that connection but also offers the opportunity to confer a blessing upon them.

Upcycled Solstice Greeting Cards

This craft allows us to not only honor our human relations, but also our relations to Mother Earth by reusing and "upcycling" old greeting cards and incorporating natural or recycled materials in the construction where possible. We will also talk about how an enchanted touch can be added with the addition of a little knot magick as well!

Supplies

Brown paper grocery bags, colored construction paper, or card stock (recycled if possible)

Old greeting cards received in past years

Holiday/seasonally themed rubber stamps and ink pad (optional)

Glitter (optional)

Crayons or colored markers

Glue

Ribbon

Paper hole punch

Scissors

Stationery envelopes ("invitation" size works best)

Instructions: The first step is to fold, cut, or trim your choice of paper so that the closed/folded card is the size you desire. You can make any size card you wish, however, I like to aim for a card size of around 4.25 by 5.5 inches, as this will fit into most commercially available "invitation" sized envelopes. To accomplish this, begin with a standard 8.5-by-11-inch sheet of printer paper. Folding a piece this size in quarters will give you one heavier-weight card of the desired size. If you fold it in half vertically, then cut across the middle halfway down, you will have two lighter-weight cards of the desired dimensions.

The next step is to look over the old greeting cards you received in past years for images you would like to utilize and reuse. Keep in mind the symbolism behind common imagery used in holiday cards, and choose images whose messages and corresponding blessings you wish to pass along to the recipients of your creations. Here are some examples of things you may look for:

Holiday trees and evergreens: When deciduous trees are bare and green grass is hard to find, evergreens remind us the earth is

still alive and that the green of the land will return. Decorated and lit trees add the symbolism of the return of the sun.

Santa Claus: Santa Claus takes many forms in cultures around the world and is said to be a composite based upon many figures in history. However, it can be said that his jovial nature, goodwill, and giving spirit serves as a great archetypal ambassador for the season in modern times. Pagans view him as Father Yule.

Doves: In modern times, doves are a symbol that many commonly associate with Christianity. They are indeed a symbol of peace, love, hope, and devotion in Christianity. However, they also have served as a symbol for the same qualities in other cultures throughout history. For example, Aphrodite the Greek Goddess of love, is associated with doves. In China, the dove is symbolic of longevity.

Deer: In general, deer represent innocence and the wilderness. Images of stags are images of the masculine divine, and relate to the returning sun, also a symbol of masculine divinity.

Glue the cut-out images into the cover of your cards as desired. You may choose a single image and add drawn accents of appropriate symbols, runes, sigils, colors, etc., or you may also make an entire scene of the upcycled card images. This project has a lot of freedom to let your creative muse run wild! There are limitless ways to add accents to your card. You can glue pine needles to your card, use glitter for accents, or cut out tinfoil to use for a cool wintry reflective pond, moon, or snowflake. Gluing strands of yarn on top of tree images as garland adds a nice textural element to the mix. Take the opportunity to make every card an original one-of-a kind piece of art.

Once you have the cover art of your card finished, let's add a little spellcraft element to this homemade holiday greeting. Take a hole punch and make a hole in the upper inside corner of the back of the card, near its crease. Cut a piece of ribbon six inches long. You might like to choose a color associated with the season such as green, red, silver, or gold. Now read the incantation below, and tie the knots in the ribbon, use the third knot as the knot that ties the ribbon to the card, through the punched hole—effectively performing the spell as you do.

With knot one, we honor the returning sun.

With knot two, blessings of health, peace, and prosperity flow to you.

By knot of three, may you share these blessings to everyone around thee!

Blessed be! So mote it be!

Now that you have carried out the spell, either write the incantation above inside the card or type, print, and glue it inside the card. Below it you can include your holiday greeting of choice such as "Blessed Solstice" or "Merry Yuletide!" You can dress up the inside with stamps, glitter, and artwork all you like. When finished, tuck the ribbon inside the completed card like a bookmark.

Slip the card into an envelope, address it, and send a little handcrafted holiday magick to your loved ones! These upcycled cards offer a greener way to participate in a traditional holiday custom. As the wheel continues to turn, by stopping to create these cards, you are taking the time to stop and pause for a few moments to honor and enjoy your connections to the important people who bring light your life. Merry Yuletide indeed!

Time to complete: 10 to 20 minutes per card (depending on elaborateness)

Cost: $10.00 to $15.00 (makes several cards)

For Further Reading:

Andrews, Ted. *Animal Speak: The Spiritual & Magical Powers of Creatures Great & Small.* St. Paul, Minnesota: Llewellyn Publications, 1993.

Tresidder, Jack. *The Complete Dictionary of Symbols.* San Francisco: Chronicle Books, 2004.

All One Family

Kerri Connor

WHILE SOME PAGANS CELEBRATE both Christmas and Yule (personally I can't think of anything much more Pagan than a giant magical elf with flying reindeer), some of them do only celebrate Yule. Whatever you celebrate, these two holidays do have several concepts in common, such as family get-togethers, the birth of an important son/sun, and even the giving of gifts.

While people tend to like both giving and receiving gifts, we also know how stressful shopping—picking out that special gift and then actually paying for it—can be. Shopping malls and stores are crowded. What if you pick out the wrong gift? It might be the wrong size, something they already have, or something they just plain don't like. And then there is the fact that gifts cost money. Even if you set limits on how much people can spend on gifts, it may be hard to stay within that budget or that budget may even still be too much for your wallet.

There are ways around the gift-giving fiasco that can bring back some of the fun and lessen some of the pain.

Gift-Giving Rules

We have instituted the one-gift-per-person rule by drawing names. At Samhain, everyone's name gets put into a hat. Each person will draw a name and then only buys a gift for that one person. We put an age limit on this. Perhaps you say once kids are in high school, get a job, or turn eighteen, then they are old enough to draw a name. You work out the age limit however you want. Of course, kids under that age limit may still get gifts from multiple people.

There are many ways to spice up gift giving on a budget. You can plan gift giving with different themes in mind. Perhaps your group decides everyone must find a gift that begins with the first letter of the recipient's name. Being creative and coming up with something different, something unusual, will show you put plenty of thought and imagination into someone's gift.

Perhaps your group decides all gifts have to be smaller than a shoebox, useful in some way, and to make it more interesting—purple. Again, you will need to put some time and effort into coming up with a gift that fits the description.

We have also gone with the more silly side and stuck with a white elephant kind of gift. Check your attic, basement, or local thrift stores. If you're looking for a white elephant, the worse the gift is, the better! Look for the most outrageous, oddballish items you can find. They will at least be sure to get a good laugh.

You can also do gifts inexpensively and still make them useful. Instead of buying gifts, have each person give something of themselves. Does someone need babysitting time and you have plenty of time to spare? Give them a couple of hours. Maybe give them time working in their garden, painting a room, or cleaning the garage.

Take pressure off of the price of the gift by focusing on the intent of the gift instead. Set a low dollar limit, such as $5, or come up with a homemade nature-themed gift instead. If you plan this early enough, you can spend some time out in the natural world looking for supplies such as nuts, seeds, bark, leaves, dried or pressed flowers, even things like antlers or animal bones can be used to make items. I had a friend find a leg bone from a deer once, his brother was able to sand and polish it into a gorgeous bone athame. You could make jewelry, a wreath or other wall hanging, some type of statue, decorations for a wood box, or other adornments for an altar. When people put a lot of thought and time into handmade gifts, they often become ones that are cherished for years to come. These type of gifts can be functional, practical, useful, spiritual, and beautiful all at the same time. Because they are made with natural items, these kind of gifts can help the receiver as well as the giver reconnect with elementals and other aspects of nature at the same time.

Intangible Gifts

Yule is also a great time for sitting around the fire and singing together. If you listen to some Christmas songs, you can pick out ones that have extremely Pagan verses. Many Pagan musical artists area also creating more and more Yuletide songs that can be sung at this time of the year. Don't be shy—create your own. You can start by using existing music and just rewrite the words for now, these are for your own private celebration. Look at "Greensleeves" and "What Child Is This?" Same music, two very different songs. You can make an annual competition out of it adding your favorites to your repertoire each year.

One of the greatest gifts you can give yourself, your family, your friends, everyone on your list any year is simply the gift of simplicity. Once upon a time, a simple orange was a wonderful present for children to find in their stockings on Christmas morning. While different stories tell of where the tradition and importance of a Christmas orange came from, perhaps it is time for us to celebrate each Yule morning with an orange of our own. An orange—a bright, round, golden orange fruit, that resembles the very sun itself. On Yule, the longest night of the year, what could be more promising than to wake up with our own little replica of the sun? Something that reminds us the sun is always there, even if it's a cloudy, cold, or blizzardy day. Something that reminds us the sun gives us life, as we peel our orange, break it into sections, and savor each juicy, energy-giving bite. Perhaps it is time we forget about electronics and games and whatever the latest craze is, and really remind ourselves, and our families, of the simpler things of life. Those things, that when it really comes down to it, are the only things that really matter at all.

❦

On this, the longest night of the year, it's important to remember what it was like for our ancestors. For those who did not have computers and video games—or electricity for that matter. They didn't have grocery stores or cars, and running water was the river on the outskirts of where their tribal village stood. This night that was so long could have been very scary for them as they awaited to see if the sun would rise the next morning and had to have faith in their gods that it would do so. Spend some time in the dark with your family this longest night. Give yourself a taste of what it was like for our ancestors and then be ready to be thankful for all that you have when the lights are able to go on again with the simple flip of the switch.

Now is the perfect time to work on teaching children all about appreciation. These exercises should help you get your point across.

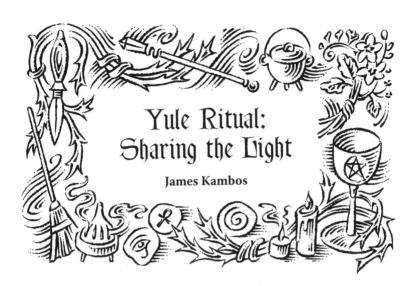

Yule Ritual: Sharing the Light

James Kambos

Items Needed

Pine garland—enough to mark out a ritual circle on the floor; this
will symbolize the wheel of the year and eternity

Four red candles, for each quarter

One Yule log, with three holes drilled in it to hold the candles

Three candles for the Yule log, one red placed in the left hole, one
white for the middle hole, and one green for the right hole

One gold candle to represent the Sun God

Altar cloth in red, white, or green

Incense: select something seasonal such as pine, cinnamon, or
frankincense, or use a simmering potpourri blend of orange
peel, cinnamon, and clove

Sprigs of holly (one for each person)

One cauldron

Pine cones (one for each person)

Items that have been collected for donation

A small Yule tree decorated with white lights and whatever else you
wish, surrounded with the donated items—to be lit at the end of
the ritual

Items for Cakes and Ale, or Your Celebration:

Sweets such as sugar cookies, snickerdoodles, or baklava

Beverages: could include eggnog, or a sparkling beverage

Small gift exchange if you wish

Music: I suggest any of the seasonal holiday songs and recordings
by Celtic artists, many of the traditional ones are Pagan in origin
and should fit into a Winter Solstice/Yule celebration

Preparing for the Ritual

A ritual for the Winter Solstice is both solemn and joyful. It's a time
to move from darkness to light, and from the shadow of death to rebirth. Although this sabbat is the second of the Pagan year, it is the
last sabbat of the modern calendar year. This being the case, I feel
that a Yule ritual should look to and remember our past (the darkness), as we move toward the future (the light).

This ritual is meant for a small group or coven and should be
performed after dark. Since this ritual is about sharing the light and
giving, I hope your group will collect toys, food, clothing, etc., to be
given to those in need. How you do this is up to you. You may select
a family/person you know, or you may get names from local agen-
cies. How you choose is up to you. Whatever you do, keep it organized and deliver the items in a timely manner. Naturally, this part
of the ritual will take place outside the sacred space you've created,
so as you deliver your gifts, feel the spirit generated by the ritual still
working with you.

For your ritual space, make a magic circle using a pine garland.
This will represent the eternal cycle of the seasons, the wheel of the
year, and life everlasting. In essence, it will be a large wreath. At
each of the four directions, place a red candle. The altar should face
East and be draped in red, white, or green. In its center set the Yule
log with the three candles placed as I described earlier on the items
list. The red candle will represent the blood of our ancestors, white
will symbolize new beginnings and green for eternity. In front of the
Yule log, set the gold Sun God candle.

The incense choices I suggest aren't only seasonal, they're also cleansing. Or you may choose the simmering potpourri, which is also cleansing, and the orange will represent the Sun.

The cauldron, holly, and pine cones can be set off to one side of the altar. At the appropriate time, each participant will use the holly during meditation. The pine cones will be used later in the ritual as a sign of new growth. Add any other seasonal decorations to the altar you wish.

I've also suggested using a small Yule tree decorated with white lights. This isn't always done, but I've included it for three reasons. First, you may want to place your donated items around it. Second, when the tree is lit after the ritual, it will symbolize the return of hope, and light to the world. And most important, evergreens were the first symbol of Yuletide to be venerated by ancient Pagans. So why not include a Yule tree in your ceremony? The tree needn't be in the magic circle, but should at least be in the same room.

For cakes and ale, the sweets I selected are some of my family favorites, but any sweet you desire is fine. Eggnog is a natural choice as a beverage, but sparkling cranberry juice would also follow the seasonal theme. The type of music for the occasion (if any at all) is completely up to you.

However, for me the Celtic Yule music seems to capture the spirit of the season. There are many selections available and they're all pretty good.

The Ritual

First, mark your magic circle by arranging the pine garland on the floor. Once the sacred space is ready, the group leader should stand before the altar facing East. All others should stand behind the leader. Together say:

On this night we stand between the realms of darkness and light. We have reached the depths of darkness, but no darkness is eternal. The light is about to return. The Goddess will give birth to the infant

Sun God. Just as the Goddess shares with us the light of her son, we wish to share this light with the world.

Now the leader, or someone who has been chosen to do so, will begin to light the quarter candles starting at the East and say:

Guardians of the East, help us strengthen the light of the returning Sun.

Light the South candle and say:

Guardians of the South, help us strengthen the light of the returning Sun.

Light the West candle and say:

Guardians of the West, help us strengthen the light of the returning Sun.

Light the North candle and say:

Guardians of the North, help us strengthen the light of the returning Sun.

The group leader will now light the incense. In silence he/she will carry the incense around the circle as they walk clockwise, and return to the altar.

Next the Yule log candles will be lit. The leader will first say:

A new cycle of life begins.

Moving from left to right, light the candles, and as each candle is lit say:

I light a candle for our ancestors. (red)
I light a candle for a new beginning. (white)
I light a candle for eternal life. (green)

After the Yule log candles are lit the leader will light the gold Sun God candle and say:

As the Divine light of the Infant Sun God grows,
that same light grows in each of us.
It's time for us to come out of the darkness.
Let us release any pain or fear that we've held onto from the past.
Let's meditate on what we wish to release.

At this point, everyone should approach the altar and receive a sprig of holly. Upon returning to their place, they may meditate on any issues they've carried with them over the past year. The holly is purifying and the points on the foliage will catch and prevent negativity from growing. When each person feels ready, they'll come to the altar and drop the holly into the empty cauldron in a symbolic gesture of letting go. Then everyone should pick up a pine cone to take with them. This will serve as a symbol of fertility and growth. The pine cone will remind everyone of this ritual every time they use it in their magic. The group leader will now raise the Sun God candle, and as this is done everyone will recite:

The dark season may obscure the Sun,
But its power will never be undone.
The infant Sun God is born again,
As his light grows, the darkness ends.
Beneath the light of his shining rays,
The great wheel turns as we find our way.

Everyone including the leader will hold hands as they stand around the circle and say:

This circle was cast in peace.
This circle is now released in peace.
We leave the circle in happiness on this night,
And wish to share our love and light.

The sacred part of the ritual is concluded. For safety, snuff out all candles.

Turn the lights of the Yule tree on and celebrate. Exchange gifts and play music if you want. Serve the sweets and beverages. And as soon as possible deliver the items you've collected.

To repurpose the materials used in this ritual you could decorate with the pine garland then burn it in a ceremonial fire. The holly should be cast into a ritual fire before New Year's as a banishing rite. The Yule log can be saved for next Yule, or burned. Its ashes may be used for protection or fertility magic. The Sun God candle and Yule log candles may be saved for next year or used in other magical rites. The pine cones can be used for growth and expansion spells.

The ritual may be over, but let the warmth and light of the season remain with you throughout the year.

Notes

Notes

Imbolc

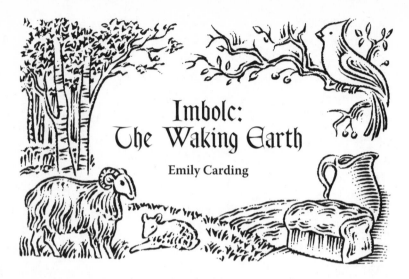

Imbolc:
The Waking Earth

Emily Carding

AFTER THE JOYOUS CELEBRATIONS of Yule have passed, it can seem a long, cold wait before we start to feel the sap rising and see the green shoots of life return to the land. The reborn Sun's growing strength is seen in the lengthening of days, but the presence of Sol Invictus, the Unconquerable Sun, cannot truly be felt until we reach the festival of Imbolc. Also known within different traditions as Bride or Candlemas (though some may see this as a concurrent yet different festival), Imbolc is the first of the four crossquarter festivals and is traditionally celebrated on the first or second day of February or whenever the first signs of green life return to the land. The etymology of the name *Imbolc*, which is of Irish-Gaelic origin, has been long disputed, meaning variously "ewe's milk" or "in the belly," both of which resonate with the meaning of the festival.

At this time of year, we start to feel the shift from the internalized contemplation of the dark days into a more active and creative state, a reflection of the outer world. After the long sleep of winter, just as the life that has been gestating in the womb of Earth begins to push through from the dark into the light, so the thoughts and ideas that have gestated in our own inner realm can be brought into the first stages of manifestation. The festival of Imbolc is an opportunity to consciously embrace these potential energies as well as to honor the divine forces behind them.

Brigit

As is hinted at in the alternate name of "Bride" for this celebration, the Irish goddess Brigit or Bride, who also has a closely connected Christianised form in St. Bridget, rules Imbolc. Indeed the whole month of February was traditionally associated with this highly significant goddess of smithing and poetry. Over recent years, she has taken on many of the qualities that were originally attributed to the Catholic St. Bride, so that she is most frequently honoured as a fire goddess. This seems appropriate for a time of year when the world moves from darkness into light and the fiery, solar power of the god grows stronger. She is also thought to rule over holy wells, a quality that is less well known, but one that is deeply significant to the celebration of her festival at the beginning of February.

The Holy Well

Here in Cornwall, which lies in the very southwest corner of England, we are known for our abundance of holy wells, as well as other ancient sacred sites scattered across the largely unspoilt landscape. When my family and I first moved down here, we had a very cold but beautiful winter. The snow covered the moors and frost glazed the bony trees with an ethereal shimmer. Toward the end of January, I had been told of a little-known holy well that was incredibly close to my home, a short five-minute walk across a field and down into the valley by the river, yet hidden from everyday view (a benefit of being off the trodden path). When I first met this well, I was overwhelmed with the magic of the place. Not only did it feel like the most wonderful blessing to have something so sacred practically on our doorstep, but on this beautiful crisp and clear day in the midst of icy winter, a single white flower was growing from the side of the well. There was a mist emerging from the well itself, and I realised that although it was not exactly a hot spring, the temperature of the water coming from within the earth was warmer than the air above, so steam was rising! The white flower was in fact wild garlic, which covers this land in the spring, but usually doesn't start flowering until April. I felt that I was witnessing a minor miracle.

It's no coincidence then, that traditional Cornish celebrations of the fire festival of Candlemas are held around the nearest holy well, as not only are the wells sacred to Brigit, as has already been noted, but they are the gateway through which life from the Under-world may reach the surface and vice versa. In Cornish traditional witchcraft, this energy is seen as a great dragon or serpent that is awakened with gifts and ceremony at this time of year, emerging from the wells and other openings into the earth to restore life to the land. Similar themes can be found recurring throughout world mythology, most notably in the Persephone myth of ancient Greece, where the young bride of Hades is permitted to return to the surface for half the year, resulting in the arrival of spring.

Initiation

Though in many Pagan practices the festival of Imbolc is much ne-glected, with more emphasis placed on the other crossquarter days of Beltane, Lammas (to a lesser degree), and Samhain, it has always held a strong personal resonance for me. Not only is my birthday in February, but my daughter Willow was also born in February and it was early February when I received my ordination as a priestess. Within Wicca it is a traditional time for initiation, and I would en-courage anyone to use this time to rededicate yourself to your path, consciously joining with the growing fiery energies both within and without yourself and the world. Although to undergo initiation ne-cessitates joining a coven or group, it is possible to self-dedicate and even write your own ceremony for this purpose if you follow a solo or individual path.

By dedicating (or rededicating) yourself or undergoing initiation at this time, you are aligning yourself with the energetic cycles of the land. Just as a seed planted in the ground grows in power whilst hidden safely in the womb of the land and is born into the light in these earliest days of spring, we too can ride on the current of this energy to bring our own wisdom from the darkness into the light. Each of us carries an inner flame at our center, a divine spark that connects us to all life within the web. When we attune ourselves to the cycles, we can feel this light growing within us, and with it, the power to manifest through Will. The long months from Samhain, through Yule, and approaching Imbolc should be a time of reflection, absorption, and contemplation. Over this span of time, we have the opportunity to choose not to wallow in our regrets and losses, but to honour them as lessons learnt and cut away all that hold us back. Tribute is paid to the ancestors, and we acknowledge their ever-present support as we move forward through the wheel of the year. Bad habits, old fixations, past wounds, even just silly mistakes can be swept away, so that by the time we get to Imbolc we can emerge just as the fresh green shoots do, leaving past baggage behind and shifting into an active, creative phase where we can step forward into the world in truth, love, and beauty.

Symbols and Traditions of Imbolc

The colours of Imbolc are green and white, symbolising the first green shoots emerging from the frozen, snow-covered landscape. Echoing this colour symbolism, snowdrops are the plant-life most associated with Imbolc, as it is around the beginning of February when they flower in the UK and Europe. Some Pagans who prefer to live by the cycles of the evident world around them rather than fixed dates, choose to celebrate Imbolc around the day when they first see the snowdrops flowering, which can vary annually between mid-January to mid-February. Ivy and violets are also associated with this festival and you may wish to use these plants on your shrine or altar for Imbolc.

British folk traditions of Imbolc include welcoming the Goddess into the home or heart of the community in the guise of a green-cloaked maiden. Under her dark green cloak, she wears a dress of white to symbolise the new life that is emerging. She carries a white candle, again a symbol of the growing light within the land. From this candle, all the candles of the different households of the community are lit, bringing the light and blessings of the Goddess into each home.

It is also traditional at Imbolc to offer the last seeds of the harvest to the gods and spirits of the land in the hope for good harvests in the year to come, but also as symbols of our hopes and plans in their latent form, ready to grow in potential with the growing light of the year ahead.

As Candlemas, which is celebrated within both Pagan and Christian traditions, it is a customary time to bless the candles that you will use in the year ahead, anointing them with appropriate magical oil and singing or chanting a blessing into them. These may also be given as special gifts to loved ones.

A Time of Potential

It is worth considering that it is nine months from the union of the Lord and Lady at Beltane to around the time of the festival of Imbolc, so there may be an influx of Pagan babies at this time of year, if people have had enjoyable Mayday celebrations. In this, we see that our celebrations are far more than a set of rituals and symbols. They are firmly aligned with the very fabric and cycles of life.

What child do you hope to bring into the world this Imbolc? What inspiration have you nurtured in the dark womb, waiting for its chance to be born? As the first lambs of the season take their first tentative yet joyous steps into the world, so the path opens up before us to take the first steps toward a bright and productive future.

Cosmic Sway

Corrine Kenner

ON THIS HOLIDAY, AS we eagerly await the change of seasons, we find Uranus living up to his reputation—at odds with almost every other planet in the sky.

As a result, you can expect the rebel planet to provoke you, too. He'll try to prod your assumptions, poke holes in your beliefs, and prompt you to make changes in your own life and in the world around you.

Does that come as a surprise? It shouldn't. Wherever Uranus pops up in an astrological chart, you can expect the unexpected.

Understanding Uranus

Uranus is the planet of revolution and rebellion. It's the planetary ruler of Aquarius, so it rules radical ideas and people, as well as uprisings and upheavals.

Imbolc, of course, is commemorated when the Sun is in Aquarius, the sign of social groups of causes.[1] The Sun's passage through

---

The eight sabbat holidays are astrologically linked to the Wheel of the Year. We celebrate half of them—Ostara, Midsummer, Mabon, and Yule—at the start of each new season, when the Sun moves into cardinal signs Aries, Cancer, Libra, and Capricorn. (Those dates also correspond with the solstices and equinoxes.) We mark the crossquarter

Aquarius heralds a monthlong focus on friendship, interpersonal connections, and innovative thinking.

This year, as we celebrate Imbolc, Uranus will be in an uncomfortable square with Venus, Jupiter, and Pluto, as well as an awkward semisquare with Saturn.

Squares and semisquares are always tense, because they represent forces that work at cross-purposes. In this case, Uranus will be at odds with Venus, the goddess of love and beauty. She wants nothing more than to float blissfully on clouds of affection and desire—but Uranus will force her to look carefully at any object of her desire. Little things about her beloved will rub her the wrong way. When Venus is forced to think with her head, and not just her heart, you might find that you also question your own judgment in the realm of relationships.

Uranus will have the same effect on Jupiter. The Great Benefic wants to shower his children with gifts and good fortune—but first, Uranus will force him to slow down, consider whether those gifts are deserved, and decide if they'll do any good. When that happens, you might find yourself reassessing where you put your time and energy, too.

Uranus' square with Saturn, the ringed planet of limitations, restrictions, and boundaries, brings foundational principles into question. Left to his own devices, Saturn wants to conserve his strength, consolidate his power, and maintain the status quo. Uranus, the rebel planet, will force him to question the very bedrock of his beliefs and operating principles. The interaction could even lead to an overthrow of any establishment that has outlived its usefulness.

Simultaneously, Uranus will find himself in an almost perfect conjunction with the Moon. Both planets are in Aries, the sign of independence and self-determination. That combination can be exhilarating—or terrifying. You'll have total and complete freedom over your own feelings and emotions—but you'll also be expected

---

days—Beltane, Lughnasadh, Samhain, and Imbolc—when the Sun reaches the halfway point of the fixed signs Taurus, Leo, Scorpio, and Aquarius.

to accept the corresponding responsibility for your actions. For a few brief moments, the conjunction might seem overpowering—but ultimately, it could be liberating.

Question Your Beliefs

Use this holiday to reassess the values and beliefs you hold dear. Start by listing ten truths you hold about yourself. Simply write them down, in the form of a numbered list. Write freely and openly, starting with, "I believe…" Be honest. No one needs to read the list but you.

With Uranus' powerful energy on your side, some of the beliefs that pop up will surprise you. Are they positive or negative? Do they help you, or hinder you? When you see them in black and white, do they ring true?

You can choose to reaffirm the values and beliefs that work for you, or reject those that hinder your growth. In that case, like Uranus, you can declare your independence from negative patterns of thought.

Planetary Positions

While the Sun is in Aquarius, three other planets are moving through Pisces: Mercury, Neptune, and the Moon. Their placement in the watery sign suggests an emphasis on deep spiritual connections and intuitive understanding.

Mercury moved into Pisces on January 31. On Imbolc, it makes a close conjunction to Neptune. The connection could help dissolve the boundaries between the head and the heart—but that dissolution can also lead to confused thinking.

Any possible confusion is compounded by the fact that Mercury will enter one of its infamous retrograde periods on February 6. When Mercury is retrograde, it's not uncommon for communication to break down. The messenger planet will continue to move backward for the rest of the month, until it starts moving forward again on February 28. During that time, Mercury will even make a return visit to Aquarius, so he'll be spreading confusion across two signs. Mercury won't make it back into Pisces until mid-March—just in time for St. Patrick's Day, which could put even more of an emphasis than usual on mind-altering activities.

Venus is currently in Capricorn, but her work here is almost done. She turned direct at the end of January, and now the goddess of love and affection is looking forward to her movement into Aquarius on March 5. At the moment, she's in an uncomfortable square with Uranus, but Venus moves quickly—and in a few days, she'll be in Uranus' realm, Aquarius, the sign of social groups and causes, and Venus will be far more comfortable when she can relax and socialize with friends. At the moment, however, she's consolidating her power in a conjunction with Pluto.

Both Venus and Pluto are 180 degrees from Jupiter, in an opposition that opens channels of good fortune. They're in an uncomfortable square with Uranus. While Venus moves quickly, sliding gracefully out of the awkward situation, Pluto and Uranus will be locked in the square for the foreseeable future.

Mars is in Libra, the sign of marriage and partnership. It's not a comfortable fit, because the ancient god of war is weak and debilitated in the land of love.

Jupiter continues to move backward through Cancer, square Uranus.

The Phases of the Moon

A rare Blue Moon in Aquarius on January 30 initiated a period of friendly camaraderie and fellowship. That affectionate energy will feel even more stable on February 6, with a first quarter Moon in Taurus. Passions will reach a fever pitch on February 14, when a Full Moon in Leo lights the night sky on Valentine's Day. Expect the heart to wander, however, when the waning crescent Moon moves into Sagittarius on February 22.

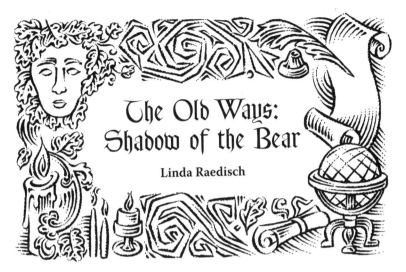

The Old Ways: Shadow of the Bear

Linda Raedisch

TERRIFYING. CUDDLY. ENEMIES. BROTHERS. Humans have long been conflicted about bears, especially when we're eating them. Chances are you've never tasted bear meat, but if you can trace your roots to anywhere within the Northern Hemisphere, then you can be sure you're descended from people who not only ate bears but who slept in their skins and wore their teeth and claws around their necks. They rendered and combed the bear's subcutaneous fat through their hair, mixed the fat with red ochre and slathered it over their bodies. Most importantly, they worshipped the bear.

Punxutawney Phil, the Pennsylvania groundhog who, each February 2, uses his shadow to measure the remaining days of winter, was preceded by the Candlemas Bear, who announced the arrival of spring in the Old World by either looking for his shadow or releasing a burst of flatulence into the snowy woods. In southern France, the eventual scarcity of Eurasian Brown Bears led latter-day devotees of the Candlemas Bear cult to replace the real thing with a man in a bear costume. In Germany, the badger was promoted to the bear's station. When Germans arrived in the New World, they allowed the more affable groundhog to take the badger's place.

A handful of shadowy episodes in the literature of the Western world give us some idea of the powerful impression the bear made on our ancestors. The one with which I grew up is the Grimms' fairy tale, "Snow White and Rose Red," in which two virtuous young sisters befriend a large bear. After spending the winter on their hearth rug, the bear disappears into the forest to protect his treasure from the wicked dwarves who are just emerging from the thawing crust of the earth. The only clue the girls have that this is no ordinary bear (in addition to his ability to speak and his disinclination to ravage their pantry) is the glint of gold Snow White spies when their friend accidentally tears out a hunk of fur on the door knocker on his way out. Of course, it turns out that he is actually a man under a curse, and by the end of the tale he is able to step out of his bearskin, a prince all dressed in cloth-of-gold. There is a double wedding for Snow White, the golden prince, his brother and Rose Red, the happy ending made possible, no doubt, by the fact that at no point in the story does anyone, much less his beloved Snow White, partake of the prince/bear's flesh.

☙

The much older love story of Bera and Björn, contained in chapters 18 to 22 of *The Saga of King Hrolf Kraki*, does not turn out so well. Bera (whose name means "she-bear") is a fetching commoner. Björn (whose name means "he-bear") is a prince of the Norwegian highlands. Despite the difference in their stations, Björn and Bera hit it off right away. Before they can plan the wedding, however, Björn runs afoul of his stepmother, Queen Hvit. Queen Hvit turns out to be a witch, which is not surprising because she comes from Finnmark in the north. When Björn rejects her amorous advances, Hvit turns him into a bear and compels him to prey upon his father's flocks, which situation inevitably results in a bear hunt. Björn is able to revert to human form only at night. As a man, then, he is able to consummate his relationship with Bera, impregnating her with triplets and counseling her not to eat his flesh when he is killed but only to take the ring that she will find under his skin when he is butchered.

All this comes to pass, with the evil Queen Hvit forcing Bera to swallow two morsels of her lover's flesh at the celebratory feast. Consequently, Bera's first two sons are both monstrous in form and somewhat lacking in character. It is the third son, Bodvar, who inherits the ring as proof of his royal parentage (along with a bear's claw on one toe, according to another version of the story) and who avenges his father by thrusting a bag over Queen Hvit's head and beating her to death—the most effective method of killing witches from Finnmark.

⚜

It is to Finnmark and points east that we must now proceed for a more vivid glimpse of the ancient bear cult. Many are the tales of half human/half bear children roaming the Scandinavian forests and of "Lapp" or Sami men who could transform themselves into bears at will. The Old Norse stories make it clear that the line between man and bear was often indistinct, but for the West Siberian Ostyaks and Voguls, peoples distantly related to the Sami, Finns, and Hungarians, the bear was nothing less than a god. For them, the hunting, butchering and consumption of the bear were sacred acts governed by specific rituals. After a feast of bear meat, which was as much a religious observance as a meal, the bear's skeleton was painstakingly put together again and interred, ready to be reanimated by the sky god Num-torem. Only the skull was kept back. This was either placed in the crotch of a tree or mounted on a stake.

At one time, the sight of a bleached white bear skull resting on a forked branch would have been a familiar one all along the circumpolar rim. The Ainu, who now reside principally on the island of Hokkaido, had been enacting such "bear-sending" ceremonies ever since they first arrived on Sakhalin, the Kuriles and the isles of Japan thousands of years ago. They placed the slain bears' skulls on forked sticks within the *nusa*, an outdoor altar, while encouraging the freed god's spirit to return the mountains from which it had descended. By the eighteenth century, what had once been a simple ritual of thanksgiving had evolved into the dramatic centerpiece of Ainu society and culture. The *iyomante* or Bear-Sending Ceremony, began with the capture of a newborn cub early in the spring. Back in the village, the cub, that is, the *kimun-kamuy* or "mountain god," was indulged as if it had been a human child. The elderly women of the community were officially in charge of its upbringing, but young mothers were enlisted as wet nurses and took over much of the cub's care, providing it with toys, playmates, and choice morsels. Once the cub had passed its first birthday, it became more difficult to manage and had to be restrained either in a cage or with long poles. The *iyomante* was at hand.

After much singing, storytelling and the firing of blunt-tipped "flower arrows," the young *kimun-kamuy* was taken from its cage and "put to sleep" by being choked between two logs. At this time, the younger women of the village were confined to their houses, ostensibly because their bodies were ritually impure, but also, perhaps, so they would not have to witness the brutal end of the cub they had nursed along with their own babies. For the Ainu, however, there was nothing cruel about the *iyomante*; it was an occasion of great joy for both the cub and the humans involved. The flesh of the bear—which after all, was not a bear at all but a god in bear's clothing—was transformed into a delectable feast while the head and skin were adorned with *inaw*, sacred shaved-wood sticks, and dressed in an appliquéd Ainu-style kimono. Inside the fence enclosing the *nusa*, the bear's remains were presented with gifts of saké, tobacco, dried salmon, and porcelain and lacquer bowls. All these were placed in the *nusa* so they could be "beamed" to the mountain god's home. There, the *kimun-kamuy* and his fellow gods would enjoy them at a party of their own. Hopefully, the *kimun-kamuy* would speak well of his human hosts. For themselves, the humans retained possession of the bear's skull which would adorn the *nusa* during future ceremonies.

Curiously, at the time the Bear-Sending Ceremony was evolving into the most important festival of Ainu cultural life, bear meat was no longer an Ainu staple or even a significant source of nutrition. Why, then, did the bear remain foremost among the Ainu gods? It could be because the *kimun-kamuy* dwelt at the headwaters of the salmon rivers and thereby controlled an important food source. It could also be that, of all the creatures the Ainu were used to hunting, the bear most resembled a man.

❦

For the past twenty-five years here in the Watchung Mountains of northern New Jersey, the American Black Bear has been appearing on a fairly regular basis. When the bears first started to make their presence known, the powers that be responded with their own version of the Bear-Sending Ceremony: each ursine offender was shot with a tranquilizer dart, loaded into a pickup truck, and driven to the mountains of Pennsylvania. My own community has come a long way since then. Two years ago, when the police put in a call to Fish and Wildlife because a young male cub had decided to tour the local schoolyards, the response was, "Well, is it bothering anybody?"

In the end, the bear was allowed to shuffle off to parts unknown— possibly the nearby Great Swamp Wildlife Refuge—but not before someone had snapped a picture of him gazing calmly out of a tree. The local paper ran the photo on the front page. Snuggled in the tree, the handsome young rascal wears a half-smile that seems to say, "We're here. Don't fear. Get used to us."

I clipped the photo and kept it on the refrigerator door for the duration of the summer, taking care to remind my daughter of the three most important rules concerning black bears: running is pointless, playing dead is also a very bad idea, and the worst idea of all is to carry fresh lox and bagels through a wooded area. In fact, your best chance when encountering a black bear is to speak in your most stentorian voice while walking slowly backward. The bear will decide you're just too much trouble and saunter off to the nearest dumpster. (Or, he'll swipe the bagel out of your hand, along with however much of you comes with it, and *then* saunter off.) The important thing is that you both get home safely to tell your stories. If the sun happens to be shining, and if you still have your wits about you as you watch him go, you might notice that the shadow of a bear looks very much like the shadow of a man.

For Further Reading:

Byock, Jesse L., translated and with an introduction. *The Saga of King Hrolf Kraki*. London: Penguin Books, 1998.

Fitzhugh, William, and Chisato O. Dubreuil, eds. *Ainu: Spirit of a Northern People*. Washington D.C.: Arctic Studies Center, National Museum of Natural History, Smithsonian Institution.

Griffin, Robert H. and Ann H. Shurgin, eds. *The Folklore of World Holidays*. Farmington Hills, MI: Gale Research, 1999.

Leach, Maria, editor. *Funk & Wagnalls Standard Dictionary of Folklore, Mythology, and Legend*. New York: Harper & Row, 1972.

Lindahl, Carl, John McNamara, and John Lindow, eds. *Medieval Folklore: A Guide to the Myths, Legends, Tales, Beliefs and Customs*. New York: Oxford University Press, 2002.

Sideman, Belle Becker, editor. *The World's Best Fairy Tales*. Pleasantville, NY: The Reader's Digest Association, 1967.

Feasts and Treats

Dallas Jennifer Cobb

WITH WINTER STORES NEARLY depleted at this time of year, our ancestors made meals from what remained at hand—dry goods, grains, preserves, and salted meats. Honor the moon with moon-shaped pancakes, and celebrate the "light in the darkness" by smothering those pancakes in dark maple syrup and preserves. Indulge in a sweet feast this morning as you honor fore-parents, invoke the Goddess, who not long ago gave birth to new life, and now mindfully nurtures herself. Take time to nurture yourself and give thanks for "another sweet"—the promise of spring, and the near end to winter.

Alita Dolcia

Pancakes are common to almost every culture, with slight variations in consistency, spices, and sweetness. Easy to prepare, they are versatile, combining with savory toppings and ingredients, or with sweet. In ancient Rome, pancakes were called *Alita Dolcia*, "another sweet." At this sabbat, we remember the Goddess who is recovering from giving birth. She can now turn her energies back to nurturing herself, the earth resurrecting into "another sweet" growing cycle.

Preparation Time: 15 minutes
Cooking Time: About 5 minutes to make 3 large pancakes
Serves: 3 people

1 cup of flour (I like oat, but you can use wheat, buckwheat, or spelt)
1 teaspoon baking powder
¼ teaspoon baking soda
1 egg
¾ cup milk (or substitute yogurt for thicker, fluffier pancakes)
2 tablespoons oil or melted butter or fat

Sift together the dry ingredients in a large bowl, then add wet ingredients and stir with no more than 25 strokes, so there are still a few lumps left in the batter. Let sit for 5 minutes while you heat an oiled, cast iron skillet (like the cooking griddles of old) on medium heat. It's hot enough when a drop of water sizzles.

Pour one-third of the batter into the pan, making a large circle. Let cook until batter bubbles, and when the bubbles pop they form a crater. Turn once and let the other side cook for about 2 minutes. Place pancake in centre of plate. Serve with Canadian bacon, maple syrup, and seasonal preserves. Recipe makes 3 large pancakes.

Peameal Bacon

Made from boneless pork loin, cured in brine, and rolled historically in ground yellow peas, currently in cornmeal, this healthier version of breakfast meat is also known as Canadian bacon. Hung in the storehouse, Peameal bacon would last the winter, the ground peas drawing the moisture out of the meat and preserving it. With the salt that came from the brine, the taste of Peameal bacon contrasts with the sweetness of pancakes.

Ideally, you can prepare your Alita Dolcia batter, and while it sits, get your Peameal in the pan. While it cooks, tend to your pancakes.

Slice Peameal ⅛-inch thick. I recommend 2 slices per person. Fry at medium heat for 5 minutes, turn, cover, and simmer on medium-low heat for 3 more minutes.

Milky Masala Chai

As a sabbat that incorporates light and dark, bitter and sweet, masala chai is the perfect drink for Imbolc. This traditional drink from India incorporates stimulating spices, black tea, and milk, and is a perfect morning pick-me-up. The inclusion of black pepper makes this drink a "warming" drink that helps elevate the metabolism. Containing protein, vitamin D, and calcium, milk provides nutrition and often stimulates strong associations with comfort and security and was a traditional ingredient at Imbolc, which literally translates to "ewe's milk." Sip, and celebrate taking care of yourself, and the sustenance of new life.

Preparation time: 1 minute
Cooking time: 8 Minutes
Serves: 4

2½ cups water
1 whole star anise
1 stick of cinnamon
1 pinch black pepper
4 cardamom pods, cracked open or crushed
4 orange pekoe or English breakfast tea bags
2 cups whole milk
¼ cup sugar (optional)

Put water on to boil in a saucepan. Crack the cardamom pods, then add them, the tea bags, black pepper, cinnamon, and star anise to the water and bring to a boil again for 3 or 4 minutes until it is very dark. Turn heat down and add milk, watching the light and dark combine. Heat until steaming, then strain and serve with sugar to taste.

Maple Syrup and Seasonal Preserves

Staples in northern households year-round, jars of preserves provide us with sweet treats throughout the barren winter. Raid your pantry and find some preserves to serve with pancakes. Alternatively, you can use low-sugar jam or frozen berries.

Maple syrup, produced from the sap of the sugar maple tree, had been used as a sweetener long before we had access to sugar. Filled with the nutrients manganese and zinc, maple syrup is tasty and healthier than sugar.

Serve these two with warm pancakes and Peameal bacon.

Crafty Crafts

Blake Octavian Blair

IMBOLC FALLS ON FEBRUARY 2 in most traditions, when in many places winter is still in full force and for some, it is at its coldest. However, the holiday brings with it the inspiration and promise of the growing light as we near spring. This is the time of year when the signs of this increased light tend to become noticeably visible and provides us a wonderful time for introspection and to take care of ourselves with a bit of healing work. The Celtic goddess Brigid is widely associated with Imbolc for her connections to healing, light, and the transformative element of fire.

For all the beauty to be found during this quiet time upon the earth, the winter cold can bring about or exacerbate aches, pains, and old injuries for many people. Perhaps you have an old back injury, a weak knee that is rearing its ugly head, or you strained yourself by pushing your snow-shoveling efforts a little too far. Have no fear, this sabbat craft is just the ticket as it is designed to call upon and honor the themes of healing and the element of fire in the form of healing warmth to honor this holiday and the goddess Brigid.

Healing Rice Bags

Fire is often viewed as an element of purification, cleansing, healing, and manifestation. However, fire can be represented in many forms aside from the literal burning flame. These representations include our ever-present electric light bulb, crystal, plant, and animal beings with solar and fire elemental associations, and the quality of heat. The gentle heat of these healing rice bags will provide a soothing touch to ailing bodies while invoking the fires and light of Imbolg. One advantage these bags have over the conventional electric heating pad is that the rice bags more easily conform to the area of the body you wish to treat. The supplies are simple and you may already have many of them around your home.

Supplies

Fabric (scraps work great, and a half a yard should make at least a few bags)

Dry, uncooked white rice (do not use instant or minute rice)

Dried herbs with healing properties and aromas

Essential oils

Needle

Thread

Funnel (optional)

Instructions: Cut two pieces of fabric to desired size and shape. A good all-purpose size is about six inches square, however, feel free to custom size one to fit any desired area of the body you'd like to apply the heated bag to for relief. I prefer to use 100 percent cotton fabric as it is hypoallergenic for most and allows the bag to breathe more easily than synthetic fabrics. Don't forget to incorporate your color-magick skills and other symbolism into your fabric choice as well! Purple is a favorite of mine and is a wonderful healing color choice with a very soothing energy. Fabrics with prints that include animals you associate with healing are also perfect. For example, snakes are well grounded as they travel with their bellies to the Earth and they shed their old skins that no longer serve them. Butterflies are also fun as they represent transformation! Choose something that calls to you. If your skills are beyond basic with needle and thread, you can also stitch or embroider a healing rune or symbol onto the side of the bag. (If your skill level with a needle and thread is less than awesome, a magic marker works great too!)

Stitch the two pieces of fabric together inside out with your needle and thread. For now, only stitch up three sides, leaving the fourth open to allow you to stuff the bag. Only basic sewing skills are necessary—it need not be fancy or perfect. Next, turn the bag right-side out through the fourth unstitched side.

Gather your rice, herbs, and oils desired for stuffing materials. Here are some ideas for essential oils and dried herbs along with their magickal properties:

Lavender: healing, peace, and purification

Orange: solar/fire energy, its scent uplifts mood

Mint: healing, its scent is both energizing and many report it relieves headaches

Vanilla: helps to restore lost energy, has a very loving vibration, and its scent is very soothing

Valerian: purification and aids in sleep (Note: the smell of valerian can be quite strong, so use a very small amount in proportion with a more pleasant aromatic oil/herb.)

Begin by filling each bag half full with dry rice. Proceed to add desired amounts of each herb and/or oil you wish to include. I suggest using 5 to 10 drops of any particular essential oil as a baseline. You just want enough to scent the bag, not to saturate it. The contents of the bag should still be relatively dry after the oil is mixed in. Adding a tablespoon or two of each dried herb you wish to include should be more than enough. You want to be careful not stuff the bag too tightly. You want to leave some room for the ingredients to shift around to allow it to conform to the body. As you add each ingredient, hold it in your hands before adding it and meditate on the qualities of each ingredient, and your intent for it as part of this bag.

When you are finished with the filling process, it is time to grab your needle and thread and stitch your healing rice bag shut. Shake the bag gently, as this will help to further mix the filling. This completes the technical assembly of the bag.

How to Use

Simply put your rice bag in the microwave for 1 to 3 minutes. Test the heat of your rice bag before applying it to the body to prevent skin burns, as the rice can become very hot, very quickly. The bag should heat up, but remain dry. The bag should not contain enough moisture to cook the rice. If the bag should ever become damp, soggy, wet, or smell rancid, dispose of the bag and make a fresh one. Do not apply rice bags directly to broken skin or over open wounds. As with any complementary or alternative therapy, it is wise to consult medical professionals before using heated rice bags on those who are pregnant, very young, or elderly. It is best to be sure there will be no adverse effect as these persons can have extra sensitivity to heat therapies. Also, rice should never be eaten after it has been used for heat therapy.

Important: The bags are only meant for use on humans and not animals.

Healing rice bags are not only handy to keep around the home for when the need arises, but they also make wonderful gifts for loved ones with chronic ailments or those share an interest in natural home remedies. I suggest conducting a simple blessing ceremony for your bags upon the completion of their construction. Simply gather the bags together in a bowl or basket and place upon your altar or hearth. Light a candle on your altar in honor of Brigid and Imbolg. Visualize the healing light from the candle surrounding yourself, the basket of bags, and the altar area. Ask Brigid to lend her light, warmth, and energy from her healing fires to bless your bags and those who will use them.

Time to complete: 45 to 90 minutes depending on number of bags and sewing speed. (Hand sewing will add time as opposed to machine sewing.)

Cost: $5.00 to $20.00 for a few bags (depending on how many of the supplies you already have on hand and what herbs and oils you wish to use).

References:

Cunningham, Scott. *Cunningham's Encyclopedia of Magical Herbs.* St. Paul, Minnesota: Llewellyn Publications, 1985.

All One Family

Kerri Connor

IMBOLG, IS USUALLY CELEBRATED as the time of year to start waking up the earth, to start calling the sun back to warm the earth, to call the Goddess back to spread vitality and fertility. Many of you may still be buried under several feet of snow. This "awakening" of the earth may not happen where you live for another month or two. Just as the groundhog usually tells us, there are always six weeks until spring.

Many people may be getting cabin fever, and what they would give for a day warm enough to open the windows and air out the house!

Though most often you won't be able to go out and start planting a garden, Imbolg is a great time to start blessing seeds and getting plants started that will later be transplanted into the ground. Small shelving-unit greenhouses can be purchased cheaply ($20) and placed in front of a large window to give those plants a great start. Even people without yards can do container gardening on decks, balconies, or porches. Tomatoes, peppers, and even lettuce can be grown in close quarters. This is a great project for kids. They can each be given their own containers—empty milk cartons work great and can also be cut and decorated by each child—to start their own plants from seeds. These plants and the produce grown from them can then be shown later in the year at your own Lughnasadh country fair.

It's also a great time to start making a list for what you would like to grow inside of yourself—what you would like to accomplish over the next year. During the dark half of the year, we often work on our internal selves, so we have a good idea of which goals to work on during the light half of the year. These plans are somewhat similar to what some people come up with back in December for New Year's resolutions, yet with the backing of your own spirituality, they tend to be much more successful! This is a great way to explain to kids that we never stop growing or learning. Everyone will always have things they need to work on, or things they want to accomplish in their life.

Use this time to start a scrapbook of your goals (or just a notebook if you like). Even small kids can do this, though you may help them define their dreams to something reasonbly attainable. Kids may include goals such as grades, reading a certain number of books, making a sports team, or joining a club. Younger kids may want to learn to dress themselves, tie their shoes, or how to read. Make sure they have some type of spiritual goals as well. Maybe they would like to start a yoga or meditation practice. Maybe they are involved in a spiritual scouting program and would like to complete certain badges. You may choose for each person to do their own scrapbook, or you may do one for the entire family. Perhaps you do a family scrapbook for more public goals and a private notebook for each person for their more private goals. Whatever the goals are, make a list of them at the beginning of the scrapbook. Young children may need you to write their list or at least "interpret" it in case they would like to draw their goals instead.

As the year turns, add updates to your goals at appropriate milestones and, obviously, when you complete one. Include pictures and journal entries. This book is a record of your accomplishments for the year. It's something to be proud of so take your time with it and track your progress, even if you have backslides. It's important to see even the smallest steps forward when we do backslide so keeping track of everything can help you move forward even when you feel it is most difficult.

You can begin these books while planning your Imbolg ritual, so that during your ritual time you can bless them and bring your goals to you deities to ask for their support and guidance. You may even have certain goals that you want to share publicly at ritual so you can ask your family/fellow practitioners for support in achieving them.

Honor Brighid

For many people, Imbolg is the celebration of the Goddess Brighid, and is often celebrated by making Brighid's cross or by placing a Brighid doll in a basket in a basket by the hearth.

Brighid is a goddess over many aspects, including smithing and poetry. Though you might not have the actual equipment to try to learn such things as metalsmithing, there may be other options you can look into. Check around and see if you can find people who do things such as leather work, silversmithing, even glass blowing. Though you might not be able to learn these skills yourself, perhaps there are demonstrations available somewhere near you where you can at least spend a day actually watching it in person. Smithing can cover a broad range of creative skills, so look into things that interest you and do some research. At the very least, you are sure to find some videos on the internet.

With Brighid as the goddess of poetry, now is also a great time to either catch up on new poets, reminisce with some of the classics, or perhaps even read them for the first time. There are even great poetry books for kids (Shel Silverstein will always be a favorite), so this isn't an adults-only project. Use this time of year to broaden your skills and knowledge. Each year give yourself something new to learn or try. Once you get yourself involved in learning about new things, you will be surprised how fast the time will fly by and bring spring in with a full bloom.

Adding these activities to your Imbolg celebration helps you to get a start on your growing season—both your physical and emotional ones, at that. If we take our cues from the earth, we must remember that every year, we need to have new growth.

Imbolc: Ritual of the Emerging Flame

Emily Carding

IMBOLC, IN THE FIRST days of February when life starts to awaken within the land, is the perfect time of year to start acting on those long-held plans, tuning in to the energies to give our creativity and productivity a boost. This is the focus of the following simple ritual, which can be performed with your family, including children, or a small working group. This ritual uses primarily the elements of fire and water, combined with a hint of earth. Though many see the elements of fire and water as being unfavourable in combination, (more than partly due to the Golden Dawn system of elemental correspondences), we can learn far more from observation of Nature than from rigid man-made systems. Fire and water may in some instances cancel each other out, but they can also create steam, a force which can propel our dreams forward. The addition of the element of earth, through the use of the first green shoots of spring, brings the ability to manifest those dreams into physical reality.

This ritual also uses the system of the Seven Directions. In addition to the traditional four directions of north, south, east, and west and their corresponding elements of Earth, Fire, Air, and Water, we also call upon the celestial realm Above, the ancestral and Faery realm Below, and the divine spark Within. As you are lighting the seven candles, bear these directions in mind, and how each of us is a star at the centre of our own universal web of connections.

Items Needed

Water (from a natural source if possible, ideally from a Holy Well or spring)

A large ceramic bowl or dish. (This should be black, green, or white ideally.)

One consecrated red candle

Seven consecrated white candles and holders. (Tealights are fine, but for safety reasons make sure they are in suitable holders or on stone.)

One flower or bud from your local landscape per person. Snowdrop is traditional, but if these do not grow near you, then whatever is the first green life to emerge.

Green, white, or green-and-white altar cloth, (optional)

A glass bottle with stopper or screw top—green or colourless is preferred

Wine and cake/bread for offerings

Part One: Giving and Receiving

As a family or group, go to your nearest wild area or green space, taking your offerings with you. Find a place that resonates with your energy—you should be able to feel it or just find yourself inclined to pause there—and give your offerings to the land with these (or your own) words:

Spirits of this place, heart of the land, we honour you. We share these our gifts with you and ask that as the light grows and life renews, that you will walk with us in love and truth. We ask to take a token from the place as a sign of friendship, as we leave you these offerings as signs of ours.

(It is important to note at this point that after leaving your offerings, if you feel the strong sensation that it is not appropriate to take anything from this place, you should respect that and simply move on to another place, with further offerings.)

Once the offerings have been left, each person should allow themselves to be guided to a place where new life is shooting and take a very small shoot or flower from a place where it will not cause damage, thanking the plant as you do so.

Part Two: Preparation

As a group, create sacred space by whichever method you usually use. If you are uncertain, there are a number of simple yet effective methods featured in *Faery Craft* (Llewellyn, 2012). Pour your water into the bowl and place in the centre of the altar, (this may be placed on the ground if you prefer), on top of the altar cloth if you have one. The seven candles should be placed equidistant in a circle around the bowl. You will need your red candle and a method of lighting it to hand, as well as your glass bottle. Each member of the group should wash beforehand, wear clean clothing or robes, and have with them their green life taken from the land.

Part Three: The Ritual

If you do not have a clear leader in your group, elect someone to act as Priest or Priestess. You may divide the wording as you see fit, according to experience and number of group members. It is also effective as a solo ritual.

Powers of life emerging, we call to you on this your feast to aid us in our endeavours. As the green life once more pushes through the darkness into the light, so let our deeds shine forth and produce shoots of abundance. As above, so below!

(Light the red candle.)

By the power of the Sun, we ask that our dreams grow in truth and honour towards manifestation.

(From the flame of the red candle, light the first white candle.)

By the grace of the Moon, we ask that our dreams grow in magic and mystery towards manifestation.

(From the flame of the red candle, light the second white candle.)

By the divine light of the Stars, we ask that our dreams grow in universal connection towards manifestation.

(From the flame of the red candle, light the third white candle.)

By the strength of Earth, we ask that our dreams grow in stability and trust towards manifestation.

(From the flame of the red candle, light the fourth white candle.)

By the sweet breath of Air, we ask that our dreams grow in knowledge and wisdom towards manifestation.

(From the flame of the red candle, light the fifth white candle.)

By the transformative heat of Fire, we ask that our dreams grow in inspiration and will towards manifestation.

(From the flame of the red candle, light the sixth white candle.)

By the healing flow of Water, we ask that our dreams grow in passion and joy towards manifestation.

(From the flame of the red candle, light the final white candle.)

Now in the centre, the place of balance between the seven directions, the great well of the deep, gateway to the underworld through which all birth occurs, we give our dreams into your keeping.

Each member takes it in turn to breathe into their green shoot or flower, holding a clear image of their hopes for the future as they do so, then taking it in turns to place it into the water, expressing their dream in their own words if they wish, or in silence. The group stands in a circle around the symbolic well, holding the energy for a time that feels appropriate.

We thank the powers of the elements and above, below and within for your blessing this night. As the light grows, so may our dreams manifest in love and truth, with harm to none and health and abundance to all! As above so below, so mote it be.

Leave the bowl surrounded by the lit candles for an hour (or until they naturally extinguish themselves), under supervision— responsible group members can take it in turn if necessary, and it provides a good opportunity for meditation on the subject of manifestation of dreams. When the hour has passed, extinguish the candles one at a time, thanking each power as you do so.

Leave the bowl with the shoots/flowers immersed in it for a whole day and night, in a window if possible so it also holds the energy of the sun and moon's light. Once this time has passed, you can bottle the water (in numerous small bottles if needed for each group member), and return the green shoots or flowers to the land.

This water can now be used to bless any new projects or plans that you wish to manifest. Just a few sprinkled drops will do. May the luminous powers of Brigit and Sol Invictus walk with you on your path to a thriving future!

Notes

Notes

Ostara

Eostre, Jesus & the Big Bunny

Melanie Marquis

WHETHER WE'RE PAGANS, CHRISTIANS, Atheists, or any other persuasion, we can't help but experience the physical and spiritual effects of spring's arrival. As winter is bidden farewell and we step out into the equinox sunshine to greet a lighter and brighter day, we find ourselves transformed, right along with the rest of nature. With the arrival of spring comes the birth of many animals, the return of the growing season, and the promise of an easier time surviving as the sunlight's energy warms the earth and our bodies as well. We become more energetic, ready to crawl out of our winter caves and find a bit of fun, just as a groundhog might pop out of its hole eager for adventure and perhaps a newborn sprig of greenery to nibble. We feel renewed, rejuvenated, excited for new experiences and filled with a fresh sense of hope. The resurrection of the natural world is apparent as flowers blossom, trees bud, and the living earth springs back to life after the cold and dreary death of winter.

It's only natural that our religious myths and traditions would be designed to parallel and mirror the changes we see not only in the world around us, but that we also feel within ourselves. While many Pagans this time of year celebrate the resurrection of Nature, or the grace and light of the goddess Eostre, many Christians celebrate the resurrection of their man-god Christ. While Pagans place flowers on their altars, so too do Christians decorate their sacred places with springtime blossoms. In both Pagan and non-Pagan seasonal decorations and traditions, baby animal symbols abound. While Christians might see a little lamb as a symbol of a resurrected man-god, a gentle and loving sacrificial lamb of sorts, Pagans might associate lambs with the season due to their softness, or their quiet and graceful cuteness, quite in tune with the energetic flow of nature's springtime tide. While a Pagan may associate a baby bird with the goddess Eostre, a Christian may see a baby bird as a representation of the new life and hope inherent in the Jesus resurrection story. The backstory behind our individual practices may differ, but at the heart, it's all the same: an expression of faith and joy in the arrival of spring and all that it symbolizes—new life, new hope, salvation from the certainty of death.

While I might not feel the urge to head down to the local Christian church for an Easter morning sunrise service, I recognize in this practice a goal quite similar to my own as I sit quietly in my own backyard awaiting the vernal equinox and the renewed sense of balance and enthusiasm that comes with it. Whether our personal myths and traditions include Jesus, Eostre, an unnamed deity, or Nature itself, the message of salvation and renewal is crystal clear: all is well; we survived the physical and spiritual winter and we can trust and see with our own eyes that the world will indeed go on. While individual dogmas can obscure our similarities, the power of spring itself sweeps away the shadows and illuminates a united purpose: to rejoice in life.

This joy comes naturally if we let it. It's when our spiritual practices become far removed from our true beliefs that we find our happiness hindered. We might feel obligated or expected to celebrate spring in ways that just don't ring true for us, and if we fall into this trap, finding the joy in the season can be much more of a challenge.

As a child, I was allowed to formulate my own spiritual beliefs, and as a result, my faith was strong. I counted on the spring being a time of great cheer, and I didn't need dogma or religion to teach me that. Just like a wild animal, when spring arrived I could feel it. When I was growing up, my family was never religious, but we celebrated religious holidays just the same. Never wanting to miss out on a chance for celebration, we enjoyed the fun of holiday tradition while leaving out the strictly religious elements that tend to interfere with and confuse the more entertaining aspects. We didn't attend church services or mention reanimated corpses at springtime, and we didn't perform any sacred rituals in honor of the Goddess, but we did color eggs and leave out baskets in hopes that the Easter Bunny would fill them with treats. We would have multiple egg hunts, taking turns hiding the eggs for all the rest of the family to find. I've come to realize that this secular-style family fun was our religion, but at the time, I didn't see it that way. I just knew that spring meant more fun, more sunshine, and the Easter Bunny, and that those were all things I really, really liked.

I remember wondering as a child why people made such a big deal about this Jesus character every springtime, when clearly the Easter Bunny was the star of the show. Perhaps this was more apparent to me because the Easter Bunny was one of the primary members of my personal pantheon, the holy trinity comprised also of Santa and Mom.

The Easter Bunny encompassed everything that was springtime—unexpected surprises, sunshine, flowers, excitement, and life. The big bunny gave us a reason to come together as a family, to color eggs the night before the big day, and to take turns hiding and finding those eggs on Easter afternoon. My siblings and I would leave our empty baskets on the table the night before Easter, and, lo and behold, by morning a miracle would occur—and the baskets would be found filled with chocolates, jelly beans, stuffed animals, and other little prizes. How a belief in the miracle of Christ's resurrection compares, I'll never know, but I have a feeling it's quite similar in terms of instilling joy and wonder in our hearts and minds, strengthening our faith in the good, and fostering a hope that the bad will get better.

☙

As a Pagan all grown up, I see more clearly the spiritual aspects of our springtime celebrations, and I've found ways to combine my old family traditions with more sacred activities and magickal practices. For example, I usually enjoy a private ritual to mark the vernal equinox. This is typically very simple, an intimate rite between just me and the maiden goddess of spring, a time to recharge, regain balance, and rejuvenate, a time to say thanks for the renewal of our Mother Earth. I accomplish this by taking a walk alone in the sunshine or by lying outside in the grass of my own backyard, just taking the time to think, to reflect, to regroup, and to rejoice as I await the dawn. I like to mark the occasion with a bit of magick, too. Sometimes I light a circle of candles, and in the middle I plant some seeds to help manifest my springtime wishes. On each seed, I draw a symbol or write a word to represent my goal, whether it be balance, energy, courage, or cheer. Other times, I'll take advantage of Ostara's balancing energies and perform a charm to set chaos to rights. I'll choose a symbol of the area of my life that has fallen into disarray, and I place it between two naturally magnetic lodestones, using the moment of equinox to restore equilibrium magickally. Often I'll wrap up the spellwork by sprinkling around some birdseed and setting out some dishes of fresh water, expressing my thanks and gratitude to the earth and her creatures. My Ostara rituals are far from fancy, but for me, they do the trick.

Being a lover of family tradition, however, I must admit that in the springtime, it's the Easter Bunny that still takes the spotlight in my house just as he did when I was a child. While I celebrate Ostara on my own, as a family, we celebrate the Easter Bunny together on Easter. It does feel a little strange, celebrating Easter as a Pagan. Even though our Easter traditions are more in line with Pagan Ostara practices than they are with mainstream Christian

Easter celebrations, the fact that I choose to have our main family festivities on Easter rather than on Ostara, and the casualness and lack of complexity in my Ostara rites, makes me feel like a bit of a heretic. Rather than performing solemn rites to a goddess of grace and salvation, rather than attending a Christian sunrise service and singing hymns in honor of a solar god returned to life after death, my faith is still primarily in the miracle of the Easter Bunny, who I admit is decidedly a fake. It's not that I'm delusional or antireligious; I just don't personally feel comfortable with a lot of formality, and I prefer to express my spirituality through my own favorite and familiar traditions, which to me means honoring the idea of an imaginary Easter Bunny and all that is symbolized therein. Besides, as a symbol and sacred companion of the goddess Eostre, the "Easter" Bunny is arguably very Pagan, regardless of what his name might imply and regardless of what the date on the calendar might be when he hops from house to house delivering promise and chocolates to all who believe.

It's rather silly, I know, yet this Easter Bunny religion is not really so different from other Pagan and non-Pagan springtime celebrations marked with deeper reverence and greater ceremony. Our personal spiritual practices are not so much in the details as they are in the overall feelings they produce. A Pagan witnessing the vernal equinox might enjoy a renewed sense of balance and hope while contemplating the cycles of nature, a Christian might experience a feeling of new life and salvation upon witnessing the Easter dawn, and an Atheist might simply feel happier and freshly energized as the sunshine warms the land. A little kid devoid of dogmatic religion might experience a surge of joy and wonder upon discovering a magickally filled basket on Easter or Ostara morning. If we allow it, the commonalities in our many springtime traditions can bring us closer together with people who don't necessarily share all our beliefs. In looking to our similarities, we find not only common ground to stand on with our non-Pagan brothers and sisters, but also we find the common roots from which our many diverse spiritual beliefs branch. The outward trappings indeed vary widely, but behind all our different practices stands a singular belief, the idea that Nature in all its forms will take care of us. It doesn't matter whether that Nature is seen as Eostre, Jesus, or the big bunny himself: it's the spring that's the thing.

As we enter this season where colored eggs and bunnies abound, don't be afraid to honor and celebrate the spring in your own unique ways. Whether that means carrying on old family traditions, creating brand-new traditions, or combining both Pagan and non-Pagan traditions into a holiday perfectly suited just for you, the power of spring will shine through it all to remind you that at the heart of the season there is hope, love, light, and salvation. Nature has redeemed us from winter, the Easter Bunny has spared us the pain of a lack of chocolate, and that Jesus character has saved us from permanent death—however we as individuals choose to tell the tale, the story of spring is all the same.

Cosmic Sway

Corrine Kenner

METAPHORICALLY SPEAKING, THE SABBAT holidays commemorate the forces of creation. They celebrate the celestial mother and father who keep the Wheel of the Year spinning through time and space. Each year, as the earth revolves around the Sun, the god and the goddess repeat the cycle of life and reinforce the cycle of experience, as they live, love, die, and are reborn.

We celebrate Ostara on the spring equinox, when the Sun shines directly on the equator, and the balance of light and darkness tips in sunlight's favor. The date marks the return of the Sun—and the god—after a long, cold winter in the Underworld. It also marks the start of the astrological New Year.

Mars' Mischief

It's not a stretch to say that March belongs to Mars, the god of virility and strength. In fact, the whole month is named after him. Mars rules Aries, the sign of leadership and drive, and embodies the best qualities of independence and self-determination.

On this holiday, as the Sun enters Aries, Mars is in Libra—the sign of partnership. Unfortunately, Libra is 180 degrees away from Aries, so the warrior planet is weak and debilitated here.

Granted, Mars isn't in unfamiliar territory. Libra is ruled by Venus, the goddess of love. Mars and Venus are lovers—but Venus' focus on marriage and partnership makes Mars uncomfortable.

Even so, Mars wants to please Venus, so when he passes through Libra he does his best to be charming, rather than overpowering. Mars is strong-willed, which means he can be surprisingly self-controlled.

Unfortunately, the warrior planet happens to be retrograde, moving backward through the sign. He started his reverse course at the beginning of the month, and he won't stop backtracking until May 19. Mars feels trapped, so his patience is thin.

He's not comfortable—and you could feel stressed and anxious, too, especially if you're sensitive to Mars' influence. For now, you might feel stuck in your personal relationships or locked in a power struggle with close friends and open enemies alike.

Avoid the temptation to blame yourself and remember that it's not personal: in this case, the whole world will be on the receiving end of Mars' frustration.

When Mars starts marching forward again in May, the situation will start to right itself—and in July, when Mars moves into Scorpio, he'll be comfortably in command of his resources again.

The glyph for Mars looks like a spear and a shield—a reminder that war can be defensive as well as offensive, and that aggression and self-protection are two sides of the same coin. In fact, the Aries lamb that marks this season of rebirth was a sacrificial animal. It symbolizes a hero's willingness to lay down his life for those he loves, on the promise of an even greater reward in the next life.

Plant Seeds of Change

While we usually think of Mars as a hot-headed god, impulsive and impetuous, it's important to remember that he also had some visionary qualities—which could help you keep your sense of perspective. That's because Mars was also the god of agriculture. When there was no need for war, Mars turned swords into plowshares. He encouraged farmers to plant crops because he knew that an army marches on its stomach. Mars was acting out of self-interest rather than altruism, but that's allowed.

This is the time of year to plan your crops, both literal and figurative. Decide what seeds you'd like to plant, and which crops you'd like to harvest. Remember to think about your needs, as well as any extra bounty you can exchange with others.

Try to have your plans firmed up by April 8, when Mars makes a close approach to Earth. Weather permitting, you'll be able to see it for yourself that night, fully illuminated by the Sun.

Planetary Positions

Mars isn't the only planet moving backward right now. Saturn turned retrograde on March 2, and it will keep backtracking through Scorpio for the next four months. Saturn actually spends about five months of each year moving retrograde, so it's not uncommon.

Saturn's retrograde periods are good times to reassess the promises and commitments you've made, both to yourself and to other people. Make sure you haven't stretched yourself too thin, and that all of your goals and ideals are built on firm foundations.

On Ostara, the Moon will start its brief journey through Sagittarius. The Moon passes through all twelve signs of the zodiac during the course of a month, and when it moves through Sagittarius, the mood lightens appreciably. During this weekend's festivities, you'll probably feel optimistic and adventurous, and any gifts you share with others will be well received.

On Ostara, the Sun and the Moon will also be in an easygoing trine, which means your head and your heart will be in agreement—at least for the moment. Be reasoned in how you share your emotions, though. The Moon is square Mercury and Neptune, which makes it easy to reveal more than you really want to.

Mercury is in Pisces now, which means the messenger of the gods is doing his best to bring you news and information from the spirit world. It's a good time to keep your dream journal close to your bedside, so you can record any important messages that come while you sleep. Mercury will move into Aries on April 7. At that point, you'll probably be less fixated on feelings and emotions, and more focused on action and accomplishment.

Venus, the planet of love, beauty, and affection, moved into Aquarius on March 5. Here, in the sign of social groups and causes, she brings a sense of balance, grace, and harmony to your interactions with friends and community. She'll move into Pisces on April 5, where she'll deepen your sense of connection with the people who are closest to you.

Jupiter is still in Cancer, where it continues to expand your home and family life. It's also in an ongoing square with Uranus, so that expansion could take unusual form or lead to unexpected developments.

The Phases of the Moon

On March 1, a New Moon in watery Pisces ushered in the month on a note of spiritual connection and Neptunian bliss. The first quarter Moon in airy Gemini on March 8 moved the focus from the heart to the head, with an emphasis on clear thinking and communication. The Full Moon in earthy Virgo on March 16 continues that practical course, making heavy responsibilities seem bearable.

The month of March will go out like a lion, with a fiery New Moon in Aries on March 30. Its energy will be linked to Mars, the god of war and Aries' ruling planet. If that Moon leaves any hurt feelings in its wake, they'll be soothed during the first quarter Moon in nurturing Cancer on April 7. Look for a romantic, partner-oriented Full Moon in Libra on April 15—together with a total lunar eclipse that will be visible throughout most of North America, South America, and Australia. Expand your social network of connections on April 22, when a third quarter Moon in Aquarius adds a dash of fun and friendship to your everyday life.

The Old Ways: Spring Cleaning

Linda Raedisch

THE PHRASE, "DOUBLE, DOUBLE, toil and trouble," conjures up one of the best-known episodes in Shakespeare, as well as a defining moment in the common perception of Witches. But replace the "Eye of newt and toe of frog" and all those other unsavory, hard-to-find ingredients with dung, urine, fern ashes, and a dash of powdered lapis lazuli for the rinse water, and Macbeth's first, second, and third Witches might just as easily have been doing their laundry.

To our eyes, the routine household tasks of two and three hundred years ago would have looked very much like witchcraft. What would you think of a housewife who spread sand all over her best carpet, then vigorously brushed it off and out the door? In the days before vacuum cleaners, this was the best way to give a wool carpet a routine clean. If you had an earthen floor, you could usually get away with a quick sprinkle and sweep, while wood floors had to be treated with the oils of fragrant herbs such as tansy and mint. If you wanted your neighbors to respect you, you'd better not forget to wash and whiten your doorstep each morning, a practice that survived well into the twentieth century.

Unless you had a separate "copper," or bricked-in cauldron, for boiling your linens, you would have no place to cook on laundry

138

day. If you dragged the cauldron out of the kitchen, however, then you could fry a few pancakes on the hearth in between loads. And when you washed your clothes under an open sky, you wouldn't have to worry about chimney soot raining down into the wash water and spoiling the whole process. After the final rinse, some Scottish housewives brought their wet linen into the churchyard where they proceeded to beat it against the gravestones, the smooth markers taking the place of both wringers and ironing boards. To the uninformed observer, this would have presented a very witchy sight indeed.

But all this is only the stuff of an ordinary Blue Monday. Had our Weird Sisters been in the throes of spring cleaning, they would have had that cauldron upended over a fire of furze, peat, and driftwood. Then they would have dipped their long-handled mops into a bucket of tallow and passed them, sizzling, over the black shell. In this way, cauldrons were periodically sealed against rust, the heat of the fire fusing the dripping fat with the iron.

If we are to believe what we see in the movies, then the word "witch" does not belong in the same sentence as "spring cleaning." Dusty tomes, cobwebby kitchens, and pots boiling over on the stove—these are the marks of a serious Witch or Wizard. Even real-life Wiccans might agree that a Witch's broom is for clearing sacred space, not for sweeping out the garage. But are the two tasks really so different? Witches come in black, gray, and white, so why not *snowy* white? Perhaps you've met a Snowy White Witch. She defines herself as much by that extra dash of laundry bluing as by her spellwork and herbal infusions, and her besom shows distinct signs of wear. She eschews store-bought abrasives to mix up her own batch of vinegar, baking soda, and Castile soap and actually enjoys working it into the steel surfaces of her kitchen.

I think it's time the Snowy White Witch got some credit, for cleaning is both an art and a chore. Popular wisdom holds that the creative soul cannot be bothered with serious housekeeping: "Boring women have spotless homes," and all that. The truth is that cleaning is *re*-creative work, a continual reestablishing of the boundaries of the sacred microcosm that is the home. For those of us who love to clean, *spring* cleaning is our Christmas, Biennale, and Cannes Film Festival all rolled into one.

Spring cleaning used to be just about all there was. Two hundred years ago, most women were still too busy weaving, sewing, churning butter, and turning tallow into soap and candles to worry about beating carpets and washing walls more than once a year. When things like textiles, sliced bread, and carbolic soap started to appear in shops, women were expected to stay on top of the dust, dirt, and cobwebs that no one had ever really noticed before.

Even after women started cleaning on a daily basis, rigorous seasonal cleaning became more important than ever, for these were the days of the coal fire, and those cobwebs were now stained black. One could no longer get along with just a push broom and a carpet beater; a clean home required nothing less than ritual paraphernalia. Each surface had its own specialized cleaning implement. There were soft brushes, stiff brushes, sweepers, whisks, carpet brooms, and wall brooms. A chambermaid in an upper class house might have such magical tools as a "whisk banister brush," "telescopic hearth brush," or "turnover library duster" at her disposal. Not that these tools made the work easy. Spring cleaning still required that the contents of the house be emptied into the yard, the bedsteads disassembled and each crack and crevice painted with turpentine, camphor or naphtha to discourage bedbugs. The bare floors had to be stripped, scrubbed, waxed and polished, the walls brushed with a paste made of fuller's earth (a kind of clay), chalk, soap, and sodium hydroxide, a.k.a. "soda," which then had to be rinsed off again.

A world away, in the American Southwest, "spring" cleaning took place in August or September, after the summer rains had filled the cisterns. It was a process of renewing the pueblo's lease with the elements as well as of sweeping out. The walls were not just cleaned but replastered. At Taos, a new layer of adobe mixed with bits of straw was applied to the exterior of the sun-baked bricks, while the women of Acoma preferred a wash of powdered dung and gypsum with a yellow slip at the base of the interior wall. When it came to sweeping out, Puebloans had no concept of "dirt" or "garbage." In the Tewa language of northern New Mexico, one does not speak of "building" a house but of raising it up out of the earth, so when it came time to return bits of that house to the earth, they did so reverently. All those broken pots and tools, the ashes from the bread ovens and the dust shaken from the house walls were gathered up, placed on a specially designated heap and topped with a feathered prayer stick.

Most of us do not have to worry that our houses will fall down if we neglect to paint or power wash them for a few years. Soot has also become a nonissue, though we still have to worry about bedbugs. But despite the relative ease of daily maintenance, ritual spring cleaning is alive and well.

The night before Passover, many Jews engage in a house-wide search for errant breadcrumbs—as good an excuse as any for turning out the cupboards and vacuuming the refrigerator coils. Closer to Ostara is the old Tuscan tradition of bringing the *fattoria*, or main farm house, to a spotless condition in the days leading up to the Christian Holy Week. In a frenzy worthy of the Italian Witch Befana, who was too busy cleaning house to accompany the Three Wise Men to Bethlehem, the mistress of the *fattoria* cleared out the cobwebs, changed the bedclothes and polished the terrazzo floors to a high gloss. Though the ritual culminated with the arrival of the Catholic priest who blessed the eggs on the kitchen table and sprinkled holy water in all the corners, the practice was actually the late incarnation of an Etruscan fertility rite.

Too busy to clean for Ostara? Consider hosting an ancient Egyptian New Year's party in July. Before you put out the falafel and beer, wash all your windows with an ammonia-based glass cleaner. Ammonia is named for Ammon, or "Amun," one of the principal gods of ancient Egypt. Amun's desert temple was situated near a field of jewel-like salt crystals, now identified as ammonium chloride. If only the temple had had glass windows, I'm sure its ancient caretakers would have extolled the crystals for their miraculous power to create a streak-free shine.

If spring cleaning still sounds like drudgery to you, it may help to think of your housekeeping activities as an ongoing conversation with the Goddess. After all, each time you sweep, dust, vacuum, or scrub, you're renewing your contract with Mother Earth. Don't just kick the dirt out the door; take the time to admire it. Is it gritty, micaceous, or cake-flour fine? Run a finger through it—of this are your four walls made.

After so many whitewashings, plasterings, and outright repairs, many of those old Pueblo houses have been "retired," that is, abandoned and allowed to sink gracefully back into the earth out of which they were raised. However new, your home, too, is in the process of subsiding. Bricks check in the cold, paint flakes away on the wind, and the bones of the house settle deeper and deeper into the foundation. Even those solid-looking panes of window glass are oozing inexorably downward toward the sash. Each time Mother Earth sends a puff of that lovely dirt swirling in under the door, she is asking, "Have you had enough? Shall I take it from here?" Take up your broom and answer respectfully, "No, thank you. Not yet."

For Further Reading:

Bredenberg, Jeff, ed. *Clean It Fast, Clean It Right: the Ultimate Guide to Making Absolutely Everything You Own Sparkle and Shine.* Emmaus, PA: Rodale Press, 1998.

Davidson, Caroline. *A Woman's Work Is Never Done: A History of Housework in the British Isles 1650-1950.* London: Chatto & Windus, 1982.

Guiley, Rosemary Ellen. *The Encyclopedia of Witches and Witchcraft,* Second Edition. New York: Checkmark Books, 1999.

Horsfield, Margaret. *Biting the Dust: The Joys of Housework.* New York: St. Martin's Press, 1998.

Nabokov, Peter and Robert Easton. *Native American Architecture.* New York: Oxford University Press, 1989.

Romer, Elizabeth. *The Tuscan Year*. New York: North Point Press, 1984.

Seymour, John. *The Forgotten Arts and Crafts*. New York: Dorling Kindersley, 2001.

Ward, Schar. *Coming Clean: Dirty Little Secrets from a Professional Housekeeper*. Minnetonka, MN: Book Peddlers, 2002.

Feasts and Treats

Dallas Jennifer Cobb

THE SUN GROWS STRONGER and is no longer a child, but an equal to the Goddess. Day and night are equal, and for a moment and in this pause, the God and Goddess fall deeply in love. Life is sweet. Love abounds. The earth is fertile and fecund. This is a magical time. From here on, the amount of light increases dramatically each day as the Sun God waxes stronger, and the days become longer. Feasting at Ostara is traditionally accompanied by foods symbolic of fertility.

Coconut Curried Shrimp

Since it is not quite warm outside, I like to create a little heat inside by adding a little spice to life. And, if everything written about curry is true, then it has a mild, uplifting energy that helps make us happy, dispels the winter blahs, and even stimulates the libido. Enjoy this feast and internalize the growing power of the Sun God.

Prep Time: 5 minutes
Cooking Time: 10 minutes
Serves: 4

2 tablespoon olive oil
3 cloves of garlic, minced
1 medium onion, diced

½ cup red pepper, diced
1 teaspoon curry powder
1 teaspoon coriander
2 teaspoon cumin
½ cup coconut milk
1 pound of jumbo shrimp, peeled and deveined
2 tablespoons water
1 tablespoon cornstarch
2 tablespoons chopped fresh cilantro
2 tablespoons finely chopped peanuts

Heat oil at a medium heat in a large, nonstick frying pan. Sauté onion, red pepper, and garlic until soft. Add spices and coconut milk and bring to a boil. When it is bubbling, reduce heat to medium high, and add shrimp. Cook until shrimp turn a lovely pink color (usually about 4 minutes). In a small bowl, combine water and cornstarch. Mix well, then add into frying pan and cook until sauce thickens. Stir in cilantro, remove from heat. Serve on top of rice, and garnish with chopped peanuts.

Brown Rice and Broccoli

Rice is easy to cook, and while I like it best plain with a spicy dish like Coconut Curried Shrimp, I also like to add a green vegetable on the side. Prepare brown rice as you usually do, and near the end when the rice is almost done, throw the broccoli florets in on top, and let them steam gently as the rice finishes cooking, the steam bringing the broccoli to the peak of color.

Preparation Time: 10 minutes
Cooking Time: 45 minutes
Serves: 4

1 cup natural brown rice
8 cups cold water
1½ teaspoons sea salt
1 head broccoli, cut into florets

Rinse the rice with cold water for 30 seconds. Bring the water and salt to a boil over high heat in a large heavy pot with a tight-fitting lid.

When the water is boiling add the rice, stir, and partially cover. Don't completely cover or it will bubble over. Cook on medium-high heat for 30 minutes.

Drain the rice in a strainer, then quickly return to the pot and cover tightly for 15 minutes, open the pot, add broccoli florets on top, seal and steam for another 5 minutes so that the steam finishes cooking the rice and broccoli.

Use a small cup to scoop rice onto the plates in a perfect, egg shaped mound. Ladle coconut curried shrimp over top, and garnish with the steamed broccoli.

Half and Half

In honor of the balance of light and dark, make a good, strong dark coffee and serve it with *leche caliente* or "hot milk." Equal parts of coffee and milk are used, but I like to serve the cups with the coffee in it, then welcome people to add the warmed milk to the coffee themselves, observing the darkness as it shifts, and mixes with the light.

Preparation Time: 3 minutes
Cooking Time: 5 minutes
Serves: 4

5 tablespoons ground coffee
3 cups of water
1 quart of 2 percent milk
Sugar

Makes 3 cups of coffee, but uses enough ground coffee for 5 cups, so that the result is a strong, dark coffee. In a saucepan, heat a quart of milk at medium heat until steaming. Place coffee in mugs and milk in a pitcher and place on the table. Serve with sugar to taste.

Crème Brûlée

If you have been thinking, "what is an Ostara Feast without eggs," then sit back and enjoy this recipe, because they are all hidden here. This delightful combination of eggs, heavy cream, and sugar is delightful and addictive. Like many of the treats available at this time of year, crème brûlée has tons of hidden calories, but the sweet, creamy taste will awaken your senses from their slumber, and like the earth, you will be renewed to life.

Preparation Time: 10 minutes
Cooking Time: 1 hour
Serves: 4 individual ramekin (oven safe) dishes

5 egg yolks
½ cup granulated sugar, plus about ⅛ cup to brûlée (melt with fire) on top
2 cups heavy cream
1½ teaspoons vanilla extract

Whisk together egg yolks and ½ cup of sugar until smooth and creamy. Add cream and vanilla, stirring to combine. Don't mix too quickly—you don't want any air bubbles in there. Place empty ramekin dishes in a casserole dish and fill the casserole dish with hot water until it comes about halfway up the sides of the ramekins. Pour egg mixture into ramekins.

Bake for 45 minutes to 1 hour, until the egg mixture sets. Remove ramekins from casserole dish and lay on a clean dish towel to dry and cool. The crème should be cool before you brûlée the sugar.

Set the broiler to "low" setting. Sprinkle a thin, even layer of granulated sugar over the top of the cooked crème, completely covering it. Place the ramekins back into the casserole dish and stick it under the broiler for about 2 minutes, or until the sugar melts and forms a dark, bubbling layer. Alternatively, you can use a small kitchen blowtorch to brûlée the sugar.

Crafty Crafts

Blake Octavian Blair

OSTARA MARKS THE SPRING Equinox and is often a much-anticipated sabbat. Many are ready to openly welcome the now noticeably longer days and the promise of warmer weather after the dark and cold of winter. The name Ostara hearkens back to the Germanic goddess Eostre, who has associations with springtime and fertility. In many areas people are able to begin enjoying outdoor activities more regularly again and begin to plant in their gardens and planters.

Adding a bit of witchy whimsy as well as a magickal boost to your gardening efforts never hurts! This craft will allow you to do just that all while helping you harmonize yourself with the incoming energies of spring.

Magickal Decoupaged Flowerpots

Magickally minded folks are no strangers to the power of symbols. We also know that like attracts like and we use these manifestation powers of sympathetic magick in our lives. These flower pots utilize these principles to give a jump-start to our spring growing efforts.

Supplies

Terra cotta flowerpots

Decoupage glue

Small foam or other paint brush (that you will not need to reuse for anything else)

Seed packs

Scissors

Permanent or paint markers

Dried leaves/petals of the plants whose seeds you'll be planting (optional)

Images aligning with magickal goals printed out or cut from magazines (optional)

Spray varnish/sealer

You will want to begin by opening your seed packets carefully across the top with a pair of scissors. The goal is to preserve both the front and back of the packet. Empty your seeds into bags or bowls labeled with what each type of seed is. Set the seeds aside until you are ready for planting.

Now, carefully cut down the sides of each packet, separating the front and back panels into two separate pieces. You will want to put these with anything else you plan to decoupage onto your pot, such as dried leaves or petals, and any other cut-out images that align with your goals.

To decoupage your desired items onto the plant pot, you can either use a premixed decoupage glue or make your own. To make your own, simply take white school glue and mix with water in equal parts. With your paint brush, apply a thin coat of the glue to the back side of the front panel of the seed packet as well as to the pot where you wish to place the packet panel. Now, carefully press and smooth the packet panel onto the pot. Proceed to attach the back panel of the seed packet to your desired location on your pot. Including the back panel from the seed packet is incredibly useful as you will always have the growing conditions and care instructions for the plants available at a glance. The picture of the fully grown plant (possibly in bloom!) on the seed packet also will call the principles of manifestation into action so as set your garden magick into motion.

Continue this ritual of creation to decoupage your other decorations, images, and dried leaves or petals onto the pot. Remember to choose things that correspond to the magickal properties and intent for what you are planting. Below are just a few ideas of goals and correspondences of some popular magickal garden plants and herbs to help get the creativity flowing. Use them as a launching pad for decorating pots for your favorite plants.

Basil: Popular for its properties of protection, cleansing, and attracting wealth. Images of money, deities of prosperity such as Laxmi and Hotei Buddha, dollar signs, and protective symbols such as pentacles and the triquetra are good choices. Utilize the colors of green and gold in your decorations.

Mint: Also known for its prosperous and protective qualities. See suggestions for basil.

Rosemary: A favorite for protection, love, and healing. Healing symbols such as the caduceus and "healing hands" or hands in namaste/prayer position are appropriate. Healing deities such as Quan Yin or Archangel Raphael and love deities such as Aphrodite or Krishna and Radha mesh excellently with the energies of rosemary. Utilize reds and pinks for love as well as purples and white for healing to suit your goal.

Daisies: Daisy is popular for its associations with love, however, it is also powerfully connected in magick to the realm of sleep. I personally have found daisy (petal or root) to be an excellent ingredient into dream pillows and spells for restful sleep and to ward off nightmares. All love imagery applies in addition to sleep imagery. Images of comfy beds and peaceful places are appropriate as are images of the night sky and the moon. Images of sheep are also appropriate as they have become a potent symbol of restful sleep through the pop culture notion of counting them to fall asleep easily. Colors of the

night and the moon are appropriate such as white, silver, black, deep blue, and purple.

In addition to decoupaging, appropriate symbols may be drawn onto the pot with permanent or paint markers. You can also opt to paint the symbols on using acrylic paint if you wish. Once you have all symbols drawn and everything you wish to decoupage on the pot adhered, it is time to move to the final steps.

To finish creating your magickal pot, brush a final coat of decoupage glue over the top of all the artwork covering the exterior of the pot. This will help to coat and seal everything into place. Don't worry, the glue will dry clear. When the glue dries (drying time will vary) apply a coat of spray varnish to the outside of the pot. This will further add to the durability of the pot if you choose to put it on a front porch or patio and reduce wear and tear from some exposure to the elements. (Note: Indoor and shaded use will prolong the life of your artwork.)

I prefer to do the final consecration and blessing of the pot at the time of planting. Simply smudging your potting area and all the tools involved (including the pot) and saying a blessing is quite effective. Write your own or try out something similar to the following:

May this pot of my loving creation help this plant through its gestation. By soil of earth, breath of air, fire of sunlight, and nourishment of water, so mote it be!

May these magickal pots serve as a reminder to you that magick grows around you all season long and that you are part of it! Blessed Equinox!

Time to complete: About one hour (not counting drying time for glue, which can vary)

Cost: $10.00 to $20.00 depending upon supplies on hand and size of flower pot.

For Further Reading:

Cunningham, Scott. *Cunningham's Encyclopedia of Magical Herbs.* St. Paul, MN: Llewellyn Publications, 1985.

McCoy, Edain. *Mountain Magick: Folk Wisdom from the Heart of Appalachia.* St. Paul, MN: Llewellyn Publications, 1997.

All One Family

Kerri Connor

SPRING IS FINALLY HERE! (Hopefully.) While some places may even still be experiencing some snow, generally the weather is warming up, at least enough to get outside for a while and maybe crack the windows open a little bit. Flowers may be blooming. Buds and leaves are showing on the trees. If you do any gardening, it's time to start getting the ground tilled and ready to go.

Ostara is the time when life in nature is truly visible again. You can see it, and feel it. For those who suffer from seasonal depression issues, it seems like a whole new world awaits them. In fact, a new world is out there waiting for us *all* to step out in and enjoy the splendor of her beauty. The earth has renewed itself once again.

Get out and explore nature. After being cooped up for the winter, even children will appreciate a good long walk to watch the world as she reawakens. We check out local parks we haven't visited before and keep an eye out for plants and wildlife as it to comes forth to bask in the glow of the warming sun. We take pictures to include on our Ostara altar.

Of course, Ostara has many tie-ins with the Christian Easter, such as bunnies, chicks, and eggs, so decorations, toys, and games are relatively easy to buy that can cross over from one holiday to the other.

Egg hunts can take different forms. Whether real boiled eggs are hidden or the more likely plastic filled eggs, give it a spin that makes your egg hunt different. If you do hide actual hard-boiled eggs, give them special meaning by the colors or other decorations you add to them. Mark a green egg with dollar signs, or a yellow egg with "A+"s. These eggs when found will have messages for the finder. The finder of the green egg may come into some money, while the finder of the yellow egg will have success in school.

For the younger kids, it is probably best (and more fun for them!) to stick with plastic filled eggs. Filling eggs, however, does not mean you need to load them up with jelly beans or other candy. We collect spare change and then use that to help fill eggs. Stickers, small toys, and more healthy snacks can often fit into these eggs, too. You can buy prefilled eggs, but seriously, what is the fun in that? Keep your eyes open, not just at Ostara, but all year for small little items that will be able to be used in your eggs and keep a hidden stash. You can also write messages and stick those in to the eggs as well. Short words of wisdom and encouragement, even a simple "You are loved," is a pleasant treat for a kid to find.

You can mix your egg hunt with other games as well. Instead of playing "Bingo" try "Spring" cards you make yourself with construction paper, and then hide in the eggs the letters such as "S 4" or "N 42." As an egg is found with a number in it they have to run back to their card to add the number to the card. Not only will this make your hunt last longer, it will help to burn up some of that energy that has been waiting to burst forth.

This is the time of the year when the earth is really starting to warm up so a good Ostara bonfire during ritual is a great way to encourage the ground to warm even more. After the bonfire is over, we use ash from it in our garden, and while it may be messy, most kids love to help dig around in dirt and other things, so you may find them actually willing to help spread it all over the garden plot.

Confetti "Bomb Shells"

What has quickly become a favorite Ostara pastime at our rituals with kids of all ages is that of the cascarones (hollowed eggs filled with confetti). A few years ago we saw them at a major discount store for 10 cents a dozen, so we literally bought hundreds of the eggs. Each Ostara, we get out several dozen and allow the kids to have their own little cascarones battle. While cascarones might not be available at a local store, you can always purchase them on the Internet. You can also make these "confetti bombs" on your own, but it is a lot of work. The manufactured cascarones you buy are generally made of papier mâché. Making a lot of homemade papier mâché cascorones takes a lot of work, but can be a fun project if you are up for it! They can also be made from blown-out, washed out actual eggs, however, egg shells can be very sharp and may cut skin. Getting smashed over the head with one made from real eggs can be downright painful, and if there are kids involved, this method will not end well. While using the most natural, historical method to do something is nice, sometimes we just have to think about who could be affected by it.

During ritual blessings, you may want to use the real egg cascarones that have been filled with herbs and oils to pour forth a blessing upon people. When doing this, crack the end on a hard corner surface first and then gently pull it apart over the person's head who is being blessed. Do not smash it, again, egg shells are sharp and cutting the top of some one's head does NOT make them feel like they are being blessed at all! Unfortunately when we first heard about this, we didn't get any kind of a warning, and while it was still fun, people did have itchy, achy, even burning heads from the scratching egg shells mixed with essential oils. Better to just head it off and not smash anything on anyone.

Ostara is the perfect time to celebrate the Earth coming back to life, and teaching your children to appreciate that it is coming back to life. Use these activities to help them recharge both physically and emotionally, and to prepare for the season of growth ahead of them.

Ritualistic Egg Painting & the Hunt

Melanie Marquis

EGGS ARE SYMBOLS OF life and renewal, sacred to Eostre, and very fitting as focal points for a springtime sabbat. You've probably colored eggs and engaged in countless egg hunts before, but have you ever made magick a part of the process? Here's how to do it.

Items Needed
Hard-boiled eggs
Cups or bowls (different colors)
Egg-dyeing kit or food coloring
Vinegar
Citrine crystal
Glass water pitcher

Start with a batch of hard-boiled eggs, cooked thoroughly but cooled. Choose cage-free eggs if possible. Think about what you would like the eggs to symbolize. You might choose springtime energies such as rejuvenation or hope, or you might decide to focus on other goals such as wealth, love, or happiness. Select the containers in which to dye the eggs. You can make magick a part of the process here by choosing bowls or cups with color symbolism in mind: yellow for joy, hope, or confidence; pink for love or comfort; green for wealth, renewal, or healing; orange for strength or energy; blue for knowledge or power; and so on. Use whatever color symbolism feels right to you. Although it's not necessary to use appropriately colored containers, doing so will add power to the magick.

Next, add the egg-dyeing colors to each cup. The simple egg-dyeing kits you see all over the stores this time of year work great, but if you prefer, you can use plain food coloring. Place one color tablet or several drops of food coloring in each container.

Now comes the vinegar. Made from acetic acid and water, vinegar has strong energies well suited to protection or banishing magick. As you add the vinegar to each cup—a couple tablespoons in each will do—think about anything that might stand in the way of the magickal goal at hand. For example, if you've chosen to make a pink egg dye to attract romance, but you feel like your insecurities might get the better of you and hold you back from achieving that goal, envision the power of the vinegar blasting away and banishing your anxieties and negative self-talk as you add it to the color.

Once the color tablet or food coloring has dissolved completely in the vinegar, it's time to add the water. Use only fresh, clean water, and charm it first for best results. Water is very impressionable— it's easy to empower with a wide variety of energies and will readily take on whatever characteristics you choose to impart to it. One way is to make a basic solar brew. Just place a citrine crystal in a glass pitcher filled with water, set it outside in the sunlight for a few hours, and it's good to go. Another way is to contemplate the energies of spring, focusing your thoughts and emotions on rejuvenation, renewal, energy, and life. Will these vibrations into the water to create a springy potion just right for coloring eggs. If you like, you can charm the water used for each egg container separately, perhaps empowering one batch of water with a loving energy, empowering another batch with strength, and so on.

Once your water is prepared and charmed to your satisfaction, slowly add it to the vinegar and color mixtures, and stir it clockwise until it's well blended.

At last, it's time for the main event—coloring the eggs! If it suits you, hold the egg in your hand and dedicate it to the goddess Eostre. You can take it a step further and invite the goddess into the eggs if you like by reciting this simple chant:

> *Eostre, great goddess, who turned bird into bunny,*
> *Great goddess of spring, and all that is sunny*
> *I ask you a favor; great goddess, I beg*
> *Join me here now, please enter this egg.*

Place the eggs one at a time into the dye. As they absorb the colors, think about the energies you wish to impart to each egg. Envision the vibrations of the water, dye, and vinegar mixture pouring into the eggs, charging them with great power in tune with your magickal aims. When the eggs have reached the desired hue, remove them and allow them to dry.

Next, it's time to give your eggs a final touch of magick through personalization. Use permanent markers, stickers, or paint to add symbols or words to the eggs to represent your springtime goals and sentiments. Consider creating some eggs especially for a magickal egg hunt—paint a dollar sign on one egg, a heart on another egg, a sun on a third egg, a feather (or airplane or car) on a fourth egg, a star on a fifth egg, a book on a sixth egg, and a clover on a seventh egg. You might also add rhinestones, beads, or even a bit of glitter to give your eggs extra sparkle.

Once your eggs are all decorated and ready, decide how you will use them. You might place a few on your altar to attract the energies symbolized by the eggs, or you might eat them to absorb this magick into your body for more fast-acting effects. For a magickal egg hunt, you will need some friends to participate in the fun. Take the magickal egg hunt eggs outside and hide them. Give each of your friends a basket and ask them to search for the eggs to reveal their springtime fortunes. Whoever finds the egg with the dollar sign can expect greater wealth, while the person finding the egg with a heart can look forward to a season of romance. The sun egg indicates happiness, while the egg with the feather, airplane, or car predicts travel. The person who finds the star egg should expect spiritual growth this spring, while the egg with the book on it indicates a season absorbed in study. The lucky person who finds the egg with the clover symbol on it can look forward to good fortune. Once all the eggs are found, eat them to seal the deal, or offer them up to the Goddess, tossing them in a wild outdoor area for hungry animals to enjoy. The magick of the eggs will be released as the shells are cracked.

Notes

Beltane

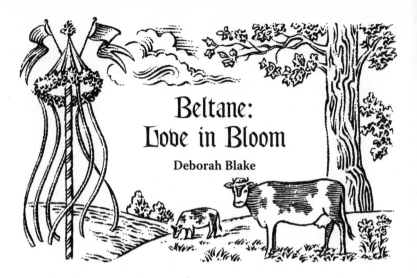

Beltane: Love in Bloom

Deborah Blake

It's the first of May, and the sun shines down on the group of men as they troop up into the woods in search of the perfect tree to form the centerpiece of the Maypole dance. Their chanting rings through the forest, soon to be joined by the clunk, clunk of the ax as each man helps to fell the tree that will serve their community. They thank the spirit of the oak for its sacrifice and tease each other about the size of their manhood and the skill with which they wield the ax. Reverence and mirth rule the forest.

In the meadow below, flower-bedecked women laugh and sing as they dig the hole for the pole to go into, making the simple act into ritual as they each take a turn with the shovel, digging away those parts of their lives that no longer work for them. One woman cradles her baby, conceived on this day, a year before. Another embraces her lover, putting a wreath of daisies into the woman's hair before handing her the shovel.

It is Beltane, and love is blooming everywhere. Birds guard nests full of eggs, rabbits chase each other through the fields, and Pagans rejoice as they celebrate the sacred union of goddess and god. For as it says in the Charge of the Goddess: All acts of love and pleasure are Her rituals, and on this day of the year, we celebrate love most of all.

Fertility, Celebration, and Bright Fires Burning

Beltane (also spelled Beltaine) or May Day is one of the eight Sabbats in the wheel of the year, a crossquarter holiday that marks the midway point between the Spring Equinox and the Summer Solstice. It is sometimes celebrated starting May Eve, or April 30, and continuing on into the next day. The astronomical date varies, but usually falls a few days later, around May 5. In the Southern Hemisphere, it is observed on November 1. Beltane is one of the major Celtic fire festivals, and a traditional time for Witches to gather together, even those who are normally solitary.

The name is derived from a word that meant "bright fire" where Beltane originated in Ireland, Scotland, and the Isle of Man. Bonfires, often called balefires, belfires, or need fires, were lit to cleanse and renew the land and people. Livestock would be driven between two huge fires to bless and protect them before they were sent out to pasture for the year. People would leap (presumably smaller) Beltane bonfires for luck, prosperity, and to show their courage. Sometimes young couples would join hands and leap the fires together.

The holiday celebrated fertility for the people and for the fields, symbolically planting the seeds for a good harvest and a healthy, prosperous year. Most cultures had some variation of fertility festivals, including Floralia in ancient Rome (observed from April 28 to May 3) and Walpurgisnacht, which was observed by early Germanic Pagans around the same time of year.

It was a natural time for a holiday for people whose lives depended on the land. After all, a plentiful harvest might make the difference between life and death for many, and so these rites tended to be raucous and bawdy, celebrating not only the end of a long and hungry winter but the anticipation of summer's growth and bounty.

In days gone by, both the rulers and the peasants put aside rigid social rules for the holiday, making love in the fields to invoke the fertility of the crops to come. Unmarried couples were allowed to spend the night in the woods "A'Maying," and married folks might take off their rings for this one time. Babies born nine months later were considered lucky.

While modern Pagans may not be quite so literal in their spreading of the seeds for a year of abundance, many of the old practices are still observed, the Maypole dance among them. The scene I described above might have taken place hundreds of years ago, but in fact, it was the joyous revelries of a local group of Pagans, with whom I have been celebrating (along with members of my coven, Blue Moon Circle) on and off for the last decade. Sometimes we stay at home to perform our own, quieter, rituals. And other times we drive the hour or so to join in with the Binghamton Pagan Community, to dig the hole, celebrate Women's Mysteries, crown the May Queen and King, and dance the Maypole dance with its intertwining ribbons and good-natured laughter. Later, there is ritual, and a bonfire, and dancing. What happens in the forest then… you'll just have to ask the faeries.

Maypoles and May Bushes

The Maypole is a long pole, usually created from a tree found nearby. Some folks prefer to use a fallen tree (so they are not killing a live one), others, like the Pagans I practice with, cut down one that is in a bad spot and would have to come down anyway. Whichever you chose, be sure to say thank you. A wreath is usually fastened to the top, with long multicolored ribbons coming from it. There should be as many ribbons as you have people doing the dance, and they should be about twice as long as the pole, since they will be woven in together. Half the dancers face one direction and the other half face the other, and they duck over and under to intertwine the ribbons in a colorful pattern.

This rarely goes off without a hitch, but that's part of the fun. If you are lucky enough to have musical folks among your community, they can play a lively tune. If not, you can use a Celtic album or sing a rousing Pagan chant for the dancers to frolic to.

In some traditions, a May Queen and a May King are chosen—largely ceremonial roles, representing the presence of the goddess and god, but one which sometimes carries responsibilities inside the community for the coming year. They are usually chosen by lot in a fun manner such as having a shiny stone hidden inside one of many cupcakes, and the Queen and King are often positioned underneath the Maypole during the dance, so the ribbons bind them together temporarily. Sometimes just the King is bound (usually to great laughter on the part of the Queen) to signify his connection to the land.

If you don't have the space, the people, or the inclination for a Maypole dance, you can have a May bush instead. May bushes were traditionally rowans or hawthorns, decorated with flowers, ribbons, colored eggs, or other symbols of the season. This is a nice time of year to plant a new bush, so you might want to pick out a particularly nice one and use it in your ritual, filling it with all your wishes for a prosperous and happy year and then planting it afterwards. Think of the nice gift this would make for Gaia!

If you are a solitary Witch, you can still have a May bush—even if it is just a tall houseplant that you adorn for the day. Put on some music and dance around, celebrating your love for yourself, your Pagan practice, and the gods you worship. This day is all about love, and you can send yours out into the universe and receive the Goddess and God's love in return.

Feed the Faeries, Feed Your Friends

Like its counterpart, Samhain, Beltane is a time when many believe that the veil between the worlds is thin, and those from the Otherworld may pass through or communicate with those on this side. Also, it is believed to be a time when the Fair Folk, or Fae, walked among us.

As part of your Beltane celebration, you may want to put a plate out for the faeries. A nicely decorated mini-cupcake or two, a few perfectly ripe strawberries, some seeds, or fresh bread will probably win you some friends among the Fair Folk. A wee sip of mead in a tiny cup will undoubtedly go over well, too. Just remember to be courteous and polite, and to thank them for coming into your life with peace and good will.

All those treats will also be well received by your friends, if you don't have faeries in your garden. If you plan to make a Beltane feast for yourself or to share with others, be sure to include some fresh fruits and a salad with the first of the summer herbs, like dill, chives, and parsley. If you're feeling brave, you can even throw some dandelion greens in there. (I prefer spinach, myself.)

Sacred Waters, Sacred Love

Beltane was also a time when people would make pilgrimages to sacred wells and bless the waters of their own wells. These days, few of us have wells (okay, I do, but the water still comes out of my sink, so there is no actual "well" to be seen), and you may not have a body of water nearby to make a pilgrimage to. But there are ways to include a water blessing in whatever rite you perform.

For instance, you can fill a bowl with water from your faucet, and bless it on your altar, thanking it for keeping you alive on a daily basis, as well as helping you to stay clean, water your plants, and all the other myriad gifts that water brings to our daily lives.

Or you can take a ritual bath (or shower, if you don't have a tub). This is nice to do before ritual, so you can add an element of spiritual cleansing as well. Mix some fragrant herbs or dried flowers (rose petals are particularly appropriate on Beltane!) with a bit of sea salt or Epsom salts, and maybe a handful of dried oatmeal. You can put these in a mesh bag, if you don't want to make a mess of your tub, or simply drop them into the water. If using the bag, you can scrub gently with it, washing away the cares and negativity of the mundane world before beginning your Beltane rites. Or you can simply sit and soak, enjoying the rare moment of self-indulgence. Remember, Beltane is as much about the love of self as it is about the love of others.

At least, that's the way I view it.

I realize that the general perception of this holiday—which is one of my favorites—is that of sexuality and male/female sexual union. But while that is a part of the tradition, and Beltane *is* in fact a time to rejoice at the union of Goddess and God, and the abundant life that returns to the fields, woods, and gardens around us, it isn't *only* about the eternal cosmic mating dance.

For me, Beltane is about love, in all its manifestations. This includes less conventional pairings (who is to say that the goddess can't love another goddess! Or the god another god!). But it also includes the love of parents for their children, family for each other (whether born-to families or the Pagan families of choice so many of us are blessed with), our love for our friends, and our love for the gods and theirs for us. And don't forget to send love inward, and love yourself. We are all manifestations of the God and Goddess here on earth, and therefore worthy of love, on this day most of all.

So light a belfire or dance around a Maypole. Feed the faeries or feed your friends. But most of all, feed your spirit with love in any and all its positive forms. For all acts of love and pleasure are Her rituals. Happy Beltane!

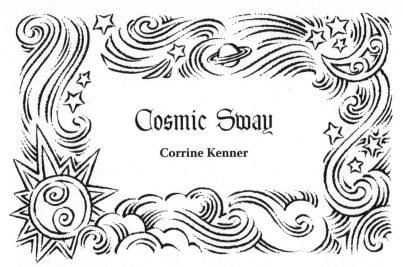

Cosmic Sway

Corrine Kenner

BELTANE BELONGS TO VENUS, the goddess of love—and on this holiday, we find her in Pisces, the sign of spiritual connection. It's hard to imagine a more perfect placement for the goddess of beauty and desire.

Beltane is a celebration of love and attraction. It's the day we celebrate the blessings of fertility, and it's the day we plant the seeds of growth and prosperity.

On May 1, the Sun will be in Venus' realm of Taurus, the sign of beauty and refinement. Taurus rules the earthly treasures that reflect our spiritual beliefs. Taurus values include money, property, and jewels, since they're the most common measure of worth in the physical world—but Taurus also rules the intangible additions that make life worth living, such as art, music, theater, and dance.

Venus is associated with all forms of pleasure, both spiritual and physical. She encourages us to follow our bliss, reach for our dreams, and live up to our highest ideals.

In an astrological chart, Venus graces everything she touches with ease and enjoyment. She's generous, almost to a fault. Like Jupiter, she's a benefactor; ancient astrologers called her the Lesser Benefic.

This year, she's perfectly poised to lend a helping hand.

Ever since Venus moved into Pisces in on April 5, she's been operating at peak capacity. Venus is exalted in Pisces. She doesn't rule the sign, like she rules Taurus and Libra. Instead, when she passes through Pisces, she's an honored guest, with power and acclaim. She's a warm and welcome queen, who bestows her blessings on an appreciative audience.

Right now, as an added bonus, you'll even find Neptune in that crowd.

Neptune is actually the ruler of Pisces. Since the planets are constantly on the move, it's not all that common to find planets in their own signs. When they do make it home for a visit, it's almost a happy accident—and they settle in, comfortably in command.

Neptune is the planet of glamor and illusion. Named for the ancient god of the sea, the watery planet dissolves boundaries, just as the constant rushing of the waves, and the ebb and flow of the tides, washes away the shoreline on the coasts.

In an astrological chart, Neptune makes everything it touches seem soft and mesmerizing; its iridescent glow casts everything in its best light.

Water takes the shape of its container, so Neptune also has shapeshifting properties. When women in need or distress call out to Neptune, he changes their forms.

Be Beautiful

The symbol for Venus is a hand mirror. (It's just like the goddess of love uses to check her appearance before she goes out in the world.) Today, before you celebrate this Beltane, take time to make the most of your appearance, so you'll be seen in the best possible light.

Start with enough beauty rest. Take a nap—especially if you've been feeling the influence of the flighty Gemini Moon. If you can't take a nap, at least take a long bath—by candlelight, if possible, with soft music in the background. Style your hair and dab cologne or perfume behind your ears. Wear clothes that feel good against your skin, in colors that compliment your complexion and styles that flatter your figure.

Once you're imbued with all the confidence and courage that Venus can offer, you'll be free to make your way into the world, where you can connect with others.

Planetary Positions

This is Venus' last hurrah in Pisces—at least for the time being. She'll start a new tour of the zodiac when she moves into Aries on May 2, and then she'll return to one of her own signs, Taurus, on May 28.

Mercury, too, is always on the move. The winged messenger will fly from earthy Taurus into airy Gemini on May 7.

The Sun will join him there on May 20. Mercury rules Gemini, which means you can expect thoughts and words to fly at a record-setting pace.

Mercury and the Sun typically travel together. Mercury is a small planet, and its tight orbit doesn't allow it to wander too far from the center of our solar system. At Beltane, both the Sun and Mercury will be in a flowing, easygoing trine with Pluto, which will lend a sense of powerful, life-affirming drama to any celebration.

During the height of Beltane festivities, however, Mars will be moving backward in Libra, in an uncomfortable square with Jupiter in Cancer. The aspect could keep Jupiter's expansive energy in check—or it might make Mars more eager to prove his own virility.

Mars' retrograde period will end on May 20. From that point on, he'll be eager to move into Scorpio, which was traditionally his own domain. The transition may seem rushed, and you might find yourself racing toward a place of personal power, too.

On May 10, Saturn will be at its closest approach to Earth, fully illuminated by the Sun. If the weather is clear in your area, you'll be able to see it yourself. On that night, Saturn will look pale yellow, and it will be brighter than almost every other star in the sky.

Saturn is currently retrograde, moving backward through Scorpio, the sign of mystery. Saturn's current focus on shared resources might prompt you to reassess your obligations to other people. If you're giving too much of yourself, for too little in return, it's a good time to stop and reverse course yourself.

Two weeks ago, on April 14, Pluto also entered a retrograde period, during which it will move backward through Capricorn. Pluto will continue to backtrack until September 23. For more on Pluto's significance, turn to the section on Mabon.

The Phases of the Moon

The New Moon in Taurus on April 29 will be accompanied by an annular solar eclipse—which promises to bring news and developments about the physical resources and spiritual values we share on a global level. We might even be moved to take dramatic action, enlightened by a fiery first quarter Moon in Leo on May 6. The Full Moon in watery Scorpio on May 14 will be primal and powerful, while a mesmerizing third quarter Moon in Pisces will bring peace and a sense of connection on May 21.

The Old Ways:
Fairy Gifts

Linda Raedisch

SOME YEARS AGO, WHILE shopping for a children's novel in the basement of a bookstore in Lübeck, a walled maze of medieval bricks and cobblestones in northern Germany, I stumbled upon an unexpected treasure. In a niche in the old wall, behind a pane of glass, sat a green-glazed mug, along with a few other humble pieces of pottery. They had been discovered in the course of scooping out the foundations of the current building and, instead of being boxed up and sent to the museum, had been enshrined right there in the bookstore, an apropos window into the city's past. Had I known then about the Danish/North German legend type, "Death of an Underground Person," I might have read much more into that little green mug.

The blueprint for "Death of an Underground Person" goes like this: A hardworking tradesman, often a tavern keeper, ventures outside the walls of the town on some errand. While he is out in the hills, he hears a voice announcing the death of one Pingel/Pippe/Prilling/Pralling—the name varies from region to region—and exhorts the tavern keeper to repeat the news when he gets home. He does so, relating the whole story to his wife in the kitchen. When he gets to the part about Pingel being dead, they both hear a cry from the cellar. Hurrying down the steps to investigate, they find a mug/silver jug/drinking horn lying on the floor near the beer tuns. Apparently, whoever had been haunting their cellar and partaking of the beer was so overcome with grief that he forgot to pick up his vessel before he rushed off to the funeral. So, had I only known about the underground folk, also called "cellar men," I could have told my then seven-year-old that the small green mug had been dropped by a dear friend of the deceased Pringel, and how this particular tribe of little people lived by tunneling from pantry to pantry, helping themselves to beer, wine, and cheese. And wasn't it a wonder that a few of their dishes had survived for us to look at today?

Beltane is one of those points in the year when we are more likely to sense the presence of the little people, hidden folk, fairies, and elves. Spring has arrived without a doubt, and we are drawn to stroll out under the moon to keep the party going all night and to open ourselves to the mysteries beyond the city lights. What better time to celebrate the gifts of the fairies? (I should clarify that, under the umbrella of "fairy gifts," I will be including that which has been lost or snatched in addition to those things which were freely given.) Nowadays, fairy gifts tend toward such abstract rewards as luck, prosperity, or a thriving garden. But only a few hundred years ago, they were just as likely to be cows, goats, hunting dogs, or objects you could hold in your hand. I can't promise you'll be allowed to touch any of these gifts today, but there are a few you can still go and see with your own eyes.

Of the four best-known Cumbrian "Lucks," two are glass vessels. In a society used to sipping their small beer from cups of horn, wood, or earthenware, specimens of blown glass must indeed have appeared to be the work of fairies. But what exactly is a Luck? In short, it's a costly object with both magical properties and obscure origins. When properly cared for, the family with which the Luck resides will prosper. If lost or damaged, then there's an end to the good fortune. Only two of the four Lucks, however, are of otherworldly provenance; the Luck of Workington, an agate cup, was the gift of Mary Queen of Scots, and the Luck of Muncaster, a green glass bowl enhanced with gilt and white enamelwork, was given to Sir John Pennington by the deposed Henry VI in gratitude for Sir John's hospitality.

At about eight hundred years old, the Luck of Edenhall, a clear glass beaker with white, green, and cobalt enamel flourishes, appears to be the eldest of the Lucks, and it was indeed the "gift" of the fairies. Cumbrian fairies are apparently more careless than the average, for they left this priceless and fragile relic perched on the edge of a well while they made merry in the grass. The beaker was discovered at the well by the butler when he came to fetch a pail of water. It is not clear if it was the butler or the dismayed fairies who first uttered the couplet, "If that glass either break or fall/ Farewell the luck of Eden Hall." The house at Edenhall is no more, but you can see the glass beaker, all of a piece, at the Victoria and Albert Museum.

The history of the Luck of Burrell Green also revolves around a well. When a maid went to draw water during a wedding reception at Burrell Green Farm, the hobgoblins who dwelt there begged her for a taste of the wedding feast. When the maid returned with cakes and wine, the hobgoblins presented her with a wide brass dish. Since brass is hard to break, the couplet running round the rim goes, "If this dish be sold or gi'en, Farewell the Luck of Burrell Green." (The dish and the farm are still there.) These are fairy tales for certain, but the Luck of Muncaster's provenance is equally dubious. The idea that King Henry, upon losing the Battle of Hexham, would have been wandering the hills with a Venetian glass bowl stuffed inside his doublet is not much more plausible than a wedding present from the hobgoblins or fairies cavorting on the green.

❧

Because elves and fairies were supposed to excel at the textile arts (while trolls patently did not), it is not surprising that a number of woven fairy flags, banners, and altar cloths have been counted as otherworldly gifts. The most famous is the Fairy Flag of Dunvegan Castle. This silk pennon has been described as green or yellow, and Sir Walter Scott, on a visit to the castle on the Isle of Skye, was able to make out a pattern of red berries against the now faded ground.

To my eyes, the silk is the color of a very old blood stain or an oak leaf that has been lying on the ground all winter. Like the oak leaf, the weave has been worn or eaten in places to a mere tracery of threads.

According to one version of the legend attached to it, the flag was a sort of christening gift from a local fairy to the infant scion of Clan MacLeod. In another, this fairy woman was the adult MacLeod's lover. (Since fairies are immortal, or very nearly so, she could easily have been both his lover and his fairy godmother.) Either way, the banner was given with the promise that whenever the MacLeod waved it, help would come. Wave it he did, on several occasions, and was saved each time, even after he had set his supernatural sweetheart aside and taken a human wife. The MacLeods were true to the flag, at least: it has never been let go from the castle.

Meanwhile in Iceland, on the altar of Hvalsnes Church, there rested a blanket woven by elfin hands. Like the Dunvegan Fairy Flag, it, too, had been used to wrap an infant in its cradle, though the Hvalsnes cloth was probably of wool, not silk. The baby was half human, and for that reason its elfin mother had brought it to the church to be baptized. When the baby's mortal father refused to acknowledge his part in the business, the spurned lady threw the blanket in through the open church door and carried the baby away again in a huff—but not before she had uttered a curse condemning her erstwhile lover to live out the rest of his days as a whale. The coverlet was said to be of a characteristically fine weave, which was probably why it was treasured for so many hundreds of years.

The Hvalsnes altar cloth brings us to the next interesting thing about these fairy flags, cups, and Lucks: many of them have strong associations with the Church. The goblin-wrought Luck of Burrell Green may once have held communion wafers for, in addition to the imprecation not to let the Luck out of the family, the brass bears the ghosts of the words, "Mary, Mother of Jesus, Saviour of Men." The inscription has been all but worn away, either by an overzealous wielder of the polishing rag or by someone attempting to destroy the evidence of the dish's original purpose. Likewise, because it used to reside in a case stamped with the Latin Christian monogram "IHS," it's quite likely that the Luck of Edenhall once held wine for the Eucharist rather than fairy ale. King Henry's Venetian glass bowl was used to baptize generations of Pennington babies, and as for those little drinking vessels dropped by the underground folk, the most precious ended up in church treasuries.

The concept of gift-bestowing fairies was already fixed in both the Celtic and Germanic Pagan imaginations, especially when it came to cups like the later Christianized Grail. But the Luck of Edenhall was made in Syria in the mid-1200s and probably brought home by a returning Crusader, as was the Dunvegan Fairy Flag, which has been traced to the Middle East in the early centuries AD. (One theory goes that the Fairy Flag once belonged to the Knights Templar, though it would already have been ancient in their heyday.) It has been suggested that when the Protestant Reformation made it unfashionable and at times life-threatening to have such relics hanging about, their owners assigned them an alternate origin in the pre-Catholic past. It was, however, hardly a time to be invoking the fairies. Fairies were equated more or less with Witches, and we know how the inquisitors felt about them. I believe that the bare bones of these stories must already have been in place, to be trotted out again in the more tolerant eighteenth century and further embroidered in the Victorian era.

However, whenever these stories arose, they eventually became fused with the glass, woven into the silk, and, quite literally, etched into the brass so that we can no longer set eyes on the pieces in questions without experiencing a little thrill. No matter what our well-informed brains might tell us, our hearts cannot help embracing the idea that here is something tangible that has slipped from fairy hands into our own.

❧

If you can't get yourself to the Isle of Skye or Victoria and Albert Museum this May Eve, consider a trip to the antique shop or flea market instead. Whatever you happen to choose—teacup, milk glass candy dish, or Japanese doll—remember that the adventure doesn't end with the sale. When you've brought your treasure home, place it provocatively on the mantel or up front in the china cabinet. Or, if you prefer, allow yourself to be discovered in the process of dusting it off as if you have just discovered it in the attic. When your children, grandchildren, nieces, and nephews start asking questions, go ahead and make something up. Whether you invoke kings, queens, goblins, or Mary Poppins, rest assured that your fairy gift will keep on giving long after you are gone.

For Further Reading:

Ashliman, D. L. "Death of an Underground Person." http://www.pitt.edu/~dash/type6070b.html#prilling. Accessed September 11, 2012.

Davidson, Hilda Ellis. *The Lost Beliefs of Northern Europe.* London: Routledge, 1993.

"The Fairy Flag." http://www.dunvegancastle.com. Accessed September 11, 2012.

Keightley, Thomas. *The World Guide to Gnomes, Fairies, Elves, and Other Little People.* New York: Gramercy Books, 1978. (Originally published in 1880 as *The Fairy Mythology.*)

Purkiss, Diane. *At the Bottom of the Garden: A Dark History of Fairies, Hobgoblins, and Other Troublesome Things.* New York: New York University Press, 2000.

Simpson, Jacqueline. *Icelandic Folktales and Legends.* Berkeley: University of California Press, 1972.

Westwood, Jennifer and Jacqueline Simpson. *The Lore of the Land: A Guide to England's Legends, from Spring-Heeled Jack to the Witches of Warboys.* London: Penguin Books, 2005.

Feasts and Treats

Dallas Jennifer Cobb

CELEBRATE MAY DAY WITH a feast of fertile foods. Celebrating the fertility of the earth this feast includes a variety of seasonally available ingredients.

If you invite friends for a big dinner, be sure to have equal numbers of men and women to invoke the energy of the past when maids ran out into the forests with young men in pursuit.

Alternatively, you could make this feast, and carry it out into the woods for a sacred picnic in the grove at dusk. Beware the magic at work in these fertile foods, and prepare for all the possible consequences of May Day frolicking.

Spinach and Cheese Quiche

Eggs and milk and cheese are all symbols of fertility, and they combine well in quiche. Like a big egg pie, quiche is easy to make, and it's portable. So if you decide to sleep out in the woods tonight, you can wrap it up and take it with you. One of the earliest greens available in the spring, baby spinach is a tender taste of fertile earth. To keep it really simple, I buy a frozen pie crust and the shredded cheese available in the dairy case.

Preparation Time: 15 minutes
Cooking Time: 35 minutes
Serves: 8

1 frozen pie crust
4 eggs
½ cup milk
½ cup cream
¼ teaspoon salt
⅛ teaspoon pepper
1½ cups shredded cheddar cheese
1½ shredded havarti cheese
1 cup fresh baby spinach greens

Preheat oven to 375 F. Place frozen crust in the oven for 10 minutes while you prepare other ingredients.

In a big bowl, combine eggs, milk, cream, salt, and pepper, and beat until well mixed.

Remove crust from oven and prick with a fork to remove air bubbles. Pour ⅓ of egg mix in crust. Layer cheeses and spinach, setting one spinach leaf aside. Pour remaining egg mix over top, and place the single spinach leaf in the middle.

Bake at 375 degrees F for 35 to 40 minutes until golden brown, and no longer runny. Remove from oven and let stand 5 minutes, then cut into wedges. Serve with mixed greens.

Spring Mixed Greens with Maple Balsamic Vinaigrette

The nutrients in the first greens of the season stimulate a cleanse of the liver and help our body adjust to the seasonal change. Our body is reminded to "spring clean" internally. If you can buy, or wild-craft, local greens, get them. Their bitter, sometimes astringent taste is medicine to our body. For urban dwellers, baby greens are readily available at the grocery store. Toss greens with balsamic vinaigrette and garnish with crushed walnuts.

Maple Balsamic Vinaigrette

Sour and sweet meet in this versatile vinaigrette. A staple around my house, I make this in big quantities, pour it into a clean bottle, and keep it for up to four weeks in the fridge. Because olive oil solidifies, remember to warm to room temperature and shake well before serving.

Preparation Time: 5 minutes
Serves: 8

¼ cup maple syrup
½ balsamic vinegar
¼ cup water
2 teaspoons mustard (can use the usual stuff, or go fancy with Dijon mustard. Both taste great.)
Salt and pepper to taste
½ cup olive oil
Walnuts, crushed

Put all the ingredients except the oil in a blender and process. Slowly add oil through the blender cap's opening, or add oil in small amounts and blend.

Love Water

Water can be transformed by intention. It has even been shown in photographs, that water changes its molecular structure after "hearing" or "reading" focused messages. Tonight, magically enhance your water with the intention of love.

Preparation Time: 5 minutes
Serves: 8

2 liters of natural water (from a spring, river, or lake, or rainwater)
Large glass pitcher

Clearing your thoughts, place your hands around the glass pitcher. Thinking of love, invoke its energy. You can think about people you love, and people who love you, things, places, and even foods you love. Let the energy of love swell with a deep breath, and feel the prickles of spirit in your scalp, then exhale and send that energy down through your heart and out your arms, so that love fills the water. Lean close and whisper over the surface of the water "Love." Protect your love water from harsh words, either spoken or written. Serve in the spirit of love, and raise a glass, toasting love.

Easy Stewed Rhubarb

The earliest fruit available in my backyard is actually a vegetable. I am always heartened when the weird green bulbs erupt from the soil after the snow has melted, and the leaves unfurl into large, fan-shaped rhubarb. Filled with vitamin C, vitamin A, potassium, calcium, and tons of dietary fiber, rhubarb is great for baking breads and muffins, delicious in pies and crumbles, and is quickly stewed.

Preparation Time: 5 minutes
Cooking Time: 15 minutes
Serves: 8

6 cups of young rhubarb stems, coarsely chopped
½ cup granulated sugar
2 tablespoons of water
Vanilla Greek yogurt

In large saucepan, combine rhubarb, sugar, and water and cook at medium heat, stirring continuously until sugar has dissolved. Reduce heat to low and simmer uncovered so the water evaporates. Stir occasionally for about 15 minutes until it becomes slightly thicker and rhubarb is in threads. Serve warm with a dollop of Greek yogurt on top.

Crafty Crafts

Blake Octavian Blair

By Beltane, spring is well underway, the flowers are blooming, and the mischievous magick of the little people is afoot. Beltane, in addition to being a fertility holiday, is also the point in the wheel of the year when people begin to sense fairy activity picking up. Fairies come in many varieties, from giant to tiny, beautiful to homely, benefic to decidedly bothersome.

Fascination with fairy beings spans cultures across the globe. Almost every culture has a version of these creatures in its lore. Historically, humans have found it a wise decision to make efforts to appease and work with the fairies rather than risk offending them and dealing with the possible repercussions. Fairies are rather fond of many plants and flowers in bloom this time of year, and will often dwell among them. In addition, and occasionally inconveniently for humans, they are also fond of shiny things such as silver jewelry and gemstones. More than one person has found that a favorite piece of jewelry or a crystal has gone missing, only to find it sometime later in a very obvious place that they had previously looked. For many, there is no doubt that these items were in the custody of mischievous fairy folk during their absence.

This sabbat craft is designed to help you give the fairy folk that may cross through your territory a place to stay and offerings of their very own, so perhaps they'll keep their eyes off of your goodies and their mischief to a minimum.

Fairy Houses

One way to show your desire to work with and to get on the good side of the fairy folk is to set aside a place just for them and with offerings for their very own. This not only shows your respect, but in giving them trinkets and pretty shiny things of their own, hopefully they'll keep their eyes off of yours!

Some half dozen years ago, I found myself completing this craft project in order to make peace with an infestation of fairies in my home. Their exact reason for taking up residence with me, I'm not sure, but they were moving, holding ransom, and making general mischief with my stones, crystals, and jewelry. These little fairy houses not only were an easy, fast, and effective solution, but they were great fun to create. And many of the décor items for your fairy house you can gathering from your yard and/or may have on hand already.

Supplies

Small- to medium-sized plain wooden birdhouse (available at most craft stores)

Gathered natural objects as desired (twigs, bark, acorns, pine cones, rocks, dried pressed/fallen leaves)

Hot glue gun or multipurpose craft glue

Acrylic paints in various colors and brushes as desired (optional)

Assorted trinkets for offerings as desired (shiny objects and beads, small polished crystals, candies, etc.)

Small saw or kitchen scissors (optional)

Instructions: The small wooden birdhouses that this craft utilizes provide a blank canvas for your crafty creative expression and the perfect château for your troop of fairies. A good place to begin work on your creation is decorating the roof. The simplest route is to paint the roof. My personal preference is to use natural colors. Or, you might forgo the painted roof in favor of something more detailed. Repurposed items from nature make an environment that beckons fairies. Perhaps you want to disassemble a pine cone and make tiny roof shingles. Or, maybe you wish to create a thatched look utilizing fallen pine needles. I also like to take a small to medium piece of branch and fashion a chimney. If your house has a slanted roof, as most do, simply cut one end at an angle to fit the slant of the roof and glue it on. If you choose to use a hot glue gun, please remember to exercise caution and use proper safety procedures.

Similar options exist for the walls of your fairy abode. Consider gluing dried, pressed flower petals and leaves of trees or herbs to the house for siding. You can arrange them in ornamental designs or completely cover the walls with them. Some plants favored by fairies you might consider are ferns, pansies, and ivy. When collecting fallen twigs and other items from trees, consider their magickal properties in relation to fairies. It is said that locations where oak, ash, and thorn trees grow simultaneously are prime fairy hangouts! Collecting pieces from these areas for use in creating your house would be very fitting. Bad-natured fairies are said to be repelled by rowan trees. Adding a touch of rowan would perhaps help to attract less mischievous tenants!

Sawing acorns in half and them gluing them to the side of the house creates a nice accent and adds the wonderfully varied properties of oak to your fairy house. Protection, healing/health, and luck are all wrapped up in this classic magickal tree. Perfect qualities for working with the little folk.

I also sometimes like to include small metal jingle bells (like those at craft stores) to fairy houses. Conflicting opinions exist in fairy lore on the use of bells and fairies reaction to them. Some say that they scare them off and work as a deterrent. Others claim that their sound and shiny appearance attract the little folk. In my ex-

perience, the fairies in my home not only enjoy the bells, but they help avert the disappearance of your own shiny items! You can use a bit of string or fishing line to hang them from or tie them to your house.

You can use acrylic paints to paint a house number for your fairies on the outside of the house. Perhaps you'd like to paint a nice homey "Welcome" sign for them. Sigils and symbols are also nice. This is the perfect time to call the seven-pointed fairy star into action!

Once your house is decorated to your taste and desire, it is time to turn your attention to the offerings you wish to leave your fairy visitors. These will be placed inside the house, through its round doorway/opening. Small acorns, polished gemstones, metallic beads, pennies and dimes, and loose jingle bells are all great options. In my experience, they also love a nice sweet treat. Leaving wrapped candies was always a well-accepted offering—red and white dinner mints, caramels, small chocolates. (I love chocolate. Who doesn't love chocolate? It is no wonder that the fairies delight in it as well!)

Place your house in the area of your home where you sense and experience the most fairy activity. Two of my favorite resting places to place fairy real estate are high up on top of bookcases and high shelves and in and among houseplants. You can put your fairy house outdoors on a porch if you choose but be aware that it will weather and that parts of it will go slowly missing as birds, squirrels, and other wildlife slowly reclaim them!

By providing the fairies a resting place in your home and giving them offerings of their own, you show that you wish to work with them, rather than against them. Also, before being too hard on the little folk, always remember that while fairies and their folklore are certainly full of mischief—so are humans! Rejoice in strengthening your relationship with the little folk this Beltane season!

Cost: $10.00 to $25.00

Time to complete: 1 to 1.5 hours (depending on ornateness)

For Further Reading:

Dugan, Ellen. *Garden Witch's Herbal: Green Magick, Herbalism & Spirituality*. Woodbury, MN: Llewellyn Publications, 2009.

Eason, Cassandra. *A Complete Guide to Faeries & Magical Beings*. York Beach, ME: Weiser Books, 2002.

Cunningham, Scott. *Cunningham's Encyclopedia of Magical Herbs*. St. Paul, MN: Llewellyn Publications, 1985.

All One Family

Kerri Connor

AT OUR BELTAINE ACTIVITIES everyone always loves to dance the maypole. Our was made rather inexpensively with a long metal pipe, some grommets, key rings, and canvas strapping in different colors. We also needed a drill. My husband drilled holes in one end of the pipe—one hole for each piece of canvas strapping he would need. Then he pounded the pipe several feet into the ground so that the holes were at the top and that the pipe was steady and barely moveable. Next he added the grommets to the canvas strapping and then using the key rings attached the canvas straps to the pole itself.

We do leave our may pole up year long and occasionally have to replace straps that have taken too much water/weather damage. Ever year we also top it with a new bouquet of flowers (generally fake ones) that are able to stick down right inside the top of the pole. The only real issue we have had with this pole is because the pole is so thin, just an inch or two in diameter, it can take a LONG time to get the dance done all the way until people have run out of their strapping. In the long run, if you try to go too fast, you'll generally end up falling down dizzy, which of course can be fun in its own way.

We usually have enough people for Beltaine that the maypole is danced several times, so everyone gets a turn. We let an adult group go first so that the kids can watch. Younger kids are often accompanied by someone older who lets them know if they need to go over or under. Sometimes we come up with the beautiful weave pattern, other times—well not so much, but the fun is in the dancing itself.

There are several types of dances that can be done on the maypole instead of just the traditional weave. We also like the spider web dance, which allows people who may want to participate but not actual dance a job to do as they sit in one spot holding the strap tightly while other people dance around them. With this dance, even those who are not very physically adept can join in on the fun.

In the past, we crowned a May Queen and a May King, but quickly learned that can actually lead to a bit of jealously among kids. So instead, we provide supplies for the girls to make flower crowns and the boys to make masks. Flowers are relatively inexpensive at craft stores even during the growing season. Black, white, or even clear eye masks can generally be found year-round at craft stores, or you can stock up before Halloween. You will want a good tacky glue for little kids or even low-temp glue guns for older ones or to help the younger ones glue their masks and crowns together.

Fertility

Since Beltaine is truly a fertility festival, we all know of the couples who go off into the woods to make their own fertility magic. Obviously, that is not appropriate with children around, but other aspects of fertility can be celebrated in mixed company.

At our celebrations, we do a full blessing of the garden plot complete with walking the boundaries of the garden while pouring milk and honey onto the ground as an offering to the gods and goddesses and asking for a bountiful harvest.

Sometimes we need fertility in other aspects of our lives. Maybe you need to produce more money, perhaps your child would like to produce more friends or better grades. Whenever you are adding to something or producing something, you are working with fertility. This activity is quick and pretty easy. You will need someone to dig a hole (we do ours in our fairy garden) in the ground. If you don't have a place to dig, just get a larger-size planter. Everyone who wants to participate takes a piece of paper and writes down a part of their life they are looking to grow. Have them try to be as specific as possible. For example, if someone needs their money to grow for home repairs, have them write that out entirely. When everyone is done, throw the pieces of paper into the hole (or planter) and cover it back up with dirt, planting it. Water it so that your wishes and needs can grow.

The Beltaine Fires

Beltaine is also the time for jumping the Beltaine fires, though I don't recommend it for young children. We always make sure that the fire jumping is done in a safe manner over a small fire that has been dug into the ground. The adult men might have their own ideas about fire jumping, but when it comes to children and teens, it's safety first.

There are plenty of other safe events that can take place around a bonfire, however. Everyone can drum. Even my granddaughter was drumming by six months of age. We have a large collection of drums, tambourines, rattles, maracas, thunder cans, rains sticks, wood blocks, cow bells, all kinds of "noisemakers" and percussion instruments that provide literally hours of entertainment around the bonfires. The music doesn't have to be perfect—it's the act of making the music together that is what counts.

If you feel more like a quieter evening, you can tell stories around the bonfire. Classic Celtic tales, tales from the Mabinogion, Irish folk tales, Native American stories of lore and legend, are all not only fun to tell and listen too, they are educational as well. Ask each adult to bring a story to tell from their own ethnic heritage, and you will be sure to have a huge variety of stories for the evening.

While many of these activities center around fertility, many also center on bringing people together in ways that are wonderful for raising energy, and of course a lot of fun for everyone involved.

Ritual: Love Is the Greatest Magick

Deborah Blake

BELTANE IS OFTEN VIEWED with an emphasis on the sexual love between a couple, but I think its message is much wider than that. (And not everyone is comfortable with the blatantly sensual or is at a place in their lives where they can identify with this kind of rite.) Pagans with small children may want a sabbat ritual they can share with the whole family, and single folks often feel left out or pressured by a holiday that is all about "hooking up." So instead, I like to focus on the general theme of love, in all its manifestations. For some, that may in fact mean an intimate relationship; for others, it is the love of family, friends, coven, animal companions, or even the love we so seldom show to our own selves—and so badly need. And, of course, it includes the love of God and Goddess for each other and for us, and the love we return to them in our worship.

Love is the Greatest Magick

This ritual is designed for group practice, but can easily be adapted for use as a solitary rite. If you are doing the ritual as a solitary, you can leave out the "welcome and explanation" speech, or read it out loud to yourself. Group instructions will be in **bold**, and can be ignored if practicing alone. Instructions are written for High Priestess

(HPS) and High Priest (HP), but if your group only has one leader, that person can play both roles. If possible, perform outside around a bonfire or portable fire pit, but you can also use a small cauldron or bowl with candles in it to stand in for the bonfire if necessary. A large houseplant can be used instead of the May bush.

Items Needed

Bonfire OR cauldron/bowl filled with sand or salt, with a few tealights inside

May bush (any small bush located in or near your circle *or* a small bush ready to be planted after the ritual *or* a tall sturdy houseplant

Colored ribbons (3 or 4 for each person taking part) in a basket

Quarter candles (1 each red, blue, green, yellow, *or* 4 white)

God and Goddess candles (1 silver and 1 gold, *or* 1 yellow and 1 white)

Sage smudge stick

Salt and water in small bowls or pitchers

Small bowl to mix salt and water in

Fun music to dance to and/or drums, rattles, or bells (optional)

Cakes and Ale (chocolate-covered strawberries or small cupcakes, mead/wine/juice—preferably something decadent and indulgent)

Speaking stick (optional, for a group)

Table to use as an altar, and altar cloth (optional)

Matches

Process into the circle or gather together inside sacred space.

Cleanse yourself and your circle space with the sage smudge stick. As the smoke is wafted from head to toe, visualize any negativity or tension floating away, leaving you clean and ready for ritual work. **Pass the sage from person to person around the circle, or have one person walk around the outside of the circle and waft**

the smoke over all those within. Take some slow deep breaths and feel yourself becoming calm and centered.

Mix the water with the salt, **[High Priest/High Priestess (HP/HPS) can say this, then bowl is passed around the circle]**:

Water into salt, salt into water; wash away all that which is negative and impure, leaving only that which is positive and beneficial.

Anoint yourself on forehead, lips, heart, belly, and groin (if desired).

Cast the circle **(HP/HPS will do this for a group)** by walking around the perimeter of the sacred space deosil (clockwise), either sweeping with a broom or pointing with an athame, sword, or fingertip. Say:

I cast the circle round and round, from earth to sky, from sky to ground. I conjure now this sacred space, outside of time, outside of space. So mote it be.

(Visualize the circle filling with a white light or glow.)

Invoke the Quarters

Invoke the four quarters by standing facing each one in turn (starting with East) and then lighting the appropriate candle after you have summoned the spirit of the element.

East (yellow candle): *I call the power of the East, the element of Air, to join* **us** *[me] in this sacred circle. Cleanse* **our** *[my] spirit with your fresh summer breezes and blow in love to fill* **our** *[my] hearts and minds.*

South (red candle): *I call the power of the South, the element of Fire, to join* **us** *[me] in this sacred circle. Shine down passion, creativity, and love like the warmth of the summer sun.*

West (blue candle): *I call the power of the West, the element of Water, to join* **us** *[me] in this sacred circle. Wash* **us** *[me] with your* *waves of cleansing and clarity, and let love fall upon* **us** *[me] like drops of blessed rain.*

North (green candle): *I call up the power of the North, the element of Earth, to join us [me] in this sacred circle. Help* **us** *[me] to be grounded and rooted, drawing up the love of Gaia from below as the trees draw in nourishment from the earth, and let* **us** *[me] be nourished as well.*

Invoke the goddess (silver or white candle): **[HPS]** Great Goddess, She who now appears as maiden, turning the land to green and growing glory around **us** [me] and who summons **us** [me] to join Her in celebrating love—I invoke you!

Invoke the god (gold or yellow candle): **[HP]** Great God, He who is lord of the beasts and consort to the goddess, whose seed brings life back to the land—I invoke you!

[Welcome speech—for group, spoken by HP or HPS] *It is Beltane, and the land around us has come back to life, blossoming with colors and fragrance, and with the rising energy of the season. That energy rises in* **us** *[me] too, and today,* **we** *[I] celebrate that manifestation of energy we call love. Love can come in many forms, wearing many faces. It has no limits: not age, nor gender, nor color, nor size. For the God and Goddess love us all equally, and bid us to love one another, and to love ourselves. It is Beltane, and the God and Goddess have come together to celebrate their love. Let* **us** *[me] celebrate with them, in joy and with open hearts, sending* **our** *[my] love out into the universe, and welcoming in all the love* **our** *[my] hearts can hold in return.*

Light the bonfire/candles.

[HPS/HP or any group member says]: *This fire represents the passion and warmth of love, which brightens the heart of the one who gives it as much as it does the one who receives it.*

Hand around basket of ribbons. Each person should take three or four ribbons. (If it is a large group, then you may want to limit each person to 1 or 2. A solitary can use as many as he/she desires.)

[HP/HPS]: *In some Beltane rituals, people dance around a May-pole to bring abundance and sacred energy to the land. In others, a May bush is used instead, and decorated to celebrate the joy of the season. Today, we will adorn this May bush with our ribbons, symbols of the love we have for those in our lives. We will take turns tying our ribbons, one by one, onto the bush, to signify the love we have... or even the love we want. You may speak of the love in your heart, or not, as you wish. And feel free to dance or chant as you hang your ribbon.*

Each person around the circle will t**ake a turn (or turns) placing a ribbon on the May bush,** speaking their love aloud if desired. If you have music, you can play it during this time, or people can drum, or chant, or sing.

Pass Cakes and Ale (first one, then the other), saying:
May you never hunger, but always have enough to eat and some-one to share it with, and *May you never thirst for happiness, but always have all the love you need.*

[Optional for group: pass the speaking stick around the cir-cle, so that each person might take a minute to speak of what is in his/her heart, while the others listen without speaking.]

Thank the god and goddess. [**HP/HPS speaks, then extin-guishes candle**]:

Great God, **we** *[I] thank you for your presence here in* **our** *[my] circle and in* **our lives** *[my life] always. Blessed be. Great Goddess,* **we** *[I] thank you for your presence here in* **our** *[my] circle and in* **our lives** *[my life] always. Blessed be.*

Dismiss the quarters in the reverse order you summoned them, and extinguish each candle in turn.

North: *Element of Earth,* **we** *[I] thank you for keeping* **us** *[me] grounded during this rite, and for joining* **us** *[me] in this sacred space.*

West: *Element of Water,* **we** *[I] thank you for your clearing and cleansing during this rite, and for joining* **us** *[me] in this sacred space.*

South: *Element of Fire,* **we** *[I] thank you for sharing your warmth and passion during this rite, and for joining* **us** *[me] in this sacred space.*

East: *Element of Air,* **we** *[I] thank you for blowing away negativity and anything that blocked the giving and receiving of love during this rite, and for joining* **us** *[me] in this sacred space.*

Open the circle by turning or walking widdershins (counterclockwise) and pointing with an athame, sword, or finger, or else [**group**] join hands and say:

Merry meet, merry part, and merry meet again! The circle is open, but never broken.

A solitary can also simply close his/her eyes and visualize the walls of the circle coming down.

You may want to have your postritual feast by the bonfire. Otherwise be sure to safely extinguish the bonfire and/or candles.

Notes

Notes

Litha

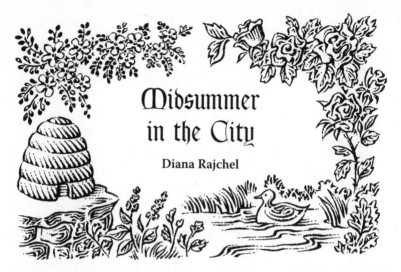

Midsummer in the City

Diana Rajchel

ONE OF THE GREAT joys of living in Minnesota is the sun that lingers until almost 10 p.m. at Summer Solstice. In winter, we yearn for it—daylight is a precious gift, and during summer, we do our best to suck up every bit of sun willing to hit us. This is true whether you live on a farm or in the most wildly urban part of the state.

The Twin Cities sit just far enough into the Northern Hemisphere to experience summer's brightness without a midnight sun, and at the Winter Solstice to have a long night of darkness—but to continue to see a sunrise every day. Sometimes we even enjoy a peek at the Northern Lights. Our relationship to the sun is one of extremes, yes, but not of absolutes. Changes of the light force changes in our daily lives. This is how we know the seasons, and understand them as a reliable constant in a state of at times wildly unpredictable weather.

In summer, days swing from cool and light to oppressively humid, with temperatures sometimes topping 100 degrees Fahrenheit. While the sweltering temperatures can break down the will to live of those with even central air conditioning, we still cherish those extremes because we all know that in Minnesota, no matter how hot it gets, in six months, we'll dream about this heat.

Even as we celebrate the heat and light, those of us in urban environments recognize that city life offers no barrier from the will of nature. Summer weather has its own severities: it brings flash floods and hail, and tornadoes that tear up cities and farms alike. The city of Minneapolis itself has seen three tornadoes inside city limits within the past five years. Flash floods annually force people from urban homes as much as they do farms. While farmers struggle with the way inclement weather can destroy crops and livelihoods, those who live within city limits must contend with losses that, while on a smaller scale than those of farms, are just as crippling. Homes, vehicles, and workplaces all face potential destruction at any time, no matter where a person lives. This is why every sabbat marks a celebration of survival. City dwellers are also the subjects of nature. The sun touches us all.

In Minneapolis, urban planners take great care to highlight the presence of nature. The Mississippi River runs through the heart of the city in a unique marriage of urban and natural landscape. A footbridge joins two sides of the city over the Mississippi River, and multiple biking and hiking trails weave between the daily automobile traffic. Minneapolis has its own unique shape, built in cooperation with nature (though it is far from the only city where nature influences its design and the reality of its inhabitants).

It doesn't matter if you live in New York City or Portland, Oregon—nature still rules you. New Yorkers may go to Central Park to get some green space, but they must also contend with nature (and with each other's human nature) on a daily basis whether riding the subway or sharing close living and working quarters with every other person in the city. Natural interaction might manifest in the form of an aggressive act, or it might appear while getting to the door of an eight-story walk-up in ninety-degree heat. Every city and every season within a city is something to be experienced differently.

Midsummer, whether urban or rural, is about light and heat. In the Wiccan wheel of the year, this sabbat marks a time of eroticism, abundance, and freedom. For all the weather's inconveniences, the heat reduces restrictions on movement, and even on time to do things. Our gardens begin blossoming or even bearing fruit, and it can seem like nature's provisions will never end. The late light and warm weather gives those with romance in mind beautiful scenery, and on a less expensive budget than an indoor date would cost.

On a spiritual level, we celebrate this abundance of light and fruit. With our rituals, we try to enhance our sense of Midsummer enough that when winter does come, we have store of that abundance within ourselves necessary to get us through the harsher, colder months. At Summer Solstice, the sun lingers the longest in the places where winter is harshest. In some parts of the world, at Solstice it shines for a full twenty-four hours, giving those people a midnight sun that compensates for the total darkness to follow in six months.

The locals may not see the seasonal changes in terms of Pagan celebration, but even so, those seasonal changes matter to anyone who lives with the seasons. Around Midsummer, the Twin Cities sees scores of festivals. Some actually overtly celebrate solstice: a ritual dance performance sometimes happens that spreads across the footbridge spannning the Mississippi previously mentioned, and the dancers appear on riverbanks, boating docks, and tall buildings within view of the bridge. Northern Spark, the Minneapolitan answer to Paris's White Night, draws artists over that bridge and on through the city. Theater lovers can watch the Mississippi River rush by from the balconies, or walk along the riverbanks after a show.

These festivals are important communal rituals that transcend religion. It's about grabbing every moment of sunlight as we can get it, and at night about grabbing that rare time of year when nature pretends to treat all of us gently. Seasonal festivals may mean the inevitable appearance of a Ferris wheel in a parking lot—but that wheel is one more manifestation of someone's wheel of the year. It means that the weather is clear enough for enough time for people to gather outdoors, to hear music outdoors, to interact outdoors. Minnesota promptly clogs the most used highways with road construction—and a running joke is that Minnesota has two seasons: winter, and road construction. While annoying because it seems rather unfriendly to pave the road with tar, the construction projects do more than reduce hubcap-eating potholes. In Minneapolis and Saint Paul, major street construction in high-crime areas often forces criminals to give up their activities or move elsewhere. Often when the criminals move, street construction will follow them. These peculiar creative changes and adaptations tell about the spirit of a city. Citizens elect officials they believe to represent them, and the people chosen often do make choices based on what they believe important to the citizens. In Minneapolis, public art and minimal potholes matter. In Chicago, fast transportation matters. In New York City, the collective island identity matters—"I'm a New Yorker" has meaning beyond what those of us who live in other cities can fathom.

While the people who arrange these events are for the most part not Pagan, they too experience these cycles of light. These celebrations, arranged by artists and atheists, Pagans and traditionalists, all serve as ways of capturing that light. There are marked ways that the urban differs from the rural in celebrating the Summer Solstice. Farming Pagans might have bonfires and outdoor circles. Many love and cherish their retreats in the woods.

In summer, it's possible for an urban dweller to have that bonfire—but the proximity of neighbors might also limit how high that bonfire can rise. Urban life comes with the double-edged sword of population density. Magical energies and events happen because cities have enough constant movement to raise energy all the time. An urban magician understands that a city has constant life in it, and that life is in near-constant motion. Even at 4 a.m., a city is never quiet. While silence is its own gift to cherish, the constant sound of a city also offers the boon—the constant reassurance of life. Summer also highlights how humans and insects are not the only ones to select an urban environment. North Minneapolis and St. Paul has seen its share of bears lumbering into neighborhoods, as well as the occasional cougar, wolf, and fox. Deer and rabbits make regular appearances in and around city green spaces, even in areas of solid cement. Rabbits bounding down the sidewalk of the warehouse district near downtown Minneapolis wait at stoplights and cross with the signals. Thanks to homesteading ordinances in some locales, many homeowners also have chickens and goats in their yards. Agriculture on a subsistence level is very common in many US cities, especially with the new growth in urban farming as a way to distribute fresher food to lower income neighborhoods.

Urban magic works from the simple philosophy of "as you seek, so shall you find." While population density presents unique problems in the form of crowding, pollution, and increased crime, it also creates opportunities and synchronicity that Pagans living in rural areas must take greater personal risks to enjoy. A thicker population means a better chance of finding a Pagan community, of encountering other types of magic workers, and of experiencing serendipity. It also means that someone you meet will likely know about the public areas safe for public ritual, or at least point you to a map where you can locate such spaces yourself. When the sun reaches its most generous point of giving to the earth, it is also a time when you can reach out and find other Pagans, made easier because of the dense population that comes with city living.

To connect to nature anywhere, and to connect to patterns of light, be out in it. In an urban landscape, you can also connect to the spirit of the city, and to the spirit of nature living in every object. The deeper you understand the immanence of nature itself, the more easily you can move in and out of ritual appreciation, no matter where you live.

Cosmic Sway

Corrine Kenner

WHEN THE SUN MOVES into Cancer on the Summer Solstice, we note the importance of all that Cancer represents—especially motherhood, home, and family. As we mark the Sun's entry to a sign ruled by the Moon, we celebrate a mother goddess who's about to give birth to a god.

The connection between the Sun and the Moon is woven through the Wheel of the Year. The luminaries are locked in a cosmic dance. The Moon is constantly waxing and waning, as she angles her face toward the light of the Sun. Whenever we see the full face of the Moon, in any sign, we know that she's directly opposite the Sun, reflecting his full strength and power.

When the Sun is in Cancer, as it is this month, the Full Moon will fall in the opposite sign—which happens to be Capricorn.

Of course, the Full Moon casts its light on just one bright night a month. In fact, the Moon moves through all of its phases and all twelve signs during the course of a month—and during this Midsummer holiday, the Moon just happens to be starting a new tour of the zodiac by moving through the first sign, Aries.

On this holiday, the placement seems especially purposeful. The Moon is a symbol of fertility, pregnancy, birth, and motherhood. A

New Moon in Aries reminds us that no woman is ever truly ready to be a mother before her first child is born—but the Moon's forward motion into Aries, the sign of leadership and initiation, is a reminder that we simply have to take each journey step by step, and eventually we'll reach our destination.

The Moon is the planet of memory, mood, and motherhood. Just as the Moon reflects the Sun's light, it also reflects our unconscious needs and desires. It reflects our fears and insecurities—as well as our desires for nurturing and safety. It describes our sensitivities: our inborn responses to emotional triggers, our instinctive responses to threats, and our immediate reactions to predatory behavior. It can relate to early childhood memories, the past, and longings for a better, more perfect life. Because the Moon is shrouded in shadows and darkness, it represents secrets and mysteries that may not be understood—or even recognized.

The phases of the Moon themselves echo its symbolic significance. Each month, the New Moon rises in darkness. As it waxes to full and then wanes to a slender crescent, its form resembles a pregnant woman—slim, then round, then slim again.

The Moon rules Cancer, the sign of home and family. The Moon also rules the fourth house of the zodiac, where modern astrologers look for information about childhood, motherhood, and nurturing.

The Moon doesn't generate light and heat of her own. Instead, the Moon reflects the light of the Sun, changing and adapting each day as it orbits around the Earth. The Moon's position is constantly changing, as she waxes from new to full and back again. And while the Moon fades from view once a month, her influence never disappears.

The Magic of Moonlight

It's easy to follow the Moon's movement through her cycles—but all too often, we forget to look up at the sky and gauge her progress through the stars.

For the next month, pay special attention to the Moon and note any correspondence between the phases of the Moon and ongoing developments in your own life. Start with this holiday, when the Moon is in Aries, and know that the Moon will spend about two and a half days in each sign. (You can check an ephemeris or an astrological calendar for the Moon's exact position.)

No matter when you start tracking the Moon's phases, know that a New Moon represents a starting point. A New Moon in any sign promises growth and change in that sign's domain. Aries, for example, rules leadership and individuality. Taurus rules values and possessions. Gemini is the sign of learning and communication. Cancer is the sign of home and family life. Leo rules creativity and children. Virgo is the sign of duty and responsibility. Libra is the sign of partnership. Scorpio rules the mysteries of sex, death, and regeneration. Sagittarius is the sign of philosophy, higher education, and long-distance travel. Capricorn rules business, career, and social status. Aquarius is the sign of friends, social groups, and futuristic vision. Pisces is the sign of mysticism and spiritual connection.

Over the course of a month, the Moon's curvy side will spell the word "dog." D is the waxing Moon, O is the Full Moon, and G is the waning Moon.

"D"—The waxing Moon grows larger, day by day, and carries the promise of the New Moon toward fruition.

"O"—A Full Moon describes the fullest potential of its sign—at least in its present stage of development.

"G"—A waning Moon symbolizes the steps you'll need to take to finish this cycle of experience, and it could suggest possibilities for a follow-up mission.

Planetary Positions

As the Sun enters Cancer on this Midsummer, it's headed toward a conjunction with Jupiter, the planet of luck and good fortune. As they connect, you might find that your home and family life finally take off in a direction you'll enjoy.

The Aries Moon will move through a brief, awkward, and uncomfortable square with that Jupiter in Cancer. You might be tempted to butt heads with someone in your household—but the feeling will pass. Aspects to the Moon are very transitory.

Mercury is still retrograde and will be moving backward all the way through Cancer and into Gemini until it goes direct on July 1.

Venus is in one of her own signs, Taurus, where she feels comfortable and secure. The feeling won't last much longer. Already, she's a little on edge, as she passes through a semisquare with Mars. In just two days, she'll leave her home behind and move into Gemini. In Gemini, she can engage in pleasant conversation. She can even seem witty and bright. Her mood, however, will be just a little on edge.

Meanwhile, Mars is in Libra, the other sign that Venus rules. It's crossing paths with rebellious Uranus—and both Mars and Uranus will be in an uncomfortable square with powerful Pluto. Either transit could trigger brief outbursts of conflict and fighting. Be patient and kind, and you can avoid getting caught in the crossfire.

Saturn, which has been moving retrograde in Scorpio since March 2, will finally turn direct on July 20. There's no rest for the weary, though: Uranus will start moving retrograde on July 22. In that respect, Uranus joins Pluto, which has been moving backward since April 14, and Neptune, which has been backtracking through the stars since June 9. Whenever you find a planet in retrograde motion, you'll often find that its energy seems focused on your inner, private life, rather than finding an outlet for expression in the world at large.

The Phases of the Moon

The last New Moon in Gemini on May 28 had a thoughtful, curious energy. It paved the way for conversation and intellectual discourse. The first quarter Moon in earthy Virgo on June 5 added a more serious, practical energy that made it easy to turn thought into action. The Full Moon in Sagittarius on June 12 was expansive and outwardly focused; its light could be seen across long distances. The third quarter Moon in Pisces on June 19 dissolved boundaries and delivered spiritual depth.

The next New Moon, in Cancer on June 27, promises to make you more intuitive. You can refine your sense of connection on July 5, with an airy and graceful first quarter Moon in Libra. By the Full Moon in Capricorn on July 12, you'll be ready to share some insights with the world at large—and that mood will be reinforced on July 18, with a determined third quarter Moon in Aries.

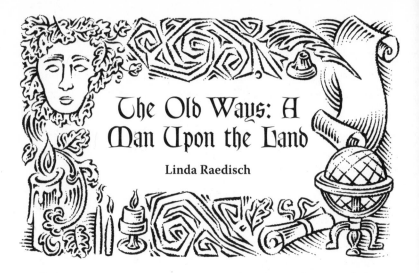

The Old Ways: A Man Upon the Land

Linda Raedisch

A MOONLIT SKERRY, A sea cave, an abandoned house overlooking the cove: these are just a few of the places you might encounter the Selkies. They are black of hair, the men's swept back into a ponytail, the women's streaming long and loose. Their large brown eyes, which stand out in contrast to their snow-white skin, suggest they are descended from some ancient pre-Celtic or even Egyptian strain. They tend to dress as if they have just come from a funeral (when they dress at all), the men in long dark coats, the women in trailing black gowns, babies held close to the breast in gray swaddling clothes spattered with silver.

Do not let their somber clothing deceive you; the Selkies know how to make merry. Should you stumble into one of those abandoned houses in which they hold their Midsummer revels, you will be surprised how well-kept the place is—the many candle flames throwing their light over the polished wood, the window glass, and the sleek, brushed hair of the dancers. It is only when you wake the following morning to the whistle of the sea wind through the empty rooms that you notice the broken window panes and the cobwebs hanging from the chandelier. It is then you realize that you have been a guest of the Seal People.

Midsummer Eve is one of only a handful of days on which the members of this mysterious here-again-gone-again tribe set foot on land. In 1959, folklorist Katharine Briggs collected the secondhand account of a woman who believed she had run afoul of the Seal People off the coast of Scotland. One summer night, the woman in question became aware of the sound of children's footsteps keeping pace with her as she made her way down to the sea for a swim. She looked around but saw no one. As she entered the water, seals appeared on the rocks all around and slipped in after her. They proceeded to mob and puff at the startled woman with what she took for belligerence until she climbed out again. It would be helpful to know whether or not this event occurred at Midsummer; if it did, we could assume the woman had interrupted the seals' solstice observance, but, sadly, the exact date was not recorded.

Compared to humans, the Seal People are a peaceful race, but it is best not to cross them. The bulls, especially, have been known to kill to protect their own, and those velvety tailcoats might conceal daggers. "I am a man upon the land, a Selkie on the sea/And when I'm far and far frae land, my home it is in Sule Skerry," proclaims the Great Selkie of Sule Skerry in the Orcadian folk ballad of the same name. "Selkie" simply means "seal" in the dialect still spoken in the Orkneys off the northern coast of Scotland. Selkies, or "Selkie-men," are not to be confused with the chimerical mermaids or with the Seelies, who are simply Scottish fairies. (Selkie might also be spelled "selchie" or "silky," but in England the latter refers to a housebound spirit in a rustling silk gown.)

The Selkie appears either as all seal—Gray or Common—or all human. His otherwordly nature is not always apparent. There are, however, clues. With his dark eyes and luminous skin, the Selkie-man is often described as inhumanly beautiful, as is the Selkie-woman. At the end of the nineteenth century, it was still generally acknowledged that certain inhabitants of the North Isles of Orkney were descended from a Norse noblewoman and a Selkie-man. A number of these descendants were ill-suited to manual labor, hampered as they were by the recurrent growth of horny tissue between their fingers and toes. Although this webbing could be sheared away, it always reasserted itself in time. The phenomenon, known as "selkie paws," was a telltale sign that there was a pinniped somewhere in the family tree.

Selkie-men were famous for seducing mortal women, but in this case, it was the Norse noblewoman, ascribed the name "Ursilla" by folklorist Walter Traill Dennison to protect the family's identity, who pursued the supernatural lover. Bored to tears by her own mortal husband, Ursilla summoned the Selkie-man in the usual way: she awaited high tide, then stood at the edge of the lapping waves and squeezed seven of her tears into the sea. We don't know if Ursilla ever laid eyes on her lover in seal form, for by the time he rose from the waves, he was already peeling off his sealskin to stand naked before her. The rich pelt must have made for a comfortable bed in the sand, for Ursilla's webbed descendants were born not from one such tryst, but from several.

Selkie females, on the other hand, rarely surface alone. They prefer to celebrate Midsummer Eve in the company of their sisters, doffing their skins to dance in the moonlight or gather driftwood to feed the blue flames that burn on the hearth of their own cottage deep beneath the waves. Many are the tales of the beautiful Selkie-woman basking under the moon with her kin only to have her rolled-up skin snatched from the shingle by a besotted crofter. Unable to reassume her seal form, she has no choice but to follow the lucky young man home and become his wife.

This Selkie bride bears her husband several children and even comes to love him, but always she is trying to sniff out the hiding place of her precious sealskin. Adding poignancy to her story is the existence of a Selkie husband and children for whom she pines, just as she must later pine for the human children she leaves behind, for she invariably finds her skin in a locked clothespress or chink in the cottage wall. It has held up well, for her human husband has been thoughtfully anointing it with sea water. Slipping it on, the Selkie-wife returns to the sea, never again to set foot on land.

The Selkie-wife's abandonment of her second set of children is not a conscious decision but an irresistible impulse. In the Faroes, one who simply could not help himself from doing something was said to be like a seal that finds its skin. Many believed that seals were actually suicides, mortals who had thrown themselves into the sea of their own volition. Only on Twelfth Night and Midsummer Eve were they allowed to shed their seal fur and enjoy the lithe bodies they had so carelessly discarded.

Post-conversion Icelanders were eager to ascribe biblical origins to these liminal creatures. According to them, the seals, whose wistful dark eyes express a world of ancient wisdom, were the descendants of Pharaoh's men—or even the men themselves—who had been swept away when the waters of the Red Sea closed up in Moses' wake. One would, therefore, expect the Selkie-man to dominate Iceland's tales of the Seal People, but it is once again the Selkie bride who does so. Was the Icelandic Seal Woman in the habit of scratching hieroglyphs in the packed volcanic soil of the farmyard? And was there ever a family of fishermen or sheep farmers whose members were christened with such unlikely names as Rameses or Nenoferkaptah? Alas, it seems not.

We now know that seals are born, if not exactly of the sea, then of the wave-washed pupping grounds at its edge. The Selkie, however, is more likely born of man's guilt-ridden imagination. Those who first told stories of Selkie-brides or sang of the Great Selkie of Sule Skerry by the light of a Midsummer bonfire were also those who, from time to time, hunted the seals for their invaluable pelts, not to mention the blubber, which could be burned in lamps, providing the light by which to sew a pair of sealskin shoes. Though driven by necessity, the hunter would not soon have forgotten the last look in the limpid brown eyes of his prey. He would have understood that to be seal and to be human were not mutually exclusive conditions.

For Further Reading:

Boucher, Alan. *Elves, Trolls, and Elemental Beings: Icelandic Folktales II.* Reykjavik, Iceland: Iceland Review, 1981.

Briggs, Katharine. *The Fairies in Tradition and Literature.* London: Routledge and Keegan Paul Ltd, 1967.

Kvideland, Reimund and Henning K. Sehmsdorf, eds. *Scandinavian Folk Belief and Legend.* Minneapolis, Minnesota: University of Minnesota Press, 1991.

Simpson, Jacqueline. *Icelandic Folktales and Legends.* Berkeley: University of California Press, 1979.

Towrie, Sigurd. "Orkneyjar: The Heritage of the Orkney Islands." www.orkneyjar.com (accessed July 15, 2012).

Williamson, Duncan. *Tales of the Seal People.* Northampton, Massachusetts: Interlink Books, 1992.

Feasts and Treats

Dallas Jennifer Cobb

THE LONG DAYS OF light make us joyous, and we celebrate into the late hours. The Sun God is at the height of his power, his chest broad and strong, his sinewy legs golden and long. Celebrate his virility today before his decline begins. Know his full glory, and eat and drink to his power. Living in a largely agricultural area, I am a local food fanatic. Always ready just in time for Solstice, asparagus and strawberries are a tradition at my Litha feasts. When we eat, we honor not just the Sun God, but the mortal gods who toil in the fields producing our food: the farmers.

Herbes de Provence Chicken

Celebrating the Sun God, I like the Litha meal to be prepared on the barbecue. Most men love to cook on the barbecue, as it hearkens back to their hunter days, and time spent around the fire with their prize game. I prepare everything, then sit back and let my partner do the cooking. Perhaps you can invite a man friend to dinner who loves fire, and likes to cook, and let him shine like the Sun God tonight.

Preparation Time: 5 minutes
Cooking Time: 12–15 minutes
Serves: 4

Herbes de Provence

1 teaspoon dried basil

1 teaspoon dried oregano

1 tablespoon dried rosemary

1 tablespoon dried lavender

1 teaspoon dried thyme

Combine all ingredients in a bowl. Mix well. Store in an airtight container in a cool place.

4 boneless skinless chicken breasts about 4 ounces each

Herbes de Provence

Sea salt

Rinse chicken, then rub with a mix of sea salt and Herbes de Provence on both sides. Grill on a hot grill for one minute on each side to sear the outside of the chicken breast, then move to top shelf of the barbecue and cook for 5 minutes on each side until chicken is done. Keep chicken warm on the top shelf while you prepare asparagus on the main grill.

Braised Asparagus

Easy to prepare on the barbecue, asparagus cooks in very little time. Stay close, and be prepared to pull it off as it reaches its zenith of color. A rich, deep green is what cooked asparagus looks like. Do not overcook it, or it will become tough.

Preparation Time: 3 minutes

Cooking time: 5 minutes

Serves: 4

1 pound of asparagus, rinsed and trimmed

Juice of one lemon

A drizzle of olive oil

Sea salt

Coat asparagus with lemon and oil, and grill for 2 minutes, turning frequently. Sprinkle with sea salt, and serve.

Elderflower Bubbly

Elderflower Bubbly is a delicious summer drink, made from the flower of the elderberry bush (*Sambucus spp*), which is common throughout Europe and North America. The American Elder is hardy to zone 4 and flowers in time for Litha enjoyment. If you don't have elderberry bushes growing near you, you could also look for Elder Flower Presse made by Bottlegreen Drinks, in your local health food store.

Preparation Time: 30 minutes and overnight infusion
Cooking Time: 10 minutes
Makes: 2 quarts of cordial

Elderflower Cordial
25 elderflower heads
Zest of 2 lemons and one orange
Juice of 2 lemons and one orange
4 cups of sugar
1 teaspoon of citric acid (optional, to prevent mold if storing)

Place flowers, lemon zest, and orange zest in a large bowl. Boil 7 cups of water and pour over top of flowers and zest. Cover and let infuse overnight.

Strain liquid through a fine sieve and put in saucepan. Add sugar and lemon and orange juice and citric acid if you're using it. Cook at medium heat, stirring constantly to dissolve sugar. Once sugar is dissolved, cook for another 5 minutes, stirring continuously. Pour cordial into sterilized bottles and seal. Keep in refrigerator.

To make Elderflower Bubbly, add one part cordial with five parts soda water, serve over ice, and garnish with sliced lemon. The taste and color are reminiscent of fine champagne added to the taste of summer—alive, bright, inviting, and magical.

Strawberries with Custard Sauce

Where I live, Solstice and strawberries are almost synonymous. Get some fresh, local berries and combine them with warm custard. Garnish with fresh mint leaves.

Preparation Time: 5 minutes
Cooking Time: 6 minutes
Serves: 4

6 cups of strawberries, hulled and sliced
6 mint leaves
Custard

Custard

I will admit I am lazy when it comes to custard. I buy Bird's custard powder at the grocery store, and following directions for "custard sauce," a thinner and easy-to-pour version. Combine Bird's custard powder with sugar and milk. I have used soy milk and cows' milk with equal success. Custard sauce can be made in a saucepan on the stovetop, or in a large glass container in the microwave for us truly rushed cooks. You can whip it up in about 8 minutes.

But if you want to make your own custard sauce, here's how.

2 cups milk
2 egg yolks
¼–½ cup sugar
½ teaspoon cornstarch
½ teaspoon vanilla extract

In a small saucepan, heat the milk until almost boiling. In a separate saucepan whisk egg yolks with sugar, then slowly add the warm milk to them, whisking constantly. Return saucepan to medium heat, stirring constantly until mixture thickens. Do not boil this or it will go lumpy! When it is thick enough for "sauce" remove from heat, add vanilla extract, and stir again. Pour the warm custard sauce over fresh strawberries, garnish with fresh mint leaves, and serve.

Crafty Crafts

Blake Octavian Blair

THE SABBAT OF LITHA, also called Midsummer, marks the Summer Solstice and the longest day of the year. This is a time to celebrate the Sun at the height of its power and the divine masculine whose energies are so closely tied to it. All of us, no matter what our gender, possess both the divine masculine and feminine within us. So when we celebrate the powers of the Sun, we celebrate as well as invoke and evoke that part of the divine within ourselves. In addition to masculinity there are many qualities associated with the planetary energies of the Sun, including creation, manifestation, health, protection, vitality, strength, and motivation, to name just a few.

This sabbat's craft will help you to honor and call upon these qualities through your own act of creation. It is no secret that Pagans love their jewelry, and when you complete this craft, you will have your own handcrafted solar talisman to wear during your Midsummer rites!

Solar Talisman Necklace

Wearing a talisman is like keeping a battery charged with a specific magickal energy with you at all times and serves as a physical reminder of its corresponding goals and properties. This easy-to-make, oven-bake clay talisman features the inscription of a solar symbol and utilizes colors and herbal ingredients with solar correspondences to provide a sunny, energetic boost for the Litha season.

Supplies

1 (2 ounce) package oven bake-polymer clay
Bamboo skewer or a nail
Loose herbs of your choice
Necklace cord (hemp, nylon, cotton, or other material of choice)
Aluminum foil
Clay tools (optional)
Rolling pin (optional)

Instructions: Before you begin your project, you will need to select a nonporous work surface such as a cookie sheet, a sheet of acrylic, or a glazed ceramic tile. An inexpensive option is to simply cover your work surface with aluminum foil. Polymer clays are nontoxic; however, if you choose to use any kitchen implements in the process such as a rolling pin or a cookie sheet, you still do not want to use it for food use after it has been used for clay work. I suggest obtaining them inexpensively from your local dollar store.

Choose a clay of a solar corresponding color. Shades of yellow and gold are excellent choices and are easy to find. Upon opening your package of clay, the first thing you will need to do is to condition the clay by kneading it. Clay straight from the package will be stiff and difficult to work with, and kneading the clay and working it in your hands will make it warmer and softer. Some people like to use a rolling pin for this. However, it can be just as effective to shape it into a ball, flatten it, and otherwise knead it like bread dough. At this time, you can also simply knead any herbs you wish to include into the clay. Focus on your magickal goals as you knead the clay to further imbue it with your intention. A thorough kneading will integrate the herbs and their properties into the clay as well as assure that all air pockets are removed. The following popular magickal herbs all have the Sun as their planetary ruler in addition

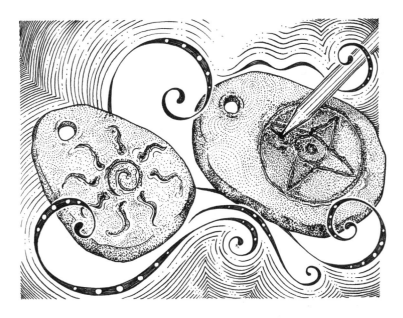

to their other properties: chamomile, cedar, juniper, marigold, sunflower, copal, frankincense, and bay. Use a mortal and pestle or an electric spice or coffee grinder to reduce the herbs into very small pieces so that they integrate smoothly into the clay. Resins will need to be powdered. Once integrated, the clay should still be smooth to work with. Stop kneading when your clay becomes warm and is soft enough to work with.

When your clay becomes workable, you can begin shaping your talisman. One block of clay will be enough to make two or three talismans, so you can tear off a piece of clay the size you want to work with. I would start with a little less than half and adjust from there. Because it will ultimately take the form of a necklace pendant, I like to make a round, flat oval shape. To easily accomplish this, roll the clay into a ball, and press down on the center of the ball with your thumb. This will roughly smoosh the clay into the desired shape. A good thickness to aim for is approximately ⅜ of an inch. I find this to be a durable happy medium between too thin and frail and too thick and chunky. Continue to adjust the pendant by shaping it with your fingers until you reach the desired shape.

The next step is to inscribe the front of the talismanic pendant with the solar symbol of your choice. Research various sun symbols and choose one that resonates with you or create your own! A simple stylized sun works just fine. There are a few different ways to inscribe this into the clay. One is to use wooden clay tools (available at craft stores), many of which have a flat edge, to press and indent into the clay. However, an effective and inexpensive version of such a tool is a Popsicle stick. The other option is to scratch it into the soft clay with a bamboo skewer or a nail.

The final step before baking the talisman is to make a hole in which to string the cord through when it is finished. A bamboo skewer or nail works well for this task also. Be sure you choose a tool that will make a hole the proper size to accommodate the diameter of the cord you have chosen. Take the bamboo skewer or nail and carefully insert into the side of the pendant, about one-third of the way down from the top. Continue to push it through until it pokes out the other side. Stop and back the skewer out of the clay from where you initially pierced it. Do not try to push or pull the entire length of the skewer through the pendant as that much handling can distort the talisman's shape. Once this small tunnel is made for threading the cord, gently clean up any rough bits round the holes with your fingers.

At this point, your pendant is ready to bake! Cover your backing sheet with tinfoil and then place your talisman face up onto the sheet. Now simply follow the baking instructions on the clay package. Each brand can vary slightly. When it is finished baking, allow the pendant to cool completely. The pendant will have hardened during baking and will be fairly durable. The pendant is now ready to have the cord threaded through. Insert a long length of your cord and adjust to the desired length. Trim and knot the cord.

Congratulations! Your solar talisman necklace is complete! My favorite way to consecrate this pendant is to place it on my Litha altar after its creation to soak up the energy of the workings and blessings that take place there and then to wear the pendant during my sabbat ritual itself. Enjoy your handcrafted talisman, as it is of your own sacred creation. May you be blessed by the powers of the Sun this Litha and all year long!

Time to complete: About 75 minutes with baking and cooling time.

Cost: $10.00 to $20.00 (makes 3 or 4 talismans).

References:

Cunningham, Scott. *Cunningham's Encyclopedia of Magical Herbs.* St. Paul, Minnesota: Llewellyn Publications, 1985.

Digitalis, Raven. *Planetary Spells & Rituals: Practicing Dark & Light Magick Aligned with the Cosmic Bodies.* Woodbury, Minnesota: Llewellyn Publications, 2010.

All One Family

Kerri Connor

WHETHER YOUR MIDSUMMER CELEBRATION focuses more on the Fey, on the actual solstice event itself, or on the battle of the Holly and Oak Kings, for those of us in the Northern Hemisphere, chances are that one thing they will all have in common is some pretty warm temperatures! Working against the heat can make people cranky and downright miserable, no matter what their age, so activities that can help you beat the heat are just what you need.

These activities are also good for helping to connect to the elements that are involved, so take some time to point this out either before or after the designated activity. If you discuss this beforehand, people will go into the activity with a different mind-set. If you discuss it after the event, you can often see the realization as it dawns on people!

These activities are also good for people of all ages, and though some adults may be more skittish than kids or teens, I guarantee they are indeed fun for all ages.

To Celebrate Air

Let's begin with a celebration of air. While this activity won't really cool you down per se, it is great fun. You will need a lot of bubble liquid and wands—if you have access to a bubble machine, even better. Split your group into two and have one group lie down on the ground looking up at the sky while the other group stands around them and blows bubbles into the air. The group on the ground can either quietly meditate on the paths of the bubbles, or playfully swipe at them. The choice is yours.

If you have a guided fairy meditation you would like to do, this would be a good setting. You could also play some type of fairy music such as a selection from Gary Stadler. Allow the two groups to switch places and perform the activity again. Once everyone has had a turn at both blowing bubbles and watching them float throughout the air, have a brief discussion about their connection with air and how this activity made them feel. This activity can also be done indoors, though you will probably want to use fewer bubbles than if you were outdoors. However, the cleanup is extremely easy—a wet washcloth will take care of any popped bubble residue on furniture or walls.

Celebrate Earth

A favorite activity at our Midsummer festival is the celebration of earth, or as we like to call it: MUD PIT! If you can't dig an actual mud pit, you can create one for about $25. (A larger pit will obviously cost more.) You will need a kiddie pool and a few twenty-five pound bags of topsoil and sand. Simply pour the sand and dirt into the pool and add water.

The mud pit we have measures about 5 feet by 9 feet. We began by shoveling out the top layer of dirt that includes any plant life. Next we use the tiller, and then shovel out everything that has been tilled up. Once the pit is empty, we till again and then shovel the removed dirt back in. Once the dirt is all back in, we add the hose to fully drench the dirt and then mix it up real good by walking around in it.

When the mud pit is all set, wrestling begins. While you have to be careful that kids and teenagers don't get too carried away; they will have the time of their lives actually being allowed to roll around in the mud. We use a kiddie pool and hose for cleanup, and of course a lot of towels, before anyone is allowed in the house to use the shower. This activity allows you to reconnect with both earth and water.

You also do not have to actually wrestle. You can simply sit or roll around in the mud. It really does feel great and if you have sand in your mix, it helps exfoliate your skin as well! If it's a particularly hot day, this activity will not only help cool people off, it's a great way to reduce stress and lift the spirits of people who are feeling crabby because of the oppressive weather. You can't help but feel grounded when this activity is complete, no pun intended!

Finger/Body Painting

An activity similar to the mud pit—in the sense that you are going to get pretty dirty—is finger/body painting. For this activity, you will need several large jars of finger paints (or find a recipe to make your own) and large sheets of paper. You can either use the special paper made for finger paints, or go larger and buy paper by the roll.

For younger children, you will probably just want to keep them with the actual finger-painting. Give them different topics to paint. You may ask them to paint the Fey, or perhaps have them paint each of the elements. This can be done as an indoor or an outdoor activity. Picnic tables and a hose make for easy cleanup after kids have finger-painting fun.

For the older children and adults, you can have them put on a swimsuit and use their full bodies to paint. Again, they can paint the same topics or allow the group to create a scene together—such as a sunset. Since the finger paints are water based—and will require a lot of water for clean up—part of the focus of this activity can be on reconnecting with water.

Reconnect with Water

Finally, another great way to beat the heat while working with the elements is also another way to reconnect with water. While many Midsummer celebrations include a mock battle of the Oak King and Holly King, you can expand on this theme and make the Oak King Team and the Holly King Team.

Instead of a scripted-out battle, perhaps fought with practice swords, between the two kings, entire teams can battle each other—in a water fight. Have plenty of water supplies on hand, water balloons, water pistols (if you don't take offense to them), water balls, kiddie pools filled with "ammo," buckets—whatever it is you want to use for your battle.

You can distinguish the teams from each other in a number of different ways. You can do something as simple as different colored T-shirts to something more elaborate such as holly head wreaths with T-shirts that have holly berries painted on them for your Holly King army, and oak leaf head wreaths with T-shirts that have acorns painted on them for your Oak King army. Though we already know which team "officially" wins, both teams are winners when they are able to cool off and raise energy and spirits at the same time with this activity. At the end of the "battle" (which could also be played out with silly string, Nerf toys, or laser tag games), be sure to crown your new king.

These are all fun ways to get family and friends to fully participate in your Midsummer festivities. You can have great fun, reconnect with the elements, celebrate, and cool off all at the same time when you add these activities into your Midsummer lineup.

Midsummer Ritual: Local Travel

Diana Rajchel

THIS RITUAL DOES NOT require an altar or tools, though you might wish to establish something as a focal point for the beginning or end of your journey. It does call for you to travel—you may want a good pair of walking shoes, and plans for what you consider necessary to feel safe as you travel. Also recommended:

- a pocket-size notebook and pen
- a fully charged phone (if you own one)
- bus fare or a mass transit pass
- a camera

On Midsummer, about an hour before sunset, visit a favorite park near a busy neighborhood. Watch the sunset. You may wish to chant as you do.

Short is the night, and long are the days—the season shifts for summer's ways.

Chant until the sun has fully set, when you see the first star or planet emerge from the darkened sky. You may want to snap a picture of it for future meditation, or just let that moment live in your memory. Begin walking. Pause every few moments to notice the subtle changes that happen when day becomes night. Feel how the air touches your skin in a different way as you cross from one street corner to another, how the temperature cools as the evening wears on, how the sounds of traffic and nature around you differ and blend. Notice how the grass smells different as more stars appear in the sky.

If you can, take mass transit—hop on a commuter train or bus. Use this as a meditative time: observe the faces of your fellow passengers, listen to the noises they make, that the vehicle makes, and look at the objects they carry. Look at the face of the driver, and consider their sacred duty to deliver large batches of people to their destinations safely.

Get off the bus at a stop you consider interesting. Find a place to sit down, to feel your location. Look into the night sky and choose one star to meditate on. Breathe the starlight into your body, and use its light to infuse your body with extra protection.

You can invoke the star with this prayer:

The light from other worlds
shines in mine,
shines in me.
From the furthest stars,
I see the universe
in its evolution
in mine
within me
throughout me.

As you repeat this verse, see yourself actually inside the star. Feel its energy pulse through your body. Relax into that feeling and then envision yourself inside your body glowing with starlight from within. The starlight pushes through your feet into the ground and through and above your head. See the light forming a knot above you and below you, sealing that energy into your body. Now encased in starlight, carry on with your Midsummer trek. All ritual and myth involves a journey. Sometimes we call the end of those journeys destinations, other times, goals. In Midsummer, the journey involves motion. People get from one place to another with more ease in the summer. To go out and walk is to celebrate a freedom granted specifically by warm weather.

The sabbat cycle marks eight points of the sun's yearly journey. You have taken in the energy of a star. Now celebrate the sun.

Surrounded by your starlight, perhaps adding an extra layer of spiky toughness outside of that shield, begin your purpose-filled walk home. Observe the people around you while doing your best to remain calm and centered. Resist the temptation to don headphones—it's important to stay connected to the outer world for this ritual. Breathe through your feet, and breathe the starlight down below you. Watch what the people you pass do and wear.

Notice how nature interacts with yourself and others. If it rains, open your arms to it (take cover in any thunderstorm). If the wind changes direction, notice which way it blows. Pause in small, safe places to make notes about shifts in wind and animals you see. You can review these later for possible omens, or at least for amusing anecdotes.

The omens you see on this journey can include plant, animal, and human activity. For something to qualify as an omen, it must have the markers of movement and/or change. Even an unusual car can constitute an omen. If, for example, a bird flies toward you, notice the bird species, the color of its feathers, and the direction it flies. Look at cats of any color that cross your path—a black cat is generally good luck for the witchy types! If a car passes you on a street that seems otherwise ghostly, notice the make and model of the car. Also, notice if it has anything unusual about the tires, and if you can catch the year and license plate. The car may represent a period in history that has lessons you can learn from in the now. If it comes up in your mind later, it likely has some personal meaning attached.

As you walk, you can stay in sacred mental space by using a litany. Because you are likely to have to move in and out of that mental space while walking through a city, these chants can help you get back into them when you do have an interruption.

Praise the Sun:
Giver of life, you fill me with you.

Connect to a Specific Sun God
Apollo, with love, I take this journey with you until the goddess Diana takes her mantle in the night.

(Apollo was the Olympian god of the sun, depicted as driving his chariot across the daylight sky.)

Helios, god of sunlight, and powerful oaths, light my countenance and reveal my truth.

(Helios was the Titan sun-god, viewed also as a charioteer but as a primal force as well.)

Ra, deliver me from chaos to order, from darkness to light, from confusion to truth. Banish my delusions that I become illuminated.

Simple Praise
Life is light and light is life.

The sun will rise again!

This is a time of bounty, and I embrace that bounty now.

You can also adjust the chant to a personal magical working. The motion of the walking, along with the constantly moving city creates energy that you can direct towards a specific purpose, such as those suggested here.

To Heal Wounds of the Soul
Midsummer sun, please fill my spirit, cleanse my wounds and close them.

To Settle an Ongoing Conflict:
Light gives truth. We see ourselves, we see what is. We see together what is right for the one, and what is right for the all, together.

To Open Your Heart to New Adventures:
Reveal to me new paths that I may safely travel.

After every ritual, it is important for your mental and physical health to return to normal consciousness. You can still do this in gentle, ritual, sacred ways.

When you return home that night, wash your feet off with a wet cloth, even if you wore shoes. You may continue to speak prayers as you wash, or you may wish for sacred silence. You have connected to the earth and carried it with you. Now you wash it down your sink or tub and give that piece of the earth back.

Once finished, find a quiet place where you can either be or see outdoors. Speak a quiet closing prayer.

Conclusion Prayer

I have walked with the sun through this night, cloaked in stars. I know well now the power of light.

Listen to the motion of the city, to the far-off shouts and sirens, and think about the city and its relationship to the sun. Consider how day differs from night beyond simple darkness. Think about the way sunlight and the lack of it changes the overall behavior of every being in the city. Go on home. Sleep well.

Living in the city does not separate you from the divine—a city is a busy, energetic, crowded manifestation of multiple divine energies and visions. Each being in it is somehow touched by Midsummer light. You can honor the ritual performed, and the sun itself, by going out and living in that city. The more you embrace the city life, the more you can benefit from it—and from bringing divine solar and starlight energy into yourself.

For Further Study:

Kaldera, Raven, and Tannin Schwartzstein. *The Urban Primitive: Paganism in the Concrete Jungle.* St. Paul, MN: Llewellyn Publications, 2002.

Penczak, Christopher. *City Magick: Spells, Rituals, and Symbols for the Urban Witch.* San Francisco, CA: Weiser Books, 2012.

Polkinghorne, Thomas. "The Urban Pagan." *The Llewellyn Journal.* http://www.llewellyn.com/journal/article/773

Kaldera, Raven. "Paganism for the City-Dweller." *The Llewellyn Journal.* http://www.llewellyn.com/journal/article/432

Telesco, Patricia. *The Urban Pagan: Magical Living in a 9–5 World.* St. Paul, MN: Llewellyn Publications, 1997.

Notes

Lammas

Lammas Rising

Elizabeth Barrette

PAGANS CELEBRATE LAMMAS ON August 1–2. In the Southern Hemisphere, some prefer to use February 1–2 instead, to correspond with local seasons. The first of the three harvest festivals, Lammas marks the beginning of the grain harvest, particularly wheat but also barley and other crops. The name comes from the Anglo-Saxon *hlaf-mas* which means "loaf-mass." Festivities customarily feature bread, beer, corn dollies, sheaves of grain, and other symbols of harvest abundance.

The Alchemy of Lammas

Lammas is a sabbat of transformation. It represents the fulfillment of expectations as spring's planting bears fruit. Furthermore it draws on the power of the sun and the element of fire, hence the bonfire or "burning man" sometimes associated with this occasion. Yet it also honors sacred beverages such as beer, cider, and whiskey, which relate to the element of water. The moon, another watery aspect, figures into the harvest because it sheds light at night thus making it easier to work after sunset. Lammas then is the holiday when fire turns to water, a transformation that can alter consciousness and bring enlightenment.

This corresponds to the process of dissolution in alchemy. The energy of the sun ripens the crops, and rain makes them swell to fruition. But too much of either can ruin the harvest and cause famine. The crops are cut in the field, a form of death; and yet the harvested grain becomes not just food for the winter but also the seed to be planted next spring. This mirrors the inner journey, giving up the busy outward activities of summer for more contemplative pursuits.

Dissolution requires both introspection and honesty. The practitioner must look inside and examine the thoughts, feelings, and decisions of the year thus far. Identify events that turned out poorly; search for the lessons in them. Acknowledge the successes and consider how to carry them forward. See how each of these have brought changes, and where the journey is headed from this point along the path. This is what provides the opportunity for transformation from within.

The symbols of fire for Lammas include the sun, the cooking fire, and the flame used to heat a cauldron. They relate to guidance and enlightenment. The symbols of water include the moon, the mirror, and the chalice. They relate to purification and deep wisdom. The sun and the moon light the way for busy harvesters. The cooking fire and chalice or cauldron represent the things made from bountiful crops, such as bread and beer, through the magical transformations in the kitchen. The mirror stands for introspection and reflection, part of the alchemical process of dissolution.

This process is ruled by the moon and Jupiter. It corresponds to the element of water and the metal tin. Within the mind, dissolution breaks down arbitrary limitations and constructs by submerging it into the subconscious. This is the intuitive, hidden part of the psyche. Here the mind releases control so it can go with the flow, allowing buried ideas to float to the surface. It also frees creativity and imagination so they can act without hindrance from outside structures. Within the body, dissolution begins in the sacral chakra, moving up to influence the spleen and lungs. As the energy channels open up, this removes blockages and revitalizes the body. On a wider basis, dissolution generally deals with breaking up and washing away impurities. So in a coven or surrounding culture, this is an opportunity to let go of the past and prepare for a time of rest and reconsideration.

The Ingredients

Certain ingredients feature prominently in Lammas foods, beverages, and decorations. These include grain, yeast, and hops. They are particularly important for the iconic Lammas products of bread and beer.

Wheat is a major cereal grain, originally from the Near East but now grown throughout much of the world. It is among the most iconic grains of Lammas; others include barley, oats, rye, and corn. The cultivation of wheat enabled the rise of cities and eventually city-states, by providing a nutritious staple food that traveled and stored well. This creates a close link with civilization—along with bread and beer, which can be made from wheat and often appear in myths about the beginning of civilization. Other wheat products include bran, bulgur (or groats), flour, malt, and semolina. These are appropriate for Lammas use; in particular, flour for baking bread and malt for brewing beer, but feel free to diversify the menu.

Wheat, like most grains, is ruled by the element of earth. Magically speaking, wheat promotes the ability to learn important life lessons, in essence, to reap what you sow. It attracts abundance and supports success. It encourages happiness and longevity. A sheaf of wheat in the field or bracketing a door will attract positive qualities and repel unwanted influences. Indoors, a corn dolly woven from wheat has the same effect. As an herb, wheatgrass is a popular dietary supplement with good cleansing powers. Sprouted wheat berries are nutritious and helpful to the digestive system.

Yeast is a type of single-celled microorganism belonging to the fungi kingdom. It feeds on sugars and carbohydrates to form carbon dioxide and alcohol. This makes bread rise and allows beer to foam. Because the process relies on tiny living creatures, requires rather finicky conditions, and still does not always succeed, it is considered magical and mysterious. The life force of the yeast remains in the final product after baking or bottling, providing extra energy. It corresponds to the elements of water and air.

Yeast may be purchased in blocks or in dry granules; this allows fine control over the specific variety, which is desirable because different yeasts yield different flavors. Baker's yeast and brewer's yeast also diverge somewhat, with the latter being used as a dietary supplement because it contains essential minerals and most of the B vitamins. A separate nutritional yeast with better flavor is also available. Wild yeast can be captured from the air by making a sourdough starter from water and flour, a traditional Lammas activity. A mixture of warm water and sugar is used to activate dormant yeast from dry granules, called "proofing" because it proves that the yeast is still viable when it foams. This is an important stage in some bread recipes.

Hops consist of the female flower clusters from the hop vine *Humulus lupulus*. They provide stability and flavoring in beer, with distinctive bitter and sour notes. In particular, they create a favorable environment for brewer's yeast to thrive while suppressing other microorganisms through antibacterial effects. The hop plant is ruled by the moon and the element of water.

As an herbal medicine, hops sooth anxiety and insomnia, sometimes combined with other herbs like chamomile or valerian. Dream pillows for restful sleep or psychic dreams often contain dried hop flowers as part of the stuffing. This approach also discourages nightmares. Similarly, hops may be added to magical floorwash for bedrooms or nurseries to promote good sleep. Lammas is an ideal time for such activities or crafts.

The Magic of Bread and Beer

Due to the interaction of grain and yeast, both bread and beer are considered magical by many cultures. Their discovery or creation often figure into important myths. They appear at feasts and festivals. Sometimes they are also used in spellcraft.

Bread

Bread begins by mixing aspects of earth (the flour) and water to create dough. The yeast adds air as the dough rises. Then the dough gets baked in an oven, which seals the transformation with fire as the dough becomes bread. In this way, bread combines all the elements. It is further seen as holding the spirit of the grain, which is why some people bake a Corn God figure made from bread as part of their Lammas celebration. Bread can also represent goddesses of bread or grain such as Brigid and Ceres.

If the dough fails to rise, it is believed to indicate malicious spirits. First check that the yeast is good and the environment properly warm and moist. But if you've eliminated mundane causes, consider that yeast is a sensitive little beast, and maybe you should do a banishing. A related custom is marking buns or loaves with a cross—usually an equal-armed cross—originally representing the four elements/directions and later picking up Christian connotations. This was said to discourage fairies or other spirits from stealing the bread. Sharing bread symbolizes hospitality, friendship, and peace. It offers a traditional way to forgive arguments and put the past behind you. Sharing bread can also embody love, if the loaf is homemade by one lover and given to the other.

Beer

Beer is typically brewed from malted wheat or malted barley in water with yeast. Hops and sometimes other herbs are added as bitters for flavoring and preservation. The yeast turns the starch into sugar, then ferments the sugar to produce alcohol. Typically beer contains about 6 to 8 percent alcohol by volume, although it can be considerably higher or lower depending on the details of the recipe and brewing process. So beer primarily relates to water, with some earth from the grain and air from the yeast action, and a little fit of fire due to heating the ingredients while brewing.

Throughout history, beer has been a sacred and magical beverage. Among the earliest written records of this is "The Hymn to

Ninkasi," both a prayer to the Mesopotamian goddess of beer and a mnemonic for a brewer's recipe. A purifying bath may be made by adding a quart of beer and a cup of sea salt to a tub of hot water. Soak for a while, then rinse off with the shower. This makes a good preparation for a Lammas ritual. Of course, the traditional "cakes and ale" still appear in many Pagan circles.

Note that if you choose to avoid alcohol, there are other options. Nonalcoholic beer and unfermented apple cider both work. If you want to keep the yeast action while avoiding alcohol, look for traditionally brewed sodas such as root beer, birch beer, or ginger beer. They have excellent flavor and harvest appeal. Root beer also has the visual effect of a dark beer while birch beer and ginger beer are pale gold. The mystical energy differs from regular beer made from barley or wheat, but it still works for magical and spiritual purposes.

Intoxication and Enchantment

Beer, cider, and other alcoholic beverages form an important part of some traditional Lammas festivities. This makes intoxication a part of the occasion also. Some people feel that altered states of consciousness open a doorway to the divine. Indeed, alcohol is counted among entheogenic substances which are consumed for ritual purposes. The original phrase for refreshments served during Pagan rituals is "cakes and ale," and plenty of covens still serve alcohol, although many have switched to other beverages.

Consider also the relationship between dissolution, dissipation, and drunkenness. The alchemical process of dissolution involves a kind of melting or washing away. Dissipation, a synonym for intoxication, evokes similar imagery. Drunkenness refers not just to alcohol, but specifically to drinking, consuming large quantities of liquid—such as those needed to dissolve something.

Alcohol itself is a strong chemical solvent. It can remove or suspend things in solution. It also conveniently lowers inhibitions and dissolves social barriers, a key reason why many people like it. Water, the prime ingredient in beer, is another important solvent.

So these things all make beer an excellent match for the Lammas tide of dissolution.

Worship often includes the use of offerings. Alcohol is popular for this, and indeed, is considered sacred in some traditions. There are numerous gods and goddesses of beer, wine, and other intoxicating beverages. Drunken revels appear in the iconography of several religions, for example, featuring Bacchus and the maenads.

Alcohol is also closely associated with magic. One reason is because intoxication feels similar to enchantment. Another is the strong magical energy generated in production, because of the live yeast, as discussed earlier. It can be used in spells, particularly in kitchen witchery.

At Lammas, beer may be served in the ritual to honor the deities of grain, harvest, and alcohol. Use it in the feast to make recipes such as beer bread, beer-battered shrimp, or beer can chicken. It can be poured over a person or object for purification, or onto grain fields for a harvest blessing. Dark beer makes an excellent liquid to fill a scrying bowl. If you brew your own beer, or know a brewer, the expended mash may be added to a compost pile to assist the transformative energies there.

Cosmic Sway

Corrine Kenner

THE SUN IS THE star of the show at Lughnasadh, when it reaches the halfway point in its passage through Leo. At 15 degrees Leo, the sign of fixed fire, the Sun seems invincible. It's at the peak of its power, burning brightly, and it shows no sign of stopping.

Ironically, however, the holiday of Lughnasadh demonstrates that life and death are indivisible. On this holiday, we commemorate the first harvest of the season. The crops are gathered up, and the god of creation is sacrificed in the process.

It's an ancient story. The Sun, which sets every night and rises every morning, is a timeless symbol of death and rebirth. In ancient times, the Sun was worshipped like a god, and most gods were imbued with supernatural gifts and talents—including the power to rise from the dead.

For centuries, people knew that the Sun was a metaphor for death and resurrection. It died each night as it set below the horizon and traveled through the Underworld. It was reborn again each morning, rising in glory and crossing the sky in a golden chariot.

In Homer's time, the Sun was Helios, who rode in a chariot by day and a golden bowl by night. From that vantage point, Helios could see and hear everything on Earth—and he could contribute to other myths and legends, too. He told Ceres about Pluto's abduction of her daughter Persephone, and he told Venus's husband that his wife was notoriously unfaithful.

As centuries passed, Helios became known as Apollo, the Greek and Roman god of music, healing, truth, and light. Apollo was the oracular god who cast light on the future. He also killed the Python, the monster of darkness that made the oracle at Delphi inaccessible.

Astrologically, the Sun is a symbol of virility, vitality, and energy. It's a depiction of inner light, and it describes the ways in which everyone can shine. The Sun also shows where each individual will expend the most energy in pursuit of his or her goals. The Sun sheds light on our sense of purpose, as well as our life's path. It's a marker of consciousness and enlightenment.

The Sun is an important focal point in any astrological chart; it represents the ego and the self. It describes confidence and self-esteem, willpower, purpose, and drive. It suggests virility, vitality, confidence, willpower, energy, and strength. It also represents consciousness and enlightenment.

The Sun's energy is masculine and direct. In a horoscope chart, the Sun often represents a strong male figure, like a father, a boss, or a respected teacher. Because the Sun is so visible, its placement can highlight areas of fame, public recognition, and acclaim. The Sun rules Leo, the sign of fatherhood and play. The Sun also rules the fifth house of creativity, recreation, and procreation. The Sun rules the heart and the spine. Both find expression in everyday language, when we describe people with courage and heart, or willpower and backbone.

As we celebrate Lughnasadh, we find the Sun in a close conjunction with two other planets—Jupiter, the expansive planet of luck and good fortune, and Mercury, the messenger of the gods. All three are in Leo, where their energy and power is funneled into dramatic self-expression.

The three planets are also in a fiery square with Mars in watery Scorpio. That could lead to a skirmish. While the Sun, Jupiter, and

Mercury are focused on self-expression, creativity, and adventure, Mars is feeling driven to acquire and consolidate his power.

The Harvest Feast

Traditionally, Lughnasadh is celebrated with a feast. This year, with Jupiter conjunct the Sun, you might want to host the biggest feast of the year. Try to hold it outdoors, in a garden or the countryside. Decorate with corn and wheat, and serve foods that are in season in your area.

It's a good time to note the sacrifice of the god by making a sacrifice of your own. Either set aside some of the bounty for needy people in your area, or arrange to make a donation to a food shelf or emergency shelter.

Planetary Positions

This is truly a month when Leo is the center of the action. The Sun is in Leo between July 22 and August 22—and on Lughnasadh, it shares the sign with two other planets, Mercury and Jupiter.

They've got energy to burn—as well as a flair for drama. If you're feeling brave—or if you could use an extra boost of encouragement—you can tap into that energy to share your passions, too. If you're in business for yourself or you're a rising star at work or school, this is an ideal time to publicize the unique gifts you have to offer.

You can also get an energetic boost from Mars, the planet of action and self-assertion. He's moving through squares with all three planets in Leo, which means he's looking for way to assert his primal drives and passions, too.

Venus moves into Leo on August 12. She's engaged in a lovely, graceful trine with Saturn, which means her visionary energy is perfectly positioned to flow into your creative work.

On that night, too, the Perseid meteor shower will start to peak. You can look for showers of falling stars through August 14. Traditionally, shooting stars were said to be the spirits of the dead, either flying through the heavens or returning to a new life on earth. Some cultures thought they were omens—both good and bad—while others believed they carried messages from the gods.

On August 18, Venus will join forces with Jupiter in a dramatic, heavenly conjunction. If the day dawns clear and bright, you'll be able to see the two of them shimmering in the early morning sky. At the same time, Venus will be moving through a square with Uranus. The planetary connection could lead you to see beauty in new and unexpected ways.

On August 29, you'll be able to spot Neptune, too. On that date, Neptune will make its closest approach to Earth, and the planet of glamor will be fully illuminated by the Sun. Neptune is moving backward through Pisces, which makes the planet seem even more mystical.

Uranus and Pluto are still moving retrograde, too. Pluto will go direct shortly, on September 23. Uranus will keep moving backward through Aries until the Winter Solstice on December 21.

The Phases of the Moon

The last New Moon in Leo on July 26 marked a night made for romance and passion. If you weren't able to take advantage of the opportunities it offered, you'll get a second chance with a first quarter Moon in Scorpio on August 3. Cooler heads—and hearts—will prevail with an airy Full Moon in Aquarius on August 10. You'll come back to earth with a third quarter Moon in Taurus on August 17.

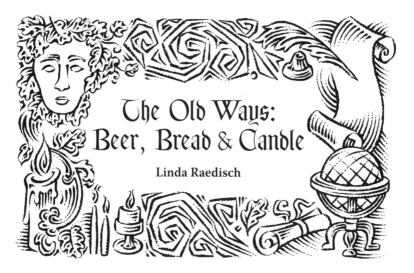

The Old Ways: Beer, Bread & Candle

Linda Raedisch

BREAD MIGHT BE THE staff of life, but when it came to the ancient Egyptian afterlife, bread was just one leg of a three-legged stool. Beer was another, and candlelight the third element necessary to keep the deceased's *ka*—spirit or essence—alive. Very few Egyptians could provide their loved ones with the "wonderful things" Howard Carter discovered upon opening Tutankhamen's tomb, but beer, bread, and the occasional candle were the bare essentials.

One of the most important occasions for presenting these offerings was at the New Year, which commenced around July 19 during the dog days of summer. This was when Sirius, the Dog Star, as the ancient Greeks called it, made a brief reappearance in the sky, rising and setting with the sun. In Egypt, these were the days when the waters of the Nile began to rise and flood the fields, which would later be sown with barley, emmer, einkorn, and spelt. The star that signaled the onset of this season of inundation was known to the Egyptians as the goddess Sopdet. When farmers looked to the dawn on the first day of the New Year, they saw not a hunting dog, but a lady striding out in a jeweled collar and the usual close-fitting linen garment, her bulb-shaped crown topped by a five-armed star. Despite this later regal appearance, Sopdet was a goddess of humble origins. Back in

3000 BC she was portrayed as a cow, which, overtaken by the rising waters, has caught a piece of riverweed between her horns. Queen or cow, her appearance in the sky was so important that the festival itself was named for her.

Though Sopdet does not exactly coincide with any of the Wiccan sabbats, the idea of an offering table will certainly resonate with modern Witches. In the days leading up to Sopdet, the priests of the jackal gods Anubis and Wepwawit were busy already preparing the offerings which dutiful sons would lay before the tombs of their fathers on New Year's Eve. Nowadays, when we picture the "false doors" of Egyptian tombs, we imagine slabs of sand-scoured rock overlooking a desert wasteland, but while those tombs were active, the false doors would have been nestled within well-tended gardens such as the tomb's occupants would have enjoyed in life. Sycamores would have shaded the offering tables set before the door while bees buzzed among the poppies and cornflowers, and flies drowned in the bowls of sweet beer awaiting absorption by the ka.

For the living, too, no meal was complete without beer, and for the vast majority who could afford neither meat nor vegetables, beer often was the meal. This is not as unhealthy as it sounds, for beer in those days was more like a foamy herb and barley soup than a party drink. It packed very little punch—children drank it—and was usually flavored with thyme and savory, both of which contain essential oils, and coriander, which aids digestion. The naturally occurring yeast was activated by adding honey or date syrup to the brew. Since the beer-making process began with underbaked barley cakes, it had long been supposed that the world's first batch of beer was the happy result of a mistake in the kitchen. But beer may actually be older than bread. Archaeological traces from Upper Egypt suggest that thirsty folk were brewing beer from mashed bulrushes and wild sorghum sweetened with chamomile and palm nuts about eight thousand years before the dawn of agriculture.

When the Egyptians did finally get around to inventing bread, they did so with panache, transforming the fields of grain into myriad breads, cakes, and pastries. At its simplest, the dough could be slapped into a flat round and left to bake in the hot sand, but in city bakeries and temples, baking was a high art. Old Kingdom bread was not baked in ovens; the batter was poured into pottery molds of all shapes and sizes, which were then arranged around a fire of wood— always scarce in Egypt—charcoal, or dung. Such breads, with a bowl of beer and a few green onions on the side, were what's for dinner in most Egyptian households. We don't know if the loaves found in tombs were identical to those eaten by the living. Since the deceased's ka did not actually taste the offerings, it was most important that the loaves looked pretty, and so they did, with circular patterns pricked out on the smooth rounds and oblongs.

Still, the most beautiful offerings of all were the candles. While the living illuminated their homes with oil-burning lamps, special molded candles were made for the use of the dead. These were made of tallow (animal fat) mixed with a little salt to reduce smoking, since smoking results in soot that would have damaged the wall paintings both inside and outside the tombs. The tallow was then cast in a cone shape, which was stuck atop a wooden, trunklike base and adorned with chains of flowers. The cones might be the yellowish white of the tallow or colored red with a dye made from the boiled roots of alkanet. Candles were not only produced at the temple; they were "pre-burnt" within the temple precincts before they were delivered to the cemetery where the wealthy often had their portraits carved and installed before the false doors of their tombs. The lighted, sanctified candles were placed before these statues to cast their glow over the cold stone and animate the features. The most lifelike ka statues would indeed have looked as if they were stepping out to wish their living relations a Happy New Year.

Sopdet falls untidily between the modern Wiccan sabbats of Litha and Lughnasadh, but the offering of beer, bread, and candle is so basic that aspects of the ancient Egyptian New Year can be incorporated just about anywhere within the wheel of the year. To toast the dog days of summer, Pagan brewmasters can experiment with the old Egyptian beer recipes, a task made easier by the many varieties of heirloom grains now being reproduced on small farms. You can bake a loaf of einkorn wheat or invoke the magic of the Black Land, as the fertile banks of the Nile were known, by hanging a wreath of Black Winter emmer stalks on your front door.

More than one Egyptologist has noted the funerary candle's resemblance to a Christmas tree. If you're an experienced chandler, you can try to re-create one for Yule. Otherwise, dress up a fat red or white pillar candle with garlands of dried cornflowers and silk poppies. Mandrake, another popular Egyptian garden flower, is harder to find, but you can make mandrake blossoms out of small squares of purple foil paper by following the instructions for an origami lily.

ॐ

But remember: most of the families observing the festival of Sopdet would have been able to afford no more than a bowl of homemade beer, a whole-wheat pita, and a simple clay lamp to celebrate their dead. If you too are strapped for cash, all you have to do is close your eyes and imagine you are standing at the edge of the desert on the ancient Egyptians' New Year's Eve. Watch now, as one by one, those thousands of lamps and candles are lit on the offering tables, transforming the cemetery into a vast lake to mirror the stars.

For Further Reading:

Gaster, Theodor H. *New Year: Its History, Customs, and Superstitions.* New York: Abelard-Schuman, 1955.

Manniche, Lise. *An Ancient Egyptian Herbal.* Austin, TX: University of Texas Press, 1989.

Montet, Pierre. *Everyday Life in Ancient Egypt in the Days of Ramesses the Great,* translated by A. R. Maxwell-Hyslop and Margaret S. Drower. Phildelphia: University of Pennsylvania Press, 1958.

Shaw, Ian, and Paul Nicholson. *The Dictionary of Ancient Egypt.* New York: Harry N. Abrams, Inc., 1995.

Tucker, Abigail. "Dig, Drink, and Be Merry," *Smithsonian,* July/August, 2011, 38.

Feasts and Treats

Dallas Jennifer Cobb

THIS SABBAT IS ASSOCIATED with many macabre elements. The Sun God continues to get weaker, and stories are told about the "corn king" mating with the Goddess and dying. As the grain corn is reaped, the image is that of a golden, virile man, who, after mating with the goddess, was slain where he stood, dying for his love. With the harvest, death and dying are everywhere, but the sacrifice is for the good of the people, so we have food to see us through the winter. So while we feel the undertone of sadness and loss, celebrate the pleasures of friends, family, and neighbors. Gather together to feast and share food, and stock not just your pantry, but your community, well provisioned for the meager days to come.

Black Beans and Greens

With harvest underway now, this dish is symbolic of the Goddess laying down her cloak of greenery and taking up the dark mantel of the Crone. The black beans represent death through harvest, and the greens represent the life being taken.

Swiss chard is a green that comes in later in the summer, lasts well into the fall, and is widely available at farmers' markets. Look for chard with gorgeously colored stalks of yellow and red.

Preparation Time: 15 minutes
Cooking Time: 5 minutes
Serves: 4

1 tablespoon olive oil
4 cloves of garlic, minced
1 medium onion, diced
A splash of Bragg's Liquid Aminos sauce, or light tamari sauce
½ teaspoon sea salt
3 drops of hot pepper sauce
10 large leaves and stalks of Swiss chard, sliced in 1-inch-wide strips
2 15-oz. cans of black beans, drained and rinsed
½ cup of water

Heat oil in a large skillet, add onion and garlic, and sauté until soft. Add chard, tamari, salt, hot pepper sauce, and water, and quick-steam the leaves until they soften slightly. Add beans, cover, and cook for 4 minutes, until hot. Serve in a big bowl with hot cornbread.

Skillet Cornbread

Made in a skillet, this cornbread is shaped like the Sun God and comes out of the oven a golden yellow. What could be more perfect than a rib-sticking slice of warm cornbread? As we eat, slowly chewing the grainy bread, we savor these tastes of summer, listening to the whisperings of the dark self, grieving as we prepare to say goodbye to our consort.

Preparation Time: 10 minutes
Cooking Time: 30 minutes
Serves: 8 hefty slices

1 tablespoon oil
1 small onion, diced
1½ cups cornmeal
½ cup flour
1 teaspoon salt

2 teaspoons baking powder
1 tablespoon honey
3 eggs
1½ cups of buttermilk
6 tablespoons butter
1 cup of sweet corn kernels
¼ cup of chopped chives

Oil the entire inside of a cast iron frying pan. Heat on medium heat. Sauté onion until soft.

While the onion cooks, prepare the batter. Stir dry ingredients together. Mix wet ingredients in another bowl, whisking to mix well. Add wet to dry and mix, adding fresh corn and chives as you do. Pour into hot pan on top of sautéed onions and place in oven at 425 degrees F for 30 minutes until golden brown.

Summer Citrus Cooler

Drink a toast to the weakening God, with orange and lemon slices floating in this cool drink, which is good with or without alcohol. I love the simplicity of this, and am always having people ask how it is made.

Preparation time: 2 minutes
Serves: 4

Juice of 1 grapefruit
Juice of 2 oranges
1 can frozen lemonade concentrate
1 large bottle of soda water
1 orange and 1 lemon sliced in thin "rounds" to use as garnish

In a large jug, mix grapefruit juice, orange juice, and frozen lemonade concentrate. Stir well to break up frozen crystals. Scoop one-eight of the mixture into a glass and add soda water to fill. If you want, you can add vodka or gin to this. Both taste great. Garnish with citrus "rounds" and serve.

Bumbleberry Crumble

All the soft fruits of summer are still available. While I can pick raspberries, blackberries, and blueberries I usually have to pull strawberries out of the freezer, but this recipe works well with frozen fruit, too. The energy of the sun is concentrated in these fruits, and when they are cooked they ooze their dark juices, the life blood of the weakening God.

Preperation Time: 5 minutes
Baking Time: 40 minutes

2 cups large-flake rolled oats
1 cup flour
1 cup demerara or raw sugar
½ cup melted butter
6 cups of berries—your choice of strawberries, raspberries, blueberries, or blackberries

In a large bowl, mix dry ingredients with a fork. Pour in melted butter and mix until things clump together. Hull berries and fill the bottom of an 8 × 8-inch cake pan. Cover with crumble mix, and bake at 350 degrees F for 45 minutes until the top is golden brown. Serve with a small scoop of vanilla ice cream.

Crafty Crafts

Blake Octavian Blair

WIDELY CELEBRATED AS THE first of the harvest sabbats and as a grain festival, at Lammas many of us adorn our homes and altars with ears of ornamental Indian corn and fill our homes with the scent of baking homemade bread (for me few scents are more comforting!). Heading into our kitchens to bake a little kitchen witchery is fitting for this sabbat, as this is generally the time when grains such as wheat and barley become ready for harvest. At this point in the wheel of the year, it is appropriate that we Pagans honor the gods and goddesses of the grain from our various pantheons and ask for their blessings upon our kitchens and the food and magick we create within it!

Mint Tin Magnet Kitchen Deity Shrine

Faiths around the world give thanks to their deities and ask for their blessing upon their food. It seems only fitting to create a shrine to your kitchen deity of choice, and the sabbat often referred to as the First Harvest is a perfect time to do so! However, many of us are limited on space or are unsure where to safely set up a large shrine practically in our kitchen. This shrine's small size provides a convenient solution by attaching to your refrigerator with magnets. This craft utilizes a small rectangular metal mint tin like the kind that popular brands of breath mints are packaged in these days. They come in various sizes, and any of them will work—it just depends on the scale you wish to work in.

Supplies
Rectangular metal mint tin
4 small magnet dots
Multipurpose craft adhesive
Scissors
Picture of deity (sized to fit inside the bottom of the tin)
Patterned or colored paper as desired
Felt as desired
Permanent markers, glitter, yarn, ribbon, sequins, and various other symbols either in miniature or in pictures cut out from magazines, almanacs, etc., associated with your deity as desired

Instructions: This is another craft in which it might be helpful to cover your workspace with a sheet of newspaper to catch scraps and assist in cleanup. When choosing your deity image for inside your shrine, measure the dimensions of the bottom of the tin. This will be roughly the dimension you want to aim for when sizing, printing, or creating your deity picture. Once you have the image, you can make necessary adjustments with minor trimming prior to gluing it inside the shrine. A note on choosing a kitchen deity:

As grains are often a staple food in our diets, if you don't already have a preferred kitchen deity, consider choosing one of the following grain associated deities in honor of the sabbat:

Amaterasu: Japanese goddess associated with the Sun and is said to be the first to cultivate rice. It is said her grandson then brought rice to Earth.

Corn Mother: A version of the Corn Mother appears in traditions and cultures around the world. Native American stories of the Corn Mother are quite prevalent through present day. The

Cherokee people honor Selu as the corn mother with a green corn ceremony.

Ceres: Roman goddess of the grain and agriculture. She often appears holding fruit and a stalk of wheat.

Laxmi: Hindu goddess of prosperity and abundance. While people may not consider her a traditional grain goddess, her track record of assisting devotees achieve abundance of the things they need, including food, has gained her enough popularity that she appears widely on rice bags and food labels all over India.

Trim the image until it fits inside the back wall of the shrine. When making the shrine, remember that bottom floor of the tin becomes the back wall of the shrine and the lid will serve as the front and door to the shrine as the tin will hang vertically on your refrigerator, lid facing out. Choose whether you want the lid/door to open to the left or to the right. Now glue the image to the back wall. Do not fear if your image is a little smaller than the back wall of the shrine, as you can add trim, ribbon, and other decorations in the extra space later, if desired.

Now, inside the front door of the shrine, as well as on the rear wall, you can glue additional images of symbols that correspond to your deity, perhaps a picture of a loaf of bread for Ceres, a few kernels of blue corn for the Corn Mother, or grains for Laxmi. Let your creativity run free and choose runes, sigils, colors, and numbers that resonate with you and the deity chosen. I suggest only putting flat decorations on the inside of the lid so that you can close your shrine door. Leave the three-dimensional decorations for the back of the tin so that the shrines depth can accommodate them without affecting the lids closure.

When you have decorated the inside, it is time to address the front of the outside of the shrine. There are a few different approaches you can take to finishing the exterior of the shrine's lid/door. First things first, you'll want to cover the branding and advertising for the mints it once housed by gluing paper or felt over the front. My preference is to use craft felt, as tin lids often have

textured and raised lettering, and the felt gives it a much smoother and nicer finish. Then, you can adorn the surface with any design or symbol you'd like. The Pentacle, Om, an appropriate rune, or even just an image of corn or wheat, it is your choice. Be as overtly or covertly witchy as you want. The small size of this shrine conveniently allows you to be as inconspicuous as you want.

Once the front of your shrine is decorated, the last step is to put the magnets on the back of the shrine. The magnet dots are easily found in craft stores and many come with self-stick adhesive on one side. If yours do not, simply use the craft adhesive you used throughout the project to glue one magnet dot in each of the four corners on the exterior of the bottom of the tin. This will allow you to magnetically hang the shrine to your refrigerator.

Whenever you wish to use your shrine for prayers, offerings, or whatever, simply open the door to your mini shrine. Use it to give thanks and offer food before serving meals or just leave it open for inspiration while cooking and practicing kitchen witchery!

Cost: $10.00 to $20.00 depending on supplies already on hand

Time to complete: 1 to 2 hours (depending on how long it takes for adhesives to dry)

References:

McCoy, Edain. *Sabbats: A Witch's Approach to Living the Old Ways.* St. Paul, MN: Llewellyn Publications, 2004.

Illes, Judika. *Encyclopedia of Spirits: The Ultimate Guide to the Magic of Fairies, Genies, Demons, Ghosts, Gods & Goddesses.* New York, NY: Harper One, 2009.

All One Family

Kerri Connor

SINCE LUGHNASADH GAVE BIRTH to the modern-day county fair, why not make a county fair of your own? Even though county fairs are often associated with being out in the country, you don't have to live in the country to pull this one off. If you don't have the land to create a mini fair, you can use a city, county, or state park. If you do happen to live in the country, you may have some extra options.

To create your own county fair, you can set up different feats of strength and physical games, mental games, and even the showing of prized animals, produce, or other grown/raised items.

If you get into planning for this early enough and you have a garden, allow each person to have their own small plot if you have room. Many vegetables can also be grown in planters, especially peppers and tomatoes, so you could also use those if you don't have enough land. This way each person can grow something to show at your fair.

Some people raise chickens, rabbits, turkeys, or other livestock, so you might be able to assign an animal to each child. You could allow children to show hamsters, cats, or dogs. Children who don't have live animals to show can always exhibit drawings, paintings, or other artwork.

Feats of strength and physical games can include many different contests. You could try archery, BB or pellet gun shooting, yard games such as lawn darts, ladder golf, bean bag toss, mud pit wrestling, tug-of-war, croquet, badminton, volleyball, egg toss, three-legged race, wheelbarrow race, potato sack race, or eating contests (watermelon, pie, or hot dog eating are popular). You know which events are most age appropriate for your children and/or other family and friends who may be celebrating with you.

For those who are more physically challenged, you can do rock-paper-scissors, thumb wars, and test your ESP. If time allows, even board games, card games, or karaoke singing can be contests that you use.

To test your ESP, you will need about twenty to twenty-five index cards. On each card write a symbol. You can use a square, star, rectangle, circle, triangle, wavy lines, or other easy to draw symbols. Each person will get a turn to try use their intuition, ESP, or other magical gifts to "see" what the card is while only looking at the back, blank side. Keep track of how many symbols each person gets right so you know who the winner is.

After all of the games have been completed, have an awards ceremony. You can go with something as simple as ribbons or you can give out trophies if you would like. You don't have to spend a fortune on trophies either. Check your local thrift stores for interesting knickknacks that will work just fine—often the sillier they are the better.

Other Activities

Lughnasadh was also the time for judgments and entering into contracts. Are there family issues that need to be solved? Do you have a group that performs rituals together that has had some problems and needs some new rules set? Now is the time to get these types of problems taken care of so that everyone can freely go into the season of Mabon with open, thankful hearts. For families, it is also a good time to reset boundaries and expectations. Perhaps chores need to be switched up a bit. The kids are a year older now—can you let them stay up another half an hour at night? You can either cover all of this ground verbally or you make it like a real contract and require everyone involved to sign their solemn oath to live by these new rules.

Another activity that you can participate in at Lughnasadh, especially if you are celebrating with a large enough group, is a trade and barter booth. The easiest way to set this up is to have a table or two set up with items people are willing to trade. These may be tangible items, or they may be services too. If it's a service, simply write down on a piece of paper what the service is. Perhaps you are willing to give three hours of free babysitting—write it down. Make sure everything is marked with the person's name who is willing to trade it. Then you allow people to "shop" and choose what they are interested in. After choosing, they then need to make a deal with the person who is offering the item or service. Maybe someone will trade babysitting for produce, or maybe exchange lawn care for children's clothes.

Some people celebrate this sabbat as Lammas instead, and in the "loaf mass" tradition, spend plenty of time baking bread and sharing it in communion with others. When baking this bread, everyone should help in some way. Depending on the kind of bread you bake, everyone involved should take a turn either stirring or kneading the dough. As they take their turn, they should infuse the dough with a positive intention for everyone that will be partaking in the bread. If you'd like, sit everyone in a circle with the bread in a large enough bowl or tub to make the stirring or kneading easy. Pass the bowl from person to person allowing them to work their magic. This can either be done silently, or each person may say out loud what positivity they are infusing into the bread. Once the bread is baked, you may want to share it in ritual, or sit back in your circle to pass it out. As each person takes their piece, they can thank the others for their good intentions and positive energies.

❧

Lughnasadh is a very community-centered sabbat and so all of these events have one major element in common—they help to build the very community that they take place in. They support the bonds of family and friendship that are already in place. If you have new people attending your celebration, these activities will help you to reach out to them and give them a chance to participate fully in the festivities.

Lammas Ritual: Reaping Ambition

Elizabeth Barrette

EVERYONE SHOULD DRESS IN autumn colors. Each person should bring a symbol of an accomplishment harvested from this year, and a symbol of something to be blessed for the future. This ritual works for variable numbers of participants. In a small group, you might want a single person or a High Priest and High Priestess to do all the parts. In a larger group, you can divide the sections among different callers so that more people can participate.

Decorate the ceremonial space with a harvest theme. Sheaves of grain or corn dollies are ideal. Use empty beer bottles as candleholders for the quarter candles; set them in candle dishes or pie plates to catch stray wax. Use pillar candles for the God and Goddess candles. For cakes and ale, have a platter of bread and a chalice of beer. Include two baskets: one for accomplishments, decorated with images of grain; and one for blessings, decorated with images of beer. (Items placed in the baskets during the ritual may be retrieved afterwards.) Cover the altar with an autumn-themed cloth if possible.

Cast the Circle: *Starting in the east, walk deosil and pour beer from a bottle to define the edges of the circle. (Indoors, sprinkle a few drops instead of pouring.) Say:*

By grain and yeast, beginning in east,
The circle is cast;
By pouring forth, finishing in north,
The magic is fast.

Call Quarters: *Starting in the east, light the candle and say the verse for each of the four quarters.*

From the east come the powers of Air,
Bringing carbon dioxide to bubble from the yeast.

From the south come the powers of Fire,
Sun to ripen the grain and heat to bake the bread.

From the west come the powers of Water,
Flowing to moisten the mash and the dough.

From the north come the powers of Earth,
Grain hanging heavy on the stalk.

Invoke the Divine: *Stand at the altar to light first the God candle and then the Goddess candle. Say the invocation:*

Come, Raugupatis, Slavic god of fermentation and yeast;
Make the mash bubble and the bread rise with tiny life.
Come, Raugutiene, Slavic goddess of beer,
Partner of Raugupatis who holds what he creates.

Come, Tammuz, Sumerian god of grain,
Cut down in the field and carried into the kitchen.
Come, Ninkasi, Sumerian goddess of beer;
In your hymn is the recipe of the sacred beverage.

Come, Silenus, Greek god of beer,
Companion of fauns and wild men of the woods.
Come, Demeter, Greek goddess of grain,
From whose boundless basket all blessings sprout.

Come, Aegir, Norse god of beer and brewing;
Yours is the gift of bragging and merrymaking.
Come, Freya, Norse goddess of bread,
Giver of the Loaf and Mistress of the Kitchen.

Give Thanks: *Lift the basket for accomplishments from the altar, and recite the verse of thanksgiving:*

We give thanks to the gods and goddesses of the harvest
For the nourishment of bread and the inspiration of beer.
As in the days of old, we come together in our circle
To honor your gifts and remember your sacrifices.

All good things come to those who work,
As magic answers to the craft of the wise.
During the year we have planted and tended and gathered in;
Now we celebrate with symbols of what we have reaped.

Place the basket back on the altar. One at a time, participants come up and deposit their symbolic objects in the basket, while adding personal words about their accomplishments if they wish.

Request Blessings: *Lift the basket for blessings from the altar, and recite the verse of benediction:*

We ask for the blessings of the divine ones
In whose hands yeast and water and grain
Pass through the mysteries and gather their energies
To come forth as bread and beer.

Now we bring forth the symbols of our hopes
To be blessed and charged for the coming year,
So that when we have sown we may reap
By the time that Lammas comes again.

Place the basket back on the altar. One at a time, participants come up and deposit their symbolic objects in the basket; if they wish, they may add personal words about what they wish to bless for the coming year.

Present Cakes & Ale: *Take the platter of bread from the altar. Beginning in the east, carry it around the circle for each person to take a piece, saying:*

May the bounty of bread always be with you.

Take the chalice of beer from the altar. Beginning in the east, carry it around the circle for each person to take a sip, saying:

May the inspiration of beer always be with you.

Devoke the Divine: *Stand at the altar to snuff first the God candle and then the Goddess candle. Say the devocation:*

Go with our thanks, Raugupatis,
For the yeast which enables fermentation.
Go with our thanks, Raugutiene,
Holder of the yeast-made beer.

Go with our thanks, Tammuz,
Grain-god sacrificed for our gain.
Go with our thanks, Ninkasi,
For singing of the creation of beer.

Go with our thanks, Silenus,
Beer-god of the wooded wilderness.
Go with our thanks, Demeter,
For the sheaves of grain you bear.

Go with our thanks, Aegir,
For your beer and celebrations.
Go with our thanks, Freya,
Bread-giver of kitchen kindness.

Release Quarters: *Starting in the north, snuff the candle and say the verse for each of the four quarters.*

Home to the north go the powers of Earth,
With our thanks for their gift of grain.

Home to the west go the powers of Water,
With our thanks for the water they brought.

Home to the south go the powers of Fire,
With our thanks for the sun and the oven.

Home to the east go the powers of Air,
With our thanks for carbon dioxide of the yeast.

Release the Circle: *Starting in the north, walk widdershins while blowing over the top of an empty beer bottle. Say:*

By blowing forth, beginning in north,
The circle's released.
By the grain and yeast, finishing in east,
Now let us all feast!

Notes

Notes

Mabon

Mabon

Suzanne Ress

MABON, AT THE AUTUMN Equinox, September 22, is believed to
go back to two ancient Welsh deities: Modron, the great mother,
and her infant son, Mabon. Mabon was taken from Modron when
he was but three days old, and brought to the underworld, much
like the Greek goddess Persephone, daughter of Demeter, the great
mother goddess. Having lost Mabon, Modron withdrew from the
earth, leaving it barren and cold. Not until Mabon reappeared as
the male fertilizing principle around Imbolc did life return to the
earth.

At Mabon, we celebrate the second and final harvest. Ripe apples, figs, and pears are gathered from the orchard; walnuts, chest-
nuts, and hazelnuts are taken from the woods, and the grapes are
plucked from the vineyard. The last cutting of hay is made and
baled. Squash, potatoes, and the final other remaining vegetables
and herbs are collected from the garden before the season's first
frost. Nights have grown chilly by now, and as a response to the
waning daylight hours, animals' winter coats begin to grow in. Hens
will have their second major egg-laying period before slowing or
shutting down for the winter, and cows' milk begins to dry up as
their calves grow big. Corn is harvested, ground for meal, and put
in storage for the winter. In leaner, more self-sufficient times extra

animals, representing more mouths to feed, would be slaughtered, and processed for meat.

Mabon can be both a sweet and bitter time of year, for it represents the end of the productive cycle, the gathering of what was produced, and taking stock of it. It can be very sweet indeed to have such an excellent harvest that one not only needn't worry about making it through the winter, but has plenty left to share with friends and neighbors, or to barter with others for luxuries.

On the other hand, if one has a disappointing harvest, Mabon could be a time of worry, even desperation. Nowadays we think of money as wealth, but there was a time, not so very long ago, when richness was measured by production of one's own basic needs and beyond. A full larder at Samhain was equivalent to a bulging bank account on New Year's Day. Humans used to live closer to nature, and it was easier to understand our place in it.

These days, when summer ends, even though we can still find all the same foods in our sterile and cold supermarkets that we found there back in May, and that we can count on finding there in January, many of us have a bittersweet feeling. We may attribute this to our memories of returning to school or of sending our quickly growing children back to school, or the end of warm late-night gatherings with friends under the stars, or the end of vacation time, a fading tan, or the first falling leaves.

At Mabon, perhaps more than at any other time of year, we realize, deep down, that we too are getting older.

In modern globalized society, growing old is considered a negative, frightening prospect, almost as bad as its alternative, death. Why is this? Is gray or white hair not beautiful? Is wrinkled skin unpleasant to behold? Is menopause an end to womanhood? Does andropause mark the finale of masculinity? Is it inevitable that our senses will fail, our bones will become as frail as sugar cookies, and our minds will succumb to senility or Alzheimer's disease? Does turning forty, or fifty, or sixty, or more, mean that we are on the downside of life's crest, and the only thing left to look forward to is a well-attended funeral? Is getting older really so bad, after all?

❧

When I was in my early twenties, I recall being in church seated in one of the back pews with my grandmother. In a whisper she remarked to me, gesturing discreetly toward a lady seated two rows ahead of us, "Doesn't she have gorgeous hair? I wish I had hair like hers!" Indeed, the woman in question had beautiful hair—thick, wavy, healthy, and pure snowy white.

In the fall of the year, we make a point of admiring the bright warm colors of changing foliage on trees—the golden yellows, brilliant reds, yellow-reds, and orange-yellows. All of these beautiful colors appear when the trees' leaves lose their green-producing chlorophyll, in preparation for winter's lean times.

Basically the same thing happens to human hair in the autumn of our lives. Our hair gets its color from melanin rather than from chlorophyll. Usually at around age forty, but often earlier and sometimes much later, melanocytes stop producing melanin, and hair loses its color and grows in gray or white. It is not known exactly why this happens!

Older people who do not dye their hair display an amazing array of lovely gray, blue-gray, silver-gray, off-white, and white hair tones. Perhaps these days we fail to appreciate the everyday beauty of gray hair, but historically, particularly in the late 1700s, white or gray hair was considered a symbol of high social economic status. Men shaved their heads bald and wore white or off-white powdered wigs, and women powdered their own hair gray or bluish gray with scented starch powder or talc.

As things age, we can appreciate their unique beauty, and this appreciation can extend to the physical appearance of ourselves and of others. Much as there is joy in the final harvest at Mabon, we cannot help but be aware that the bounty of fruit left by a plant is its legacy for the following year's growth, and in some cases signals the end of the plant's life. In all cases, the end of the growing season signals another growing cycle closer to the last and final one.

In late middle or old age, human beings undergo a sort of harvesting, or taking stock, of all they have produced or accomplished during their individual lives. A particular characteristic shared by nearly all older human beings is the ability to realistically evaluate themselves and their previously held goals and priorities. In general, the fruits of human aging include much greater peace of mind, a sense of personal completion, and a sense of self-fulfillment.

❧

Physiologically, our bodies never lose their ability to gain muscular strength, flexibility, or cardiovascular fitness. Perhaps the mistaken idea that, over the age of forty, one must resign oneself to a future with a flabby, aching, tired, and slow-moving body came about as sedentary lifestyles became commonplace.

Aerobic capacity among physically active people is about 25 percent better than that of sedentary people of any age. An active fifty-year-old can easily maintain the functional aerobic capacity of a twenty-year-old with regular exercise.[1]

Elderly men and women's body muscle strength has been shown to respond well to resistance training, at an average improvement rate of 5 percent per training session, the same as for young adults. Muscle responds to vigorous training with marked and rapid improvement into the ninth decade of life![2]

Not only does aging mean we do not need to resign ourselves to ill health, but there are several ways in which human beings, like fine wine or cheese, actually improve with age, becoming more mellow, rich, and finally achieving their full personal depth. The only way to arrive at this point of perfect maturity of the human mind is through living at least fifty years, the more fully the better.

The Seattle Longitudinal Study[3] has followed a group of men and women, starting in 1956, at seven-year intervals, to study aspects of psychological development in adults. One of the study's many findings was that subjects at midlife scored higher on almost every aspect (verbal and numerical ability, reasoning, and verbal memory) of cognitive function than they did at age twenty-five.

As we mature, perhaps partly because we can draw on many years of previous experience, we are better able to control our emotional and behavioral reactions. Part of the calmness of old age is due to a chemical change in the brain's limbic system. The amygdalae, two almond-shaped structures in the brain that generate our most intense emotional responses, show a great reduction in activity, especially in response to the negative emotions fear, anger, and hatred.

As adults age, they usually pay less attention to negative than to positive emotional stimulation, and are less likely to remember negative than positive emotional material.[4] Mather Canli's study sums it up thus: "The profile of findings suggests that, with age, the amygdalae may show decreased activity to negative information while maintaining or increasing their reactivity to positive information."

Incidentally, many people who have been myopic all their lives suddenly find they develop perfect 20/20 vision at the same time that their age cohorts are beginning to have trouble seeing clearly up close. This is due to molecular changes in the eyes' lenses that can naturally correct youthful myopia.

In both men and women who are physically active, excess body weight often disappears on its own sometime around age fifty. Many older people's weight returns effortlessly to what it was at age eighteen or twenty, and, in women, cellulite usually melts away like magic as estrogen decreases. Other liberating pluses for postmenopausal women that are rarely celebrated are the possibility of enjoying carefree unprotected sex with one's regular partner, and an end to the hassle of menstruation.

✤

Adult maturity is liberating in other ways, too. Many people find that once their children have grown up and left home, and they go into semi or full retirement, they suddenly feel free to experiment and let go of self-imposed limitations and inhibitions. Being aware that one's own death may be just around the corner may create an attitude of, "If not now, when?" Older people with a hidden creative flair may plunge into a second career as an artist, writer, actor, chef, or interior decorator. Lifelong lovers of nature and the outdoors may take up beekeeping, volunteer as ecological guards, help out in a fish hatchery, or at a wild animal rescue unit. People with highly developed manual ability may turn casual electronics, woodworking or crafting hobbies into full-fledged passions, often giving back to their communities through teaching or mentoring programs.

Frequently it isn't until the age of forty-five or so that adults, both men and women, seem to merit respect from strangers. I remember realizing this suddenly years ago when I was in the car with my father. I was home from college and had not seen him for several months. He was forty-five and his hair had recently begun to turn silvery. He pulled into a filling station, and I couldn't help but notice with what marked respect the young attendant treated him. It was something I had not taken note of before in the way strangers behaved with my father, and it was certainly different from the way they usually behaved with me.

As long as an older person continues to be curious about the world, and to think and learn, brain cells continue to sprout new connections at the same rate as a much younger person's. Amazingly, older people are also more able than young people to use both left and right hemispheres of their brains simultaneously.[5]

At Mabon we gather not only the fruits of the trees and plants we have tended through spring and summer, but we also take stock of the fruits of our own finite lives, reviewing what we have learned, produced, and contributed, and preparing how best to go forward from that point. We can do this at any age, but as we move closer to the end of our lives this taking stock becomes more significant, and should give us ever more reason to celebrate the harvest.

1. *Exercise Physiology*, 5th Edition "Energy, Nutrition, and Human Performance." McKardle, William, Frank I. Katch, and Victor L. Katch. 2001, Lippincott, Williams, and Wilkins.

2. Klitgaard, H. et al. "Function Morphology and Protein Expression of Aging Skeletal Muscle: A Cross Sectional Study of Elderly Men with Different Training Backgrounds" Acta Physiol Scand 1990; 457 (suppl.): 1

3. The Seattle Longitudinal Study: www.uwpsychiatry.org/sls/

4. Mather Canli, Dept. of Psychology, University of CA, Santa Cruz, "Amygdala Responses to Emotionally Valenced Stimuli in Older and Younger Adults" Psychological Science, April, 2004.

5. Gatz, Margaret, Psychology and Gerontology Professor, Dept. of Psychology, University of S. California.

Cosmic Sway

Corrine Kenner

EVER SINCE THE SUMMER Solstice, when we had the longest day and the shortest night of the year, we've been losing daylight. At the autumn equinox, we reach a balancing point—and an astrological milestone. On the day of the equinox, the Sun shines directly on the equator, and day and night are of equal length. At the same time, the Sun enters Libra, the halfway mark on the zodiac.

Pluto's Realm

The equinox represents a spiritual halfway point, too. Metaphorically speaking, Mabon is the second harvest festival. The god may have died physically at Lughnasadh, but he's still with us in spirit. Now it's time to send him on his way. His destination is frightfully clear: he's bound for Pluto's realm, the Underworld.

It's interesting to note that Pluto itself is making an astrological comeback. A few months ago, on April 14, Pluto went retrograde. From our perspective, the distant planet looked like it was moving backward through Capricorn, the sign of career and social status.

During any retrograde period, a planet's energy seems to focus inward. It feels more personal than usual. As Pluto moved backward through Capricorn, you may have found yourself questioning your own place in society, and reassessing your values, actions, and beliefs.

Pluto's retrograde period, however, ends on September 23. At that point, you can move forward—whether you need to reclaim your personal power, or simply make the best use of the time and talent that's already at your disposal.

Pluto is actually a secret name for Hades, the ancient Greek god of the dead. Hades was so powerful—and so feared—that for centuries, no one wanted to say his real name aloud. Even now, his realm is associated with darkness and distress, and it's said to be guarded by Cerberus, a three-headed hound from Hell.

Surprisingly, Pluto's mythic origins aren't nearly as frightening as you might think. Pluto was the son of Saturn and Rhea, an early form of Mother Earth. He's part of a family triumvirate of power: his brother Jupiter rules the heavens, and his brother Neptune rules the seas.

Pluto's reputation, however, is less than stellar. Pluto took his wife, the maiden Persephone, by force. As she picked flowers in a meadow, Pluto opened the earth beneath her feet; Pluto literally swallowed her alive. Eventually, the dark goddess Hecate rescued Persephone and returned her to her mother. The God of Death couldn't be completely stripped of his prize, however, so Persephone was still condemned to spend a third of each year in Hades. Apparently, her life there wasn't a living hell. She adapted to her otherworldly position and became the powerful Queen of the Dead.

Pluto did have one redeeming quality, as far as the ancients were concerned: as king of the lower world, he was the giver of all the blessings that came from earth, including precious gems and metals.

In astrology, Pluto symbolizes death and resurrection, forgiveness and release. It can indicate areas of testing and challenge, power struggles, and resistance. It's a planet of evolution and unavoidable change. Pluto compels us to release anything that's no longer living up to our needs or expectations, so we can recycle and reuse that energy in better ways. Pluto teaches us that endings are merely part of the cycle of regeneration and rebirth, and inevitably lead to a second chance at a new life.

Pluto has a long, slow, erratic orbit of 248 years. It spends an entire generation in each sign. In 2008, it moved into Capricorn, the sign of business, career, and social status. It won't cross into Aquarius until 2024.

The glyph for Pluto looks like someone rising from the dead; technically, it's a coin and a chalice, symbols of payment for everlasting life.

Ritual: Replace Bad Habits

Pluto typically calls for the release of old habits, patterns, and relationships that have served their purpose and now should be relegated to the pages of history. During this year's Mabon celebration, Pluto is locked in a protracted, irritating square with Uranus.

You can put that energy to good use by releasing irritating habits from your life, too—especially if those habits are unhealthy. Do you smoke? Drink? Overeat?

Banish bad behavior on September 23, when the waning crescent Moon in Virgo is hardly more than a sliver in the sky. It should be a powerful visual: the luminary will be curved like a harvest scythe in a field of wheat. In fact, Virgo is often pictured as a harvest goddess, carrying a sheaf of wheat.

Replace your bad habit with a surprising new one that your friends and relatives would never expect. If you've been sedentary, wake up a half hour early and exercise every morning. If you're addicted to chocolate, load up on fruit instead. If you suffer from a truly debilitating habit and need professional help to break it, get on the phone and schedule an appointment with a doctor, counselor, or advisor.

What's more, in true Uranus fashion, don't tell anyone about the surprising new you until you've practiced your new habit for at least a month—the cycle of one Full Moon.

Planetary Positions

At Mabon, the Sun moves into Libra, the sign of partnership and balance. Mercury is in Libra, too, bearing messages of a close, personal nature. Now's the time to tell your loved ones how you feel. In a few days, when Mercury goes retrograde in Scorpio on October 4, your heartfelt communications could be misconstrued. At that point, if you want to clarify matters, you'll have to wait until Mercury goes direct on October 25.

The Moon is in Virgo, in a close conjunction with Venus. On that night, the goddess of love will pay special attention to the finer details of her appearance, and she'll make more of an emotional investment in her connection to others.

Mars is in outgoing, adventurous Sagittarius. It's squaring off with Neptune, so Mars is going to stick to fighting battles it knows it can win.

Jupiter, the planet of luck and good fortune, is in an easy, flowing trine with Uranus. You can expect to be surprised by the twists and turns of fate. At the same time, Jupiter is locked in its ongoing square with Saturn, which reins in some of Jupiter's native enthusiasm. Saturn would simply tell you he's keeping Jupiter real.

Neptune and Uranus are still retrograde—but on October 7, you can connect with Uranus' energy directly, as Uranus makes its closest approach to earth.

The Phases of the Moon

The last New Moon in Virgo on August 25 ushered in the month on a note of practicality and dedicated effort. The first quarter Moon in Sagittarius on September 2 was outgoing and enthusiastic. The Full Moon in Pisces on September 8 dissolves boundaries and encouraged spiritual growth and connection, while the third quarter Moon in Gemini on September 15 heightened both curiosity and versatility.

Get ready for a New Moon in airy, graceful Libra on September 24. The first quarter Moon in Capricorn on October 1 is earthy and practical, grounded in physical existence and material reality. The fiery Full Moon in Aries on October 8 will be accompanied by a total lunar eclipse, which brings new freedom and independence—whether you're ready to be liberated, or not. If you weren't quite ready to go out on your own, you can go home again, during a third quarter Moon in Cancer on October 15.

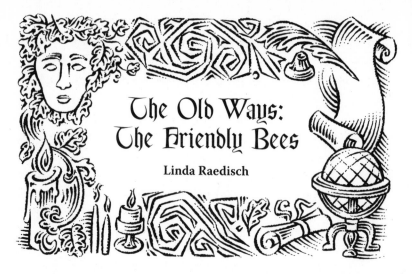

The Old Ways: The Friendly Bees

Linda Raedisch

DECIDING TO WRITE ABOUT bees was the easy part. Deciding where to put those bees was more difficult. If I placed my apiarian piece under the auspices of Ostara, I told myself, I could write about *pysanky*, Ukrainian Easter eggs dyed using the wax-resist method. Anyone who has made pysanky knows how intoxicating hot beeswax can be. To say it smells sweet or flowery does not do it justice; "carbonized mead" is a little more like it. Although I have made dozens of pysanky over the years, I'm really only so-so at this sacred, painstaking art form, and since I'm too lazy to blow the eggshells out, most of them eventually explode. To be honest, it's that clean, golden scent that keeps me pushing the hot copper stylus into the beeswax year after year. (I'm convinced that the smell of beeswax candles on the altar is what kept a lot of people coming back to church in the Middle Ages, too.)

Eggs aside, I might have made the bees the heroes of my "Spring Cleaning" article, for, in the old days, once the combs had been emptied of honey, they were melted and combined with water, vinegar, linseed oil, turpentine, and/or "curd soap," applied to a rag and used to polish the furniture. However, an even better candidate for my paean to the bees was the sabbat of Lughnasadh, because August 1 was also Old Russian Honey Day. As at the English Lammas, the first fruits were born to the church on this day along with the first dripping combs of honey. Two weeks later, on August 15, Lithuanians still celebrate the Feast of Honey and Bread (and butter, I would hope).

Then again, late November/early December is, for me, the time to make the rounds of the German Christkindlmarkts to stock up on beeswax candles for the dark days of winter. For gifts, I buy the ones that are cast in the shape of beeskeps. A beeskep, in case you are wondering, is a dome of coiled wheat or rye straw in which bees were invited to make their homes before someone invented those boring white boxes. The word comes from Old Norse *skepa*, "a bushel," via Old English *scep.* A shed full of skeps was known as a "bee bole." Obviously, there's a lot to be said on the subject, so why not celebrate the bees at Yule by the light of the candles they had helped to make?

But, really, you can buy those skep-shaped candles at harvest festivals, too. And there's something poignant about the sight of a bee dawdling among the September chrysanthemums with the first frost just around the corner. You know that soon he'll be hanging up his striped velvet waistcoat and turning in for the winter. I suppose he brings out the Beatrix Potter in me. Not that I imagine bees are cuddly; I agree with British self-sufficiency guru John Seymour (1914–2004) that bees should be left "severely alone." Still, I don't panic when a bee wanders into the house. If it has a lot of fuzz, I know it's a bumblebee and I'll help it outside before it concusses itself on the window glass. If it has a little fuzz I know it's a honeybee and I'll politely show it the door. (If it has no fuzz, it's a yellow jacket and there will be no prisoners!)

Once, when I was twelve or thirteen years old, I heard some buzzing in the folds of the living room curtains. A friend visiting from the other side of the Watchung Mountains (a mere ten minute walk, for such are mountains in north central New Jersey), said, "Don't kill it! It might be one of my mother's Italian honeybees!"

Now, if that bee had been a queen bee, and if she had decided to establish a new hive in our backyard, and if my family, my friend's family and the bee had all been Lithuanian, we would have been joined forever after by biciulyste. *Biĉiulis*, a Lithuanian word for friend, comes from bite, "bee." But biciulyste is more than friendship; it is akin to kinship. (As it turned out, we trapped the bee under a glass, let it outside and allowed it to wing its way home over the stubs of the mountains.)

In the old days, once a queen had "hived off" in your direction, there were certain things you had to do to keep her and her family happy and productive, and not just in Lithuania. The convention of informing the bees whenever there was a death in the beekeeper's family was an almost universal one, the Irish going so far as to drape the hives in black crêpe. Strict Lithuanians would sell neither their swarms nor their honey, though this condition could be gotten around by bartering. Bees liked to be told secrets and would give their blessing to those embarking on new enterprises, as long as they were kept informed. Dead bees were not to be left lying on the ground or windowsills but buried like humans.

If all this sounds like a lot to remember, you could ask Austeja, the Lithuanian bee goddess, for help. Her name comes from the verb *austi*, "to weave," as in, to dart quickly through the air like a shuttle through the warps threads on a loom. Austeja is also an all-around fertility goddess, a sort of queen bee for the human hive. The first written reference to Austeja does not appear until the sixteenth century, but, like the Lithuanian language—the oldest living Indo-European tongue—she is much older. If you are having trouble picturing just what a bee goddess should look like, I would direct you to a central Greek amphora of the seventh century BCE on which a female figure stands with oversized arms outstretched over two black beasties. She is wasp-waited, if she'll pardon the expression, with a heart-shaped face and rather sparse, kinky hair. Her fitted bodice is formed of horizontal bands of linear designs. Is she really a southern incarnation of the ancient bee goddess? No one can say for sure, but Marija Gimbutas, who was both an archaeologist and a Lithuanian, felt she might be.

❦

Maybe you'd prefer to envision Austeja as a housewife in traditional Lithuanian dress. Her sleeves, bodice, and long, fringed apron all bear horizontal bands of woven and cross-stitched geometric designs. With sage green and mustard yellow predominating, the tones are relatively earthy compared to the other folk costumes of Europe. She also wears an understated beaded crown and a necklace of polished chunks of amber, golden bright like drops of honey in sunlight. Her face is open and friendly. If she were selling her wares at a late summer festival, you would not hesitate to stop and buy a jar of honey and a pair of beeswax tapers for your Mabon table. Of course, if she really were Austeja, she would be giving them away!

For Further Reading:

Gimbutas, Marija. *The Living Goddesses*. Berkeley: University of California Press, 1999.

Leach, Maria, editor. *Funk & Wagnalls Standard Dictionary of Folklore, Mythology, and Legend*. New York: Harper & Row, 1972.

"Lithuanian Bee Goddess." http://www.thebeegoddess.com/id17 .html. Accessed September 23, 2012.

Seymour, John. *The Forgotten Arts and Crafts*. New York: Dorling Kindersley, 2001.

Travel Lithuania. "Museum of Ancient Beekeeping." http://www .way2lithuania.com/en/travel-lithuania/beekeeping-museum. Accessed September 23, 2012.

Feasts and Treats

Dallas Jennifer Cobb

AS THE DAYS GROW short and the nights grow longer, this sabbat is often the last time to enjoy an outdoor meal in comfort. Balancing the goddess and god energies, mirroring the day and the night, the light and the dark, my partner and I prepare this meal together, cooking most of it on the barbecue. The man in my life loves to huddle around his fire pit as we toast the dying Sun God. As he cooks, I watch the faint glow of the charcoal embers in his face, and say my own sad goodbye, symbolically.

Grilled Pork Chops with Applesauce

Stainless steel pots can be used on the barbecue safely, so applesauce could also be prepared there. Timing wise, start the applesauce, then tend to the pork, and the two will be done around the same time.

Resurrection Applesauce

A traditional symbol of the resurrection cycle of birth, life, death, and rebirth, apples are abundant at this time of year. This recipe can also be used to make lots of applesauce to bottle up for use in the winter and spring. Every time you pull out a jar you will be reminded of the sweet meal eaten at Mabon, the bittersweet celebration of the Sun God dying, and look forward to his resurrection.

Preparation Time: 15 minutes
Cooking Time: 20 Minutes
Serves: 8 servings or more

5½ cups peeled, cored, and chopped apples
½ cup apple juice
1 tablespoon fresh lemon juice
Sugar, honey, maple syrup or stevia to taste

In a saucepan, heat apples and both juices to a medium heat until bubbling, then turn to low and cook for 15 minutes. Use a hand-held blender to puree to a smooth consistency, adding sweetener to taste at this time. Serve warm with pork.

Butterfly Pork Chops
Preparation Time: 5 minutes
Cooking Time: 12 minutes
Serves: 4

4 medium-size (4 ounce) pork chops
2 tablespoons lemon juice
½ teaspoon rosemary, finely ground
½ teaspoon thyme, finely ground
¼ teaspoon black pepper, finely ground

Brush pork with lemon juice, then rub herbs on both sides of meat. Grill for about 5 minutes per side, until meat is well cooked, and internal temperature is 160 degrees Fahrenheit or 70 degrees Celcius.

Super Sweet Potatoes

Preparation Time: 8 minutes
Cooking Time: 25 minutes
Serves: 4

Four large sweet potatoes
Butter to taste

Rinse sweet potatoes, and then prick a few times with a fork. Place them on a plate and microwave for 4 minutes on one side, roll them over and microwave for 4 minutes on the other side. Wrap pre-cooked sweet potatoes individually in tinfoil and place on the upper shelf of the barbecue, turning occasionally. Start them before everything else, and they will be done at the same time as the pork and applesauce. Before serving, slice the top of the sweet potato and add a dollop of butter.

Warm Spiced Wine

Red wines go well with pork, and my preference is for a Burgundy or Cabernet. Because it is cool out, a warm spiced wine helps to take the chill off. The God is weakening, but as we sip, we are warmed inside, infused with the colors of the sabbat. Sometimes called Glogg, this recipe is a great way to help a cheap, or slightly bitter wine, taste better.

Preparation Time: 3 minutes
Cooking Time: 15 minutes
Serves: 4

1 bottle red wine (Burgundy or Cabernet are preferred)
3 tablespoons brown sugar
3 whole cloves
3 cardamom pods, cracked
The peel of half an orange
1 teaspoon ground cinnamon

Combine all ingredients in a saucepan and warm over medium heat. Stir to dissolve sugar. Do not boil! Strain into mugs and garnish with an orange slice or a cinnamon stick.

Now drink a toast to the weakening god.

Dark Chocolate Dipped Fruit

As you dip bananas, kiwi, pineapple, and even strawberries (if you can find them at the grocery store) into the dark chocolate, imagine pulling the Goddess's dark cloak over their luminous color. These colors of the season appear to shine more brightly as the fruit is warmed by the molten chocolate.

Preparation Time: 5 minutes

Cooking Time: 1 minute

Serves: 4

6 cups of fresh fruit, peeled and cubed

2 cups of dark chocolate chips (if you can't find dark, semisweet will do)

2 tablespoons of coconut oil

Peel and cut fruit into bite-size pieces. Place chocolate chips and coconut oil into a microwaveable bowl.

Microwave for three, 20-second bursts, stirring between each one. Place warm chocolate dip in the center of the table and let people dip their own fruit. Microwave again for one or two 20-second burst as needed, if chocolate cools.

Crafty Crafts

Blake Octavian Blair

MARKING THE AUTUMN EQUINOX, Mabon is one of my all-time favorite sabbats! Mabon is not only a celebration of the seasonal marker for the official start of fall, but it is also one of thankfulness, abundance, and balance. This is a time to acknowledge and give thanks for abundance in all areas of our life, not just that of literal agricultural harvest. This is the Pagan's thanksgiving and we celebrate family, friends, good health, prosperity (of all kinds), and, of course, food as well. With the day and night being of equal length on the equinox, Mabon reminds us to also honor balance in our lives and examine where we feel we could use more of it.

This is also an appropriate time to share our abundance with others, and we often do so through sharing food by feasting with loved ones. There is no greater way to celebrate abundance and honor balance simultaneously than giving to others when we have enough to share. However, it is important for us not forget our non-human relations as well. This craft will assist us in sharing the abundance full circle with our relations in the animal world as well.

Mabon Bird Seed Balls

As the weather turns to fall and food becomes a little trickier for our wild feathered friends to come by, it is a nice thought to honor our connection to our animal relations by providing a little food for them throughout the cold months. These birdseed balls are a fun way to share your abundance and lovingly create a nutritious treat for the wild birds in your neighborhood to feast on. (Additionally, you may indeed catch a rogue squirrel or two catching a snack as well!)

Supplies

2 cups wild birdseed
½ cup vegetable shortening
Dried fruit (optional—quantity as desired)
Rolled oats (optional—quantity as desired)
Cornstarch (optional as needed)
Cookie cutters (optional)
Wire coat hangers

Instructions: Combine birdseed, shortening, and the dried fruit and oats (if you choose to use them) in a large mixing bowl. Mix thoroughly together by working with your hands. Don't be afraid to dig right in as you will have to use your hands to shape the balls in the next step anyway. Sometimes we have to get down and dirty in our magick and this is one of those occasions! As you work the mixture in your hands, contemplate how the seed came from Mother Earth, meditate on your own abundance and on your intent to extend that back to Mother Earth through caring for and sharing your abundance with the wild birds through the winter. Feel your hands alive with energy, imparting it into the mixture as you work.

For the next step, you will want a large baking pan or cookie sheet to place the balls in as you finish forming them. For easy cleanup and removal of the balls from the pan, first lay a sheet of wax paper down on the pan. How big you choose to make the birdseed balls is up to you. I prefer to make them just a bit smaller than a tennis ball. How many balls you will get from the mixture will depend both the amount of extra optional ingredients you choose to incorporate as well as what size you make your balls. The measurements listed in the supplies list are a loose guideline. You may find you need to add a little more shortening or seed to your mixture to achieve the consistency you desire. Additionally, if you have trouble getting the mixture to stick together to form into a cohesive shape, add cornstarch as needed for a binder.

A fun variation of the standard ball shape is to use cookie cutters of various shapes. Various fall-themed shapes and symbols of the season are often available in the stores this time of year and include, acorns, leaves, and pumpkins. Lay the cookie cutter down on the wax paper on the pan and pack it tightly with the mixture and then remove the cookie cutter.

When you are finished forming the balls and treats, place the entire sheet of them into your kitchen freezer for a couple hours. Freezing the balls will help them congeal into a more solid form. While they are setting up in the freezer, take several wire coat hangers and bend them to fashion them into hangers. How you need to bend them will depend on where you wish to hang them. If you want to hang them on a fence in your yard, you can simply grab the hook with one hand, grab the flat bottom bar of the hanger, and pull in opposite directions. This makes a long narrow loop with the hook at one end. Now fold that in half and bed the hook so it will face outwards. How you can hang it over the side of the fence . You can use your ingenuity to adapt and bend the hanger as needed for other locations you may wish to put the treat. Hanging from the eaves of your house in front of a window, from a deck or porch railing, or from tree branches are all popular and excellent choices. (Note: If creating this craft with children, it is best for the adults to handle the shaping and bending of the coat hangers.)

When the birdseed balls have spent their two hours in the freezer, remove them, and simply press them onto the hook of the coat hanger holders. They should still be soft enough for them to slide on by pressing firmly. However, if they are too solid, allow

them to warm up for about ten minutes and then slide them onto the hook. It should be noted that these natural bird treats are designed for cooler weather, and may lose form a bit in warmer seasons as they are held together. If you live in a climate where fall weather has not quite arrived along with the equinox, place these treats in shadier locations rather than in direct sunlight.

Now on cool fall mornings, sit back and enjoy a mug of hot mulled cider, tea, or coffee and enjoying your abundance and celebrating balance as you watch the birds and wildlife enjoy the balance you have helped to create by sharing your abundance with them. Mabon Blessings!

Time to complete: 2.5 to 3 hours (includes freezer time)
Cost: $10.00 to $20.00

All One Family

Kerri Connor

FALL IS IN THE AIR! The temperatures are starting to cool, the leaves are slowly starting to turn vibrant colors of yellow, red, and orange, the corn stalks in the fields are drying, the second harvest has arrived, and the season for giving thanks is at hand.

Since Mabon is basically the Pagan equivalent of Thanksgiving, many of these activities will deal with just that—the giving of thanks.

If you have a digital video camera, spend some time "interviewing" each person of your family or group. Have each one really think about their answer beforehand. The question you will be asking them is, "What are you thankful for?" After you have recorded everyone's answers, use an editing program to combine the videos. You may choose to add it to music or include pictures from your ritual or festivities. Save the video to play at your next Mabon after interviewing everyone asking the same question and filming them again to make the video to play the next year. Watching these videos help bring events and situations into perspective for people. When they see what they were thankful for the previous year, they also see what they may have been neglecting the previous year as well. It's also interesting to see how priorities shift or stay the same over the years. Plus, it's fun to see how people themselves have changed in the past year—some will look exactly the same while others will have major physical changes such as weight loss or gain or hairstyles and colors that will be really noticeable and stand out. These changes alone can bring about more ideas and concepts to be thankful for. This has always been one of the favorite activities at our Mabon celebrations.

During your actual ritual, spend some time thanking the gods and goddesses for whatever you want to. We either allow everyone to take turns and say whatever comes to mind, or use the alphabet system to come up with things and concepts to be thankful for. To do this, the first person comes up with something to be thankful for that begins with the letter "A," the next person "B," next person "C," and so on, until you have made it all the way through the alphabet. Give time for a silent giving of thanks. This can be beneficial as some people may have things they want to thank the deities for but don't want everyone else to know about! Simply set aside some time for a quiet giving-of-thanks meditation. Either end this time by simply stating it is over, or ask each person to ring a bell or gong to signal that they have completed their meditation to the gods.

While all of these activities are easy enough for kids to do, you may want to add in a way that makes giving thanks a bit more fun. For this activity you will need permanent markers or paint and a pie pumpkin for each child. Allow each child to paint or draw things or concepts they are thankful for on their pumpkin. Have the kids do this activity before ritual so you can place the pumpkins on and around the altar during ritual.

Paying It Forward

Now is also a good time to pay your thanks forward. Food banks need help all year long, and while they often get a lot of donations through November and December, they are often forgotten about the rest of the year. Kids can help by going to neighbors, family, and friends to collect canned goods and other nonperishable items. If you had a garden and have extra fresh produce, see if your local pantry or a even a women's shelter can use it. Many food banks also take items other than food, such as toilet paper, shampoo, toothpaste, and cleaning supplies. Use your resources at this time of year to help others who are less fortunate than you are, and remember to thank your deities as you work on this project that you can be on the giving end instead of needing to be on the receiving end.

Other ways you can pay your thanks and good fortune forward crop up naturally. You may want to hold a coat or blanket drive before the winter weather sets in. Many homeless shelters need these donations, along with sheets, towels, and pillows. We work with our Local PADS (Public Action to Deliver Shelter) to get them donations, and to help with washing laundry.

Children's book drives are another way to really help get kids involved in wanting to help. Unfortunately, it seems there is always a school or library that has suffered from a fire or natural disaster that could greatly benefit from a book drive.

Make your plans now for what charities and organizations you are going to work with over the next year. Plan to put in volunteer hours, participate in fundraisers, or make donations in other ways.

With the cooler weather setting in, it's time to clean out dresser drawers and closets. Items that are no longer needed or wanted can be donated to different organizations. Shelters for battered women and children can often use donations of gently used clothes.

Always make sure to check with organizations about what their donation requirements are before dropping anything off. The last thing you want to do is burden them with items they don't need or can't use.

Prepare for Winter

Start preparing for the cold months ahead for you and your family as well. If you can or freeze produce or other food products, finish them up and thank the deities for the bounty you have to store. Take stock of winter supplies and make sure you have enough supplies to deal with an emergency situation. Snow or ice storms have been known to knock out electricity in some areas for a week or more. Make sure you have the supplies in place in case something like this happens to you. This includes firewood, water, food, flashlights, blankets, batteries, candles, lighters, backup generator, kerosene, and whatever else you personally need. Kids can be helpful in storing supplies and taking inventory.

Again, as you work on any of these projects with your children, emphasize the importance of thanking the deities for the bounty you have. Often we take our daily life for granted, and focus on what we don't have—let Mabon be a reminder and celebration of gratitude of all that you do have in your life and all that you and your family have going for you.

Mabon Ritual: Celebrate Decay

Suzanne Ress

THE PURPOSE OF THIS Mabon ritual is to fully appreciate how the passage of time, recognized clearly at this time of year with the seasonal change, inevitably leads to death, which then leads to new life.

All participants, even if there is only one, should assemble outdoors, preferably in a secluded location with a clear view of the sky, at any time between sunset and midnight. If there is more than one participant, and each is arriving from a different location, a specific time can be set, purely for economic reasons, so that each individual need not gather and haul all of the necessary equipment.

Brief words of greeting may be exchanged, but once the ritual begins, silence should be maintained.

Celebrants may wear their traditional sabbat robes, but if these are not normally used or are unavailable, each person should dress in gray, brown, or other drab-colored old clothes, and avoid wearing any kind of jewelry or perfumes.

Items Needed

A funeral pie (recipe on page 303)
A container of prune juice with aromatic bitters added
An old, chipped cup

A pair of scissors

A black candle and a windproof holder for it

Incense of cypress, and incense burner

Cold ashes from burnt wood, a handful in a small container

A loudly ticking clock wrapped in a towel

Additionally, each participant should bring a handkerchief or small
box containing the brown and withered seed heads from weeds
or flowers, and a small flashlight. Each participant should read
over and be familiar with the ritual beforehand.

Before starting the ritual, place the black candle securely in a lan-
tern or hurricane lamp, on a small table, rock, or other altar at the
center of where you will be working, and light it. Place all of the
other items around the candle, and light the incense, making certain it is held safely in a burner. Now turn off your flashlights and
put them away in a pocket or a nearby place outside your working
area.

Gather all participants in a circle around the altar space and,
if necessary, wind up the clock, or simply uncover it, and place it
next to the candle. Everyone present should start moving counterclockwise, at a walk, following the beat of the clock's ticking. Continue walking around the altar in this way, each person visualizing
her aura surrounding her body as a fuzzy outline of colored light,
for as long as is deemed necessary. Be aware that with every tick of
the clock, one more second of your life is over. Each person should
feel himself alone and separate from all the others present, in his
mortality.

Stop walking before you become dizzy, and stand still, meditat-
ing silently for several minutes on the passing of time. Be attuned to
the dozens, hundreds, thousands, and more moments that are forever happening, and try to feel yourself alive in each of these swiftly
passing moments as it ticks away from you. With each tick you are
growing older and moving closer to death, and ultimately, decay.
Only by living fully in each moment can life be meaningful, for its

end is inevitable. New life feeds on and is nourished by the decay of old life. The cycle is interminable.

When it seems as if enough time has been spent reflecting on these thoughts, the leader of the group, or another person moved by his spirit, shall signal to the others present, by picking up his handkerchief or box of dried seed heads, that they should follow suit.

A ritual shall ensue in which the pair of scissors is passed from person to person without making any bodily contact, and each person shall cut off a small bit of hair from his own head. These bits of hair are to be put together with the seeds from the dried heads in the handkerchief or box, and to them add a pinch or two of wood ash. All of it should be mixed up thoroughly.

Still standing separately within one's own aura, each individual should sprinkle this mixture of seeds, hair, and ash onto the earth at her feet to form an invisible circle around her. Everyone shall then close their eyes and, always aware of the clock's ticking, visualize tiny green sprouts breaking through the earth where the seed was sprinkled. Let each tick of the clock signify a minute rather than a second, and then expand it, so that each tick becomes an hour, a week, a month. While you are standing there, the sprouts grow into plants. They could be great tall strong sunflowers, or cornstalks, or viny bramble weeds that grow upon your body and cover you with their tangled leaves and thorny stems. As the months turn to years, and the years to decades, your body ages and soon dies, but the flowers or weeds growing over you cover your body with their vibrancy, taking nourishment from your decaying flesh. Perhaps you have planted tobacco or other night-blooming flowers and you can even imagine smelling their sweet scent as they devour you.

As the plants around you grow thicker and fuller, the remains of your body become less and less, until finally nothing is left. What was once your body has now become flowers, leaves, or vines.

When enough time has elapsed with this visualization, and when someone of the group feels moved to do so, still without speaking, he or she may signal to the others that each may serve himself a small slice of funeral pie, and help himself to a sip or two of prune juice with aromatic bitters added, from the old chipped cup.

Once everyone has silently finished this meager refreshment, the leader of the group, or another designated person, shall raise her voice barely loud enough to be heard over the incessant ticking of the clock, and shall repeat the following words, learned beforehand by heart:

> *Our revels are now ended: these our actors,*
> *As I foretold you, were all spirits, and*
> *Are melted into air, into thin air:*
> *And, like the baseless fabric of our vision*
> *The cloud-capp'd towers, the gorgeous palaces,*
> *Yea, all which it inherit, shall dissolve,*
> *And like this insubstantial pageant faded,*
> *Leave not a rack behind: We are such stuff*
> *As dreams are made of, and our little life*
> *Is rounded with a sleep.*
> —from William Shakespeare's *The Tempest*

At this point, the one who has spoken should silence the clock by wrapping it in the towel. She should then blow out the candle, leaving all in darkness and silence for several minutes.

The flashlights can now be retrieved and turned on, and the ritual tools put away. Participants may briefly salute each other before going their own separate ways.

Recipe for Funeral Pie

1 baked pie shell
1½ cups raisins
1½ cups plus 2 tablespoons sugar
4 tablespoons flour
3 eggs, separated
2 ounces melted butter
Juice of 1 lemon
2 teaspoons grated lemon rind

Directions: Put the raisins in a saucepan with 1½ cups water and 1 cup of the sugar and boil for one minute, then cool. In a bowl, combine ½ cup water, ½ cup sugar, the flour, and egg yolks. Blend well, then stir into the raisin mixture. Over low heat continue stirring until thickened, then remove from heat and stir in butter, lemon juice, and lemon rind. Cool.

Whip the egg whites until stiff, then whip in 2 tablespoons sugar. Pour the raisin mixture into the baked pie shell, top with the meringue, and bake at 350 degrees F for 10 minutes.

Notes

Inspiring, Practical Ways to Enhance Your Craft

*L*lewellyn's *Magical Almanac* has been inspiring all levels of magical practitioners for over twenty years. Filled with practical spells, rituals, and fresh ideas, you'll find new ways to deepen your craft and enhance everyday life.

This edition features compelling articles on carnival magic, healing waters, offerings to Faery, earth-based spirituality in the city, a Frankenstein meditation, enchanted entryways, the garage-saling witch, the animistic perspective, and more. Also included is a calendar section featuring world festivals, holidays, astrological information, incense and color correspondences, and 2014 Sabbats.

A Year of Esbat and Sabbat Rituals

It's easy to lose ourselves in the everyday business of life. One way to bring our bodies, minds, and spirits into alignment is through ritual celebrations. A vital part of Wicca and Paganism, ritual strengthens our connection to nature and helps us enter the realm of the Divine.

For Witches and Pagans of all levels, *A Year of Ritual* provides ready-made rituals for a full year of Sabbats and Esbats. Groups or solitaries can use these easy-to-follow rituals. Ideas, words, and directions for each ritual are included along with background information, preparation requirements, and themes. This unique sourcebook also explains basic formats and components for creating your own rituals.

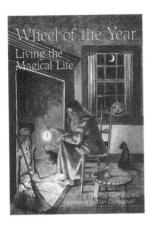

Notes

Notes